"Business as mission is an increasing phenomenon in the church. Both the nature of some closed countries and the call for all kinds of people to be involved in God's global mission has opened the door and shown the need for new ways to do mission. In *The Missional Entrepreneur*, Mark L. Russell provides a helpful guide for those willing to do more than business as usual. It will help them engage in the Father's business."

— **Ed Stetzer,** *president, LifeWay Research,*
coauthor, Compelled by Love

"Mark Russell's book is part primer and part provocateur. It raises important questions about how *business as mission* is defined and practiced and the characteristics of the more (and less) effective practitioners. It will prove especially challenging to those who assume that the motives and practices of traditional missionary work can be transferred successfully to a business context."

— **Steve Rundle,** *Crowell School of Business, Biola University;*
coauthor, Great Commission Companies

"*The Missional Entrepreneur* comes out at an opportune time as two major trends converge. More and more nations are closed to traditional preaching and church-planting missionaries, but they still welcome missionaries who can do something that the national government perceives to be 'useful'—like fixing teeth, or teaching English, or improving agricultural yield, or proliferating microbusinesses and other ways for locals to make a living.

"At the same time, more and more local churches want to make a difference in their country and in people's lives—this side of death. Mark Russell has practiced what he now preaches, and he has likely reflected upon the work of more missional entrepreneurs than anyone else. This book is destined to inspire, catalyze, and inform a generation of new-breed missionaries."

— **George G. Hunter III,** *School of World Mission and Evangelism,*
Asbury Theological Seminary

"Mark Russell's *The Missional Entrepreneur* is rooted in a holistic approach to business as mission. His analysis of two types of businesses—blessers and converters—is one of the most powerful arguments for holistic/integral mission that I've encountered. The book is worth getting for this chapter alone, although there is much more to savor as well."

— **Dewi Hughes,** *theological advisor, Tearfund*

"Mark L. Russell's global and cross-disciplinary experience enriches his book on business as mission (BAM). With great insight, he probes BAM from theological, historical, cross-cultural, and practical angles. This book is a significant contribution to the BAM movement."

— **Mats Tunehag,** *senior associate for business as mission, the Lausanne Movement and the World Evangelical Alliance Mission Commission*

"If you think you must give up your career or business to serve God, then think again. There are opportunities to use your business skills overseas, and Mark Russell will show you in Scripture both why and how you can be strategically involved in God's work. This book demonstrates that business and mission belong together!"

— **Russell S. Woodbridge,** *assistant professor, Southeastern Baptist Theological Seminary; theological educator, Kiev, Ukraine*

"*The Missional Entrepreneur* is broad in scope and yet remains accessible, providing a clear and comprehensive overview of business as mission and its significance for Christians today. Russell deftly draws together global and business realities with biblical foundations and mission strategy, constantly anchoring his text with stories and examples. Aspiring practitioners and business as mission veterans alike will find *The Missional Entrepreneur* both thought-provoking and practical. For newcomers to the subject of business as mission, this book would make for an excellent introduction."

— **Mark Plummer,** *director of the Introduction to Business as Mission course and cofounder of the Business as Mission Resource Team, Youth With A Mission International (YWAM)*

"*The Missional Entrepreneur* comes at just the right time as the business as mission movement continues to gain attention and momentum. Mark writes with clarity, relevance, and biblical wisdom, but most importantly, provides practical areas of application. Aspiring entrepreneurs, missions committees, and anyone interested in seeing business bring the good news to the world need to read this book!"

—**Peter Greer,** *president, HOPE International; coauthor,* The Poor Will Be Glad

"One might say that Mark Russell has given us the book we need on a topic whose time has come—except that actually the concept of business as mission has biblical roots as old as Abraham. In fact, this book emphasizes that the Abrahamic great commission of being a blessing to the nations can be fulfilled in as many creative ways as there are ways of doing honest business. The book is thoroughly biblical, showing dimensions of Paul's missional life, for example, that we easily overlook or misunderstand; but it is also very thoroughly researched in relation to today's globalized marketplace. Full of practical wisdom gained from wide experience in different cultures, the book is an inspiring introduction to the richly holistic understanding of mission that flows from a truly biblical integration of the creational and redemptive dimensions of our responsibility."

—**Christopher J. H. Wright,** *international director, Langham Partnership International; author,* The Mission of God

"*The Missional Entrepreneur* is a welcome addition to the exploration of the emerging concept of business as mission (BAM). Insights arising from Dr. Russell's extensive interviews of BAM practitioners are especially thought-provoking. The book's multifaceted discussion of BAM makes it indispensable reading for all interested in mission strategy."

—**Tetsunao Yamamori,** *president, WorldServe Ministries; coauthor,* On Kingdom Business

"Mark Russell has given us a vivid explanation of what business as mission is and how we can be involved. With practical and biblical insights, he shows us how to integrate work and mission, creation, and relationships. Mark's experiences and real-life stories will enlarge your vision and ignite your passion for BAM. This is a fun, informative, and easy read!"

—**Kent Humphreys,** *ambassador, FCCI/Christ@Work*

Dedication

This book is dedicated to my beautiful wife, Laurie,
the most incredible wife God could ever give me,
who has supported me in ways far too numerous to mention.
And to our children, Noah and Anastasia,
may they be missional in all they do.

the MISSIONAL ENTREPRENEUR

PRINCIPLES *and* PRACTICES *for* BUSINESS *as* MISSION

MARK L. RUSSELL

NEW HOPE
PUBLISHERS

BIRMINGHAM, ALABAMA

New Hope® Publishers
P. O. Box 12065
Birmingham, AL 35202-2065
www.newhopepublishers.com

New Hope Publishers is a division of WMU®.

Library of Congress Cataloging-in-Publication Data

Russell, Mark L., 1972-
  The missional entrepreneur : principles and practices for business as
mission / Mark L. Russell.
       p. cm.
  Includes bibliographical references and index.
  ISBN 978-1-59669-278-7 (sc)
  1. Missions. 2. Evangelistic work. 3. Business--Religious aspects--
Christianity. I. Title.
  BV2063.R79 2010
  266'.02--dc22

                              2009039289

Cover design: Arthur Cherry, www.arthuradesign.com
Interior design: Glynese Northam

ISBN-10: 1-59669-278-2
ISBN-13: 978-1-59669-278-7
N104141 • 0110 • 2M1

TABLE OF CONTENTS

ACKNOWLEDGMENTS

No book is written in isolation. Though my name stands on the cover as the author of this book, many people have helped shape and form this book in ways that have improved it tremendously.

My wife, *Laurie,* has listened to my ideas and processed my research with me in ways that helped me to articulate better what I want to say. Her wisdom enriches my life in ways words cannot express.

My brother, *Jeff,* a talented missional entrepreneur, has been my partner in many projects and has given me an understanding of the inner workings of international business, without which I could have never written this book.

Special thanks to my parents, *Lynn and Elaine Russell,* who not only helped me with time and input in the development of this book, but also taught me at an early age that this life is about so much more than money.

Dr. Terry Muck of Asbury Theological Seminary proved an exceptionally helpful mentor during my doctoral work. His input and conversations helped me to effectively process my research.

Finally, I must thank *New Hope Publishers.* Publisher *Andrea Mullins's* excitement for all things missional turned a "chance" meeting into this book. Editor *Randy Bishop's* patience and perseverance are to be commended. My thanks extend to the entire New Hope team of editors and marketers for their tireless work.

FOREWORD

Contemporary culture has become enamored with the "life coach." Many want (or are told they need) a therapist, counselor, mentor, philosopher, or leader to give them advice on particular matters. Sadly, many times these sources of advice do not dispense very good, much less Christian, counsel. It is rarely Bible-driven, God-centered, and Christ-exalting "coaching."

That is why I am happy to recommend Mark L. Russell's *The Missional Entrepreneur*. Russell serves as a reliable instructor for Christian men and women in the business world who wish to use their career and influence for God's glory and the advancement of Jesus's mission. Indeed, there are few books that address the everyday issue of how to make much of Christ in one's vocation.

One of the blessings of the Protestant Reformation was a renewed emphasis on this concept—living out one's *vocatio* (vocation) to the glory of God. For the reformers, there was no separation between the secular world and the spiritual world. They believed that one's vocation was his or her special calling. Thus, one could be called to do a variety of things, but each person was to have the great aim of glorifying God in those respected fields of service. Following the line of the reformers, Dutch theologian Abraham Kuyper much later stated, "There is not a square inch in the whole domain of our human existence over which Christ, who is Sovereign over *all*, does not cry, 'Mine!'"[1] And so, as Christ is Lord over all things, it is definitely worth our time to carefully meditate on how to glorify God in the area of work to which He has called us.

Russell writes with the analytical mind of a researcher, the business acumen of a professional, the heart of a pastor, and the zeal of a missionary.

His background, education, life experiences, and passions enable him to write authoritatively on this subject. He writes in chapter 2:

> *Recently I conducted a research survey at a large church in the south-eastern US. The results showed that 74 percent of the respondents saw little to no connection between their faith and their job. Of those who saw a connection, 64 percent were employees of a religious institution. Only 11 percent of respondents with a job in a nonreligious organization saw a connection between their faith and their employment. Furthermore, even those 11 percent reported a lack of confidence and fulfillment in their ability to integrate their faith at work.*

Based upon this research, Russell goes on to assert, "It seems that church leaders are not teaching their congregations how to integrate their faith and their job." As a pastor, I do not take offense to this. Instead, I rejoice that someone is writing about it, because it seems to be so true. While I have preached more than once on "a biblical perspective of work," I have longed for a book to put in the hands of our businessmen and women in order to help them use their "tentmaking" job for the good of the kingdom. Thanks for your ever-so-needed resource, Mark. May God continue to stir up the hearts of His people to live missional lives for His glory and the good of the lost world.

Dr. Tony Merida, *teaching pastor, Temple Baptist Church, Hattiesburg, Mississippi*

part 1

FUNDAMENTALS

chapter 1

INTRODUCTION TO BUSINESS AS MISSION

Wall Street and Main Street have not been on the friendliest of terms recently. In early 2009, with the world economy in recession, the US government dispersed more than a trillion dollars in bailout monies, only to have executives at AIG redistribute $165 million or so to themselves for what they called contractually obligated executive bonuses.

In June 2009, in a humiliating fall from grace, General Motors, the world's biggest carmaker for much of the twentieth century, announced that it would have to file for chapter 11 bankruptcy protection. The move left thousands unemployed. Investment banks are collapsing, stress is in the air, and it's everyone else's fault.

Throughout history, business has brought people together and pulled them apart. It has helped humankind progress while also revealing our darkest impulses. In the past 20 to 30 years, our world has become interdependent like never before. This recent phenomenon of incredible interconnectedness is referred to as globalization and is driven by the three ITs.

Information Technology: We can communicate further, faster, and cheaper than ever before.

Inexpensive Travel: For just a couple thousand dollars, you can go anywhere in the world in about a day or less. If that sounds expensive or slow, then you have been seriously affected by the relative ease of our world today.

International Trade: We are selling our products everywhere and are buying products from everywhere. We are in a world where international trade is now a normative part of all businesses.

The engine that drives globalization is the economy. As a result, if one cares about this world—and, hey, I know a God who loves the world—then we have to care about the economy and what its impact is. Right now, our economy is broken and those who care about this world have to care about that.

My wife, Laurie, and I lived in Munich, Germany, for several years. There, we discovered that Germans, by and large, do not have built-in closets. In place of closets they use *schranks*: large pieces of furniture that function like a closet, something like an armoire, only a lot bigger.

They are huge pieces of furniture and for novices, as we were, they are quite complex to assemble. After spending hours putting ours together we realized we had made several mistakes. Thankfully, however, the schrank was functional. Breaking it down and putting it back together again was just out of the question. It would be too much work. But over time the imperfections of our assembly job became annoying. It didn't look right and the doors were awkward.

A year later, we moved. Moving is always a lot of work and presents many challenges. But we were excited for one reason: we had a strategic opportunity to rebuild the schrank the way it should have been in the first place. Right now, our economy is broken. This is a strategic opportunity to rebuild the economy the way it should have been in the first place. But to rebuild a broken economy, we have to understand that we live in a broken world.

Four Realms of Brokenness

The Bible begins with God creating the world, giving life to Adam and Eve, assigning them tasks, and walking with them in the Garden of Eden. However, in the biblical account of events, this situation does not last very long. Deceived by the serpent, Eve eats the fruit of the forbidden tree and Adam, knowing better, follows her lead. The result is what is historically called the Fall of humankind. There were several curses that came about due to the Fall. These curses demonstrate areas of brokenness in our world. The four realms of brokenness are:

- *Abundance:* God gave Adam and Eve access to abundant resources (Genesis 1:28–29) for their well-being. With the Fall, these resources became scarce (Genesis 3:17).
- *Relationships:* God created Eve since it was not good for Adam to be alone. We were created for fruitful relationships. With the Fall, these relationships became contentious (Genesis 3:16).
- *Creation:* God created a world that was "very good" (Genesis 1:31). With the Fall, humankind's relationship with the rest of creation became antagonistic (Genesis 3:17–19).
- *Spiritual:* Adam and Eve were created to be in relationship with God. With the Fall, this relationship was fractured (Genesis 3:23–24).

These four areas of brokenness refer to, in more contemporary language, four spheres of life: economic (the provision of goods and services to humankind), social (relationship and community with one another), environmental (creation and our relationship to it), and spiritual (our unique relationship with the triune God). All of these areas are broken.

God is on a mission to reconcile all four realms of brokenness. God's mission of reconciliation has come to us through Jesus Christ: "For God was pleased to have all his fullness dwell in [Christ], and through [Christ] to reconcile to himself all things, whether things on earth or things in heaven, by making peace through his blood, shed on the cross" (Colossians 1:19–20).

Christ humbly came to earth and called us into God's mission for the reconciliation of all things, to bring forth the kingdom of God, and to ensure that God's will is "done on earth as it is in heaven." This is a *big* mission and followers of Christ should be humbled that we have the privilege of participating in it.

Figure 1.1

FOUR AREAS OF BROKENNESS AND GOD'S MISSION

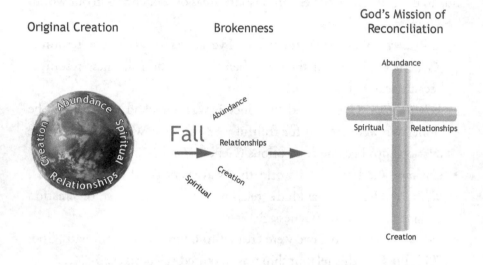

Original Creation | Brokenness | God's Mission of Reconciliation

Generally, when we talk about God's mission, there is a focus on the aforementioned spiritual aspect of the world's brokenness, namely our fractured relationship with God Himself. Churches everywhere rightly emphasize that only Christ can restore this relationship. May we never dismiss or underemphasize this foundational truth for life and eternity.

However, in many places, there is no direct talk about healing the other three areas of brokenness or any acknowledgement that this necessary healing is also part of the mission to which God has called us. And even when there is that recognition, there is often an absence of any tangible, real-life solution or response.

Thankfully, there is change in the air and much of it is good. Christians everywhere are waking up to the tremendous oppression that comes through poverty, hunger, lack of clean water, preventable diseases, absence of education, environmental degradation, and other social problems that are simply reflections of these aforementioned areas of brokenness.

Boise Fry Company

There are numerous enterprises seeking to impact these areas of brokenness, and followers of Christ are making a tremendous difference in a variety of ways. I'd like to highlight just one such business, located right where I live in Boise, Idaho. Blake Lingle has two goals for the Boise Fry Company (BFC), the restaurant he founded: 1) make amazing fries and burgers and 2) operate an ethical business that reflects his relationship with Christ. This means he tries to help the poor, protect the Earth, and treat all people — employees and customers alike — as Christ would.

How does he do it? Lingle realized that refugees are some of the poorest, most disenfranchised people in America. Since government aid stops only months after arrival, he told me, refugees who do not quickly find a job can face dire circumstances. So, he has intentionally sought out needy refugees and provided them with on-the-job training and employment at BFC.

That is not all the company does. BFC also tries to minimize its impact on the environment, God's creation. The hospitality industry is a big polluter, particularly restaurants, which buy, make, and trash lots of products. When BFC began, Lingle made a conscious decision to buy organic, sustainable, and biodegradable products in an effort to become one of the few 100 percent green restaurants in the United States. Some of their green products and equipment include: biodegradable fry cones, napkins, and to-go cups, as well as energy-efficient freezers and refrigerators and low-wattage, energy-efficient light bulbs. Furthermore, excess potatoes are recycled to grow more potatoes and used peanut oil is recycled as fuel in cars.

Lingle also believes that a healthy earth makes for a healthy body. Many modern farming practices rely on chemicals, additives, and pesticides. Nutrients can be lost from perfectly good foods. That, coupled with the preservatives added to most processed foods can make for unhealthy meals. In Lingle's opinion, pesticides and preservatives are as much to blame for the obesity epidemic as saturated fats. So, at BFC, when feasible and/or affordable, local, natural, and organic foods are purchased. Also, everything is prepared in house, which lessens the need to use preservatives. And finally, the humble fare isn't adulterated with unnecessary ingredients and fat. For example, potatoes and peanut oil are the only ingredients in the company's fries. According to Lingle, other fast-food fries are likely to contain ingredients such as partially hydrogenated oils, wheat and milk derivatives, preservatives, antifoaming agents, dextrose, and salt. As I talked with him, Lingle shared that he views these decisions as part of the mandate to love his neighbor.

Understanding and appreciating people, both employees and customers, is the cornerstone for most ethical, successful businesses. In a plethora of small ways, Lingle and his team at BFC have used a fast-food restaurant to slowly but surely restore the four areas of brokenness in their corner of the world.

Figure 1.2

BAM SWEET SPOT OF SYNERGY

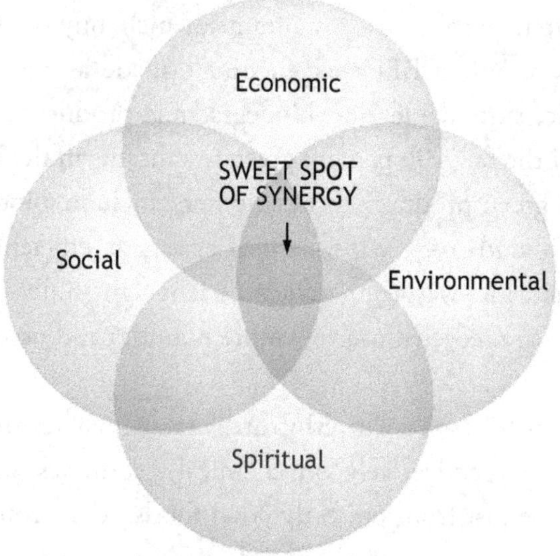

Economic

SWEET SPOT
OF SYNERGY
↓

Social

Environmental

Spiritual

Social = Hiring refugees

Environmental = Serving healthy, organic food and using biodegradable products and energy-efficient appliances

Spiritual = Loving employees and customers as Christ would

Economic = Operating a profitable and thriving business that benefits the owners, employees, and community

Reconciling these four areas of brokenness is our mission, and this book is dedicated to the unique way in which business can be an instrument of reconciliation in these areas. That is business as mission.

Never the Two Shall Meet?

As an undergraduate student at Auburn University, I felt directionless because I was simultaneously interested in the business world while sensing a strong call to vocational ministry. I was majoring in business management and, as a part of my studies, I traveled to Guatemala to study Spanish. My experience in Guatemala transformed my view of the world. I came back and changed my program to focus on international business. As quickly as I could, I returned to Latin America to the country of Paraguay where I furthered my studies. Despite my increased interest in other cultures and overseas experiences, I still had no clear direction as to where I was headed vocationally.

At the end of my studies, I went to Russia for one year through a Christian organization to teach ethics in a public school. This experience solidified my calling to overseas Christian ministry. I returned to the States and completed a master of divinity at Trinity Evangelical Divinity School. Though I was excited about this direction in my life, I continued to be dismayed and sometimes frustrated that I could not also pursue my interests in the world of business.

At this same time, my younger brother, Jeff, was approaching graduation at Georgia Tech and was experiencing the same dilemma I had faced years earlier: whether to pursue business or missions. Jeff felt directed by God to go into business but with a missional focus. He shared this sense of direction to me, and I can remember distinctly thinking that God was speaking through Jeff to me that He wanted me to work at bringing the worlds of business and missions together.

Over the years I have lived in Russia, Chile, and Germany, traveled to more than 70 countries, consulted on scores of projects, and have worked to develop various projects using business professionals in effective local and cross-cultural ministry as well as in cross-cultural overseas missions. Though I originally thought we might be the only people in the world integrating business and God's mission, I soon learned that lots of people around the world are engaging business as mission or at least attempting to do so.

Business as mission (BAM) is an emerging term and a developing concept. There has been much fascination in both missions and business circles with the concept of strategically using business to accomplish missional purposes. Conferences and consultations have been held around the world. As a frequent participant it has become clear to me that though the term is ubiquitous in missions circles, its meaning varies greatly from person to person and organization to organization.

As a result, in 2005, my exceptionally understanding wife, Laurie, and I moved to Kentucky so that I could pursue a PhD at Asbury Theological Seminary. My specific intent was to gain a better understanding of God's mission in the world and how that might relate to business. I read about the practices of business through the centuries and how theologians and church leaders treated the concept of business and its role in the mission of God.

For my PhD dissertation I did an in-depth research study of business as mission in a single cultural context, namely Chiang Mai, Thailand. This research project was a multiyear project involving 12 businesses and 128 interviews. I focused on missional entrepreneurs who were living cross-culturally in Thailand and self-identified (though not necessarily publicly) as Christian missionaries.

During my time at Asbury, I joined HOPE International, a Christian microfinance organization that works in 15 countries around the world and with more than 250,000 clients. Through my job there as director of spiritual integration, I continued to explore the possibilities of economic interventions to heal the four areas of the world's brokenness.

In conversations, I have realized that there is a lot of confusion over what BAM really is, or, perhaps better put, what it really should be. So, that is why I've written this book: to add what I hope is a clarifying and helpful voice to this important and much-debated topic.

In this first chapter, it will be useful to examine some areas that can give us a common reference and clearer understanding moving forward.

Understanding God's Mission

The words *mission* and *missions* are used interchangeably by many people, but for missiologists they carry distinct meanings.

Mission: God's overarching purposes in the world.

Missions: The local outworkings of Christians partnering with God in His mission.

To this point, I have been largely referring to mission or God's purposes and goals for this world. Some groups consider mission and missions only as church planting and evangelism (CPE) in parts of the world where Christians are a significant minority. I call this CPE missions to reflect the priority given to church planting and evangelism by those who take this approach, which reflects a primary emphasis on the spiritual area of brokenness. While I too emphasize and advocate for mission and missions to include a robust witness for Christ, I have come to see God's mission and His vision for missions to be something much bigger and more encompassing than producing professions of belief. He desires to see faith and love through our actions and that those actions produce real change for the sake of His mission of love and reconciliation to a broken world. I believe business can serve this mission.

It is also worth noting that missions is frequently used to specify work done in cross-cultural settings. Undoubtedly, there is much to be done cross-culturally and as a lover of travel, languages, and cultures, I personally default to cross-cultural ministry out of preference. But followers of Christ do not have to cross cultures to engage in God's mission. They can do so anywhere and at any time. In this book, we will look at a lot of cross-cultural situations and explore the cross-cultural implications of BAM. But I believe that BAM can be done by anyone, anywhere, and at anytime.

An emerging term in the church today that reflects my deeply held belief that all followers of Christ can and should be on mission with God is *missional*. Being missional is about living in a state of being that is at the center of God's mission wherever you are. Every Christian, every leader, and every church should be missional. A person who lives on mission and starts up a business(es) in order to live out that mission is a *missional entrepreneur.*

At times the personal mission of these missional entrepreneurs will cause them to get on planes, go to faraway places, learn foreign languages, and raise their children in different cultures. But that is not necessary. You can be a missional entrepreneur anywhere. There are many missional entrepreneurs where I live in Boise, Idaho. I admire and respect them tremendously.

I know missional entrepreneurs in Kabul, Cairo, and the Congo. Every place has needs and missional entrepreneurs can rise to the occasion and meet those needs wherever God leads and directs them. Thankfully, God is working through His church in many ways. I take it to be a spiritual indicator that He wants us to take business seriously as an instrument to be used for His glory and the restoration of a broken world.

What Is Business as Mission?

Several terms are used for business as mission, generally referred to by the acronym BAM. Here are seven existing paradigms of BAM:[1]
- Business *and* mission — two separate activities.
- Business *for* mission — funding mission through the profits of business.

- Mission *in* business—seeking to lead unbelieving employees to faith in Christ. This reflects a CPE understanding of mission.
- Business *as a platform for* mission—work and professional life as a means of channeling mission throughout the world.
- Business *in* missions—business as a means to proclaim Christ in cross-cultural settings. This reflects CPE missions and a preference for working in unevangelized parts of the world.
- Business *as a cover for* missions—business as a means simply to obtain a visa. No real business is actually operated. This reflects a CPE missions mind-set. (The dangers of this approach will be discussed extensively in chapter 9.)
- Business *as* mission—business as a vehicle of the mission of God in the world.

My preference for the term *BAM* is that it be reserved for the understanding that business has a tremendous role to play in God's mission to reconcile the four areas of brokenness in our world. However, I understand that many of my brothers and sisters in Christ have different understandings, which is why I find the categories above helpful. Rather than using one term for seven different things without clarification, it is better to specifically state and define the different understandings people hold.

Holistic Thinking

I believe more and more followers of Christ are realizing that God calls us to be salt and light and to be on mission with Him everywhere. This includes the marketplace. Even though there has been an ongoing recognition throughout church history that Christians are called to do this, there is an upsurge in activity in recent years that makes one wonder what God is up to? Even before we delve too deeply into our topic, I believe it may be helpful to consider what the future might hold for BAM. Where are these waves of changes taking us?

We are living in times of major socio-cultural change. This is so obvious and well documented that it does not need to be elaborated on here. These changes are not just in the travel, communication, and technology sectors of life, but are also affecting people's religious perspectives and changing their religious preferences and orientations.

One of the primary changes occurring today is in how people view life. As our world has rapidly become a global village, ways of thinking are being exposed, analyzed, and changed. Particularly in the Western world, in the period of modernization, people once viewed life in terms of categories. Among the many changes brought by the emergence of postmodernism and globalization is the shift to noncategorical thinking. In the future, people's worldviews will be increasingly holistic. Actually, this holistic worldview is often already characteristic of many non-Western cultures. People of all backgrounds are likely to see life in a more integrated fashion in the years to come.

Revolutionary Everyday Faith

Researcher and author George Barna has examined many of these trends and how they may specifically affect the church in the US. In his book *Revolution* he writes that his research indicates there is a growing subnation of more than 20 million people who are devout Christians but "have no use for churches that play religious games." They can no longer stand for lifeless, fruitless, Spirit-less worship and ministry.[2] He adds that 91 percent of Americans who identify themselves as born again "possess a patchwork of theological views and rarely rely upon those perspectives to inform their daily decisions."[3] These statistics point to a seeming disconnect between religious faith and real life in practice and teaching that has produced a significant sense of disenchantment with "traditional church."

Nevertheless, Barna says that about 70 percent of all Americans still rely on a local congregation as their primary source for their spiritual life. He says about 5 percent of the population relies on an alternative faith community, 5 percent on their family, and approximately 20 percent have turned to various cultural sources such as the media, the arts, or other institutions to satisfy their spiritual needs. What is most interesting is where Barna thinks this is heading. He projects that by 2025, only about one-third will rely on local congregations.[4] Barna cites our insistent desire to have "customized experiences" as the primary motivation.[5] But he also adds that people are searching for "practical faith experiences, rather than generic, conceptual faith; a quest for spiritual depth and breadth, rather than settling for one dimension or the other."[6]

Here, it seems to me, Barna is touching on something significant. As our culture is changing, it is exposing and magnifying some of the weaknesses of many Christian faith traditions, particularly that church and religion have been promoted as an important *part* of people's lives as opposed to a *way of life* that is integral to all spheres of one's existence.

This is why a lot of business professionals are drawn to the concept of business as mission. They have a tremendous level of discontent with a "church on Sunday, rest of life on Monday" type of approach. They want to live their faith every day including through their professional work. Business as mission is a strategic framework for the church to engage and empower business professionals.

In the future, people will not be content, nor should they be, in living a fractured life of church on Sunday and employment throughout the week. If the church fails to act, its ability to impact society and transform lives will significantly decrease. However, if we develop empowering frameworks that help people integrate their faith with their jobs, then we are likely to not only see more people interested in our faith, but also a more accurate and compelling outworking of the ideals of the faith in the routines of life.

We have an opportunity to expand our understanding and capacity of what we mean by religious leadership. This is the occasion to which God is calling the BAM movement. BAM is about expanding our understanding of God's mission and expanding our vision for who should be engaged in God's mission.

Principles for Business as Mission

Chapters 2–4 are an abbreviated theology of business. Business has a spiritual mission, and God has special purposes for it. These chapters explore how business can be an instrument in providing for humanity, an avenue to serve others, a place to exercise one's gifts and skills, and a vehicle of reconciliation. Obviously, business can be an instrument of evil and exploitation. But this is all the reason why we need to understand God's purposes for it. We cannot simply let business remain in its broken state.

In chapters 5–7 we will look closely at the life of the Apostle Paul. Most church folk have probably heard somewhere that Paul was a tentmaker. But it is not something that many people have reflected on very much. In these chapters, we will look at Paul's world, his life, and the meaning of his work as a tentmaker. Paul was an evangelist and a church planter, but what emerges from these chapters is a picture of an entrepreneur who was on mission with God. Though his personal mission was to introduce the gospel in new locations, he was a missional entrepreneur who understood the importance of work and business in people's lives and for the young Christian church.

Figure 1.3

PRINCIPLES AND PRACTICES FOR BUSINESS AS MISSION

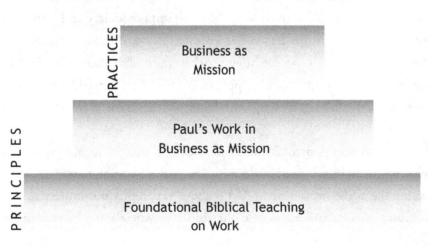

Practices for Business as Mission

From there we move to a more concentrated focus on best practices for BAM today. In chapter 8 I examine some historical precedents for BAM activities. These provide an almost continual lineage from the Apostle Paul to us today. We will also look at some of the contemporary and emerging developments in BAM. In chapter 9 we will shift to exploring why many missionaries as well as business professionals choose to launch entrepreneurial business ventures in foreign lands. What are their motivations? And how do those motivations influence their activities and results? In this chapter we will also discuss the pitfalls of using fake or "cover" businesses simply as a deceptive means to obtain a visa.

In chapter 10 I present models of two missionary families engaged in BAM. Though the names and details are changed, these families are essentially composites of real-life missionaries whom I studied as a part of my PhD research in Chiang Mai, Thailand. In chapter 11 we will explore the reasons why the two families had different experiences and see how that relates to their motivations and their understanding of mission. It will be important to note the differences between blessers and converters.

In chapter 12 we explore the importance of defining goals, vision, and strategy and what those look like in missional entrepreneurial ventures. We will explore many of the pitfalls in strategy, including the absence of a strategy. Since so much BAM takes place in cross-cultural contexts, it is necessary to take a serious look at what it means to work cross-culturally, which we will do in chapter 13. My experience and research have shown that only a minority of missional entrepreneurs in cross-cultural settings have a deep understanding and ability to articulate the differences between cultures, much less actually make effective adaptations in behavior to their new culture. Yet this is a pivotal ingredient for success.

In chapter 14 we explore many of the inherent challenges in doing business in foreign cultures with multiple goals as well as multiple competitors. What are we to do when followers of Christ are in competition with one another? In many parts of the world, because of a fondness for particular business strategies, missional entrepreneurs find themselves with lots of competition. I conclude this part of the book in chapter 15 by examining some issues relevant to BAM and missions agencies. Missions agencies around the world are actively launching businesses and promoting entrepreneurial activity. While this is exciting, it is important to think through our motivations, as well as a number of potential challenges and problems, and to reflect deeply on the consequences of our decisions and actions.

Missional leadership needs to be understood in order to be a missional entrepreneur. In chapter 16 we look at the biblical purposes for leadership and how this should shape the missional entrepreneur. Finally, in chapter 17 we will look at the issue of offshoring. We are living in global times, and we are in an interconnected and interdependent world. The contemporary trend of BAM has often been focused on business activity in foreign countries. Offshoring is a confusing and controversial topic. It is therefore, worthwhile, to look at this unique issue from a biblical perspective and see what conclusions can be drawn.

Questions for Reflection & Discussion

1. How should we view work considering that the Bible opens with God working?

2. How has work become distorted as a result of the Fall?

3. How can business manifest the original purposes of work?

4. How has business become distorted as a result of the Fall?

5. What is our primary mission as followers of Christ?

chapter 2

THE FOUNDATIONS OF BUSINESS

"I don't know if it's fair. I don't make the rules."

Those were the words of then AT&T CEO Robert Allen in response to a reporter's question regarding the company's 1995 reorganization, which resulted in the firing of approximately 40,000 workers. One can be empathetic to Mr. Allen's situation and the difficulty of managing such a large organization during a financial downturn in which decisions have ramifications for thousands and repercussions for years. With a bit more time and thought, perhaps Mr. Allen could have phrased his response a little better.

Sadly, his comment seems to reflect the level of thinking most people give to the virtue of their on-the-job decisions as well as to the inherent value of their work. Through the years I have worked in various countries with scores of businessmen and women. My primary desire has been to understand their world better so I could help them integrate their Christian faith with what they did on a daily basis. It has been my experience that most people, when initially faced with the question, "How does your faith relate to your work?" respond in a fashion not dissimilar to that of Mr. Allen. The typical gesture is a blank look or shrugged shoulders. Common responses are "I just work here" or "I need the money."

Recently, I conducted a research survey at a large church in the southeastern US. The results showed that 74 percent of the respondents saw little to no connection between their faith and their job. Of those who saw a connection, 64 percent were employees of a religious institution.

Only 11 percent of respondents with a job in a nonreligious organization saw a connection between their faith and their employment. Furthermore, even those 11 percent reported a lack of confidence and fulfillment in their ability to integrate their faith at work.

It seems that church leaders are not teaching their congregations how to integrate their faith and their job. Robert Wuthnow in *God and Mammon in America* cites an informal poll of church members in which 90 percent of the people reported they had never heard a sermon relating faith to employment. Only 40 percent of those surveyed for the more systematic Economic Values Study had been inspired to work harder through a sermon within the past year.[1] Wuthnow also finds that when clergy do discuss work, it is viewed as a place for self-expression rather than an opportunity for serving or loving others.

Authors Laura Nash and Scotty McLennan find that clergy tend to juxtapose happiness in one's faith with happiness in wealth and success: "Most conceptions of religious happiness [articulated by clergy] turned out be subtractive in form: spending less time at work and more with family, needing less money, buying fewer consumer items. At no time were the potential contributions of business seen as a path to faithfulness or the happiness of faithfulness."[2]

Nash and McLennan conclude that the sum of these perceptions results in a large gap between clergy and business professionals, which prevents a shared understanding about religious faith and business. I think it can be accurately stated that many clergy tend to minister as if they believe that the church has no business discussing business.

A purposeful discussion is therefore necessary to bridge this gap and to develop a meaningful way for clergy and business professionals alike to interact with one another and to integrate the apparently dichotomized but actually interrelated spheres of faith and business. It has become increasingly clear to me that thoughtful reflection and dialogue on these themes must exponentially increase for the church to serve its members and for Christ followers to meaningfully integrate faith and work.

A Spiritual Life

Through the years religion and economic enterprise have had a strained yet sometimes inappropriately strong relationship. Think about Jesus's outrage when He threw over tables and cleared the money changers from the temple (Matthew 21, Mark 11, John 2). In light of His unwillingness to fight against those who captured and crucified Him, even to the point of rebuking Peter for doing so (Matthew 26, Mark 14, Luke 22, John 18), as well as His general peaceful demeanor and refrain that peacemakers will be children of God (Matthew 5:9), it is noteworthy that economic exploitation in a religious setting drove Him to such an outburst.

Unfortunately, the Christian religion through the centuries has not always rejected what Jesus rejected. One of the motivating factors for the Crusades was to bring wealth and resources back to the "Christian countries." Martin Luther later protested the profits the church made from acts of penance. Turn on your television right now (well, wait till you're done reading) and you'll probably find some preacher promising prosperity in exchange for a relatively small financial donation to his or her ministry. (If you can't understand what he or she is saying, look for the message with the phone number scrolling across the bottom of the screen.) These abuses certainly contribute to people's generally negative reaction to mixing religion with money and business.

There is also a further complication that I have faced when discussing business in the context of religion. Frequently when I mention to someone that I am working on faith and business issues, the common assumption is that I am attempting to develop a new way of financing the church's activities, such as a fund-raising technique or strategy. As needed as this is, it is not my present concern. My focus is how our faith is expressed through and empowers business, not vice versa.

A mission is an assigned task, duty, or calling. It is my contention that business as a whole has assigned tasks, duties, and callings. Furthermore, these assigned tasks, duties, and callings are spiritual in nature. To be spiritual in nature means to *live out the highest purpose(s) and deepest meaning of an activity in such a way that aligns our ethical understanding, moral conscience, and actual behavior with our created design.* Business is a product of our natural, created order and should be carried out in such a way that it fulfills its spiritual purpose.

Really What Is Business?

Business is a common term with broad meaning. However, it can be, at times, more exclusive than inclusive in nature. For instance, I've noticed when I speak on business in diverse settings that most people think the term does not relate to them. At times, people whom I consider business professionals, because they work in a for-profit business, have asked me what "businesspeople" think on certain issues. When I've told them that they should tell me since they are a "businessperson," frequently they respond with something like, "Oh, I'm not a businessperson; I'm just an engineer." Such comments imply a too narrow view of business, as if it only includes certain functions such as sales, marketing, and perhaps consulting.

At other times business is discussed in such a way that is assumed to be the functional equivalent of work, employment, or other organizational systems. This is too broad. To have a meaningful discussion of the spiritual mission of business it is, therefore, necessary to define precisely what one means when the term *business* is employed (pun intended).

Business is as ubiquitous as it is amorphous. It is difficult to define because it is everywhere. It is probably easiest to start with saying what it is not. Business is not synonymous with work, though work is clearly integral to the functions of business. Work, as a topic, is clearly more broad than business. Work relates to all types of human activity directed toward making or doing something. This is a part of life that is important to all, whether they be scientists, politicians, doctors, or business professionals. Business, of course, is consumed with work and theological discussions of its nature will tend to have extensive overlap with similar conversations on the theology of work. However, there are aspects that are unique to business and distinguish it from the more general category of work.

Work and business are also not the same as employment. Employment is usually understood to involve financial payment. Business pertains to many jobs functioning as a collective whole. Employment relates to a singular job. Furthermore, many people have meaningful employment in areas that are not related to business, such as educational institutions, nonprofit organizations, and government agencies. Therefore, theological discourses on business will, again, broadly extend into the same territory as employment, yet they should remain distinct.

While we are at it, it is also helpful to distinguish between work and employment. My mother, who has not been employed since my oldest sibling was born, is one of the hardest workers I have ever known. She cared for my three siblings and me, and, if you knew my two brothers, you would realize that this was no small task and took immense work. (I of course made life quite easy for her.) Furthermore, she helped maintain our small family farm in humid Mississippi through the boiling summers, feeding horses and the like. She wrote Bible studies (more work) and taught at church (tough work). She functioned as a taxi driver taking us to an assortment of childhood activities (lots of work). All the while, my father drove to a university where he, among other things, sat in air-conditioned offices, chatted with colleagues at the coffee pot, and made money doing things I never really understood, like writing textbooks on thermodynamics. To be fair, my father definitely worked, but so did my mother. Work is not the same thing as employment.

In summary, business is related to but not synonymous with work and employment. It is also so broad and expansive in nature so as to evade easy definition. This paradoxically means it is perceived sometimes quite narrowly, as only relating to certain types of organizations or jobs.

So, let's say what business is. Business is, at its most fundamental level, the creation and distribution of goods and services. But this is also the broadest definition and, in that sense, is not altogether helpful. A theological educational institution is also about the creation and distribution of goods and services. In this sense it is a business. But its nonprofit status and emphasis on education make it different from what is commonly thought of as business. The same is true of hospitals, government agencies, and other nonprofit organizations. So, for our purposes we will limit the scope of business somewhat and define it as *an organization that creates and/or distributes goods and/or services and relies on financial profit for survival, success, and expansion capability.*

I have included the aspect of financial profit because it is an important facet that distinguishes businesses from other organizations. Business is about creating wealth. This is one of its most fundamental attributes as well as its most controversial. The creation of wealth and the concept of profits produce an internal tension that is felt by most spiritually inclined people, whether they are ministers or business professionals. Jesus expressed the inherent tension when He said, "No one can serve two masters. Either he will hate the one and love the other, or he will be devoted to the one and despise the other. You cannot serve both God and Money" (Matthew 6:24). This tension must, and will, be dealt with in order to reach a rich understanding of the spiritual mission of business.

Work: What Is It Good For?

Jesuit priest Pierre Teilhard de Chardin reportedly said, "We are not human beings having a spiritual experience. We are spiritual beings having a human experience." This statement reflects my fundamental assertion: Business should not be viewed as a tool to get through life, rather it should be considered an opportunity for spiritual living. We need to reorient our natural inclinations from the visible realm to the invisible one and realize that our faith and spiritual mission are integral to the visible human world.

Understanding the concepts of *fundamental* and *instrumental* value is critical to what I'm saying. Something of fundamental value means that it has inherent worth and its worth is not dependent on what it can do. Having instrumental value means that something's worth is solely determined by what it does or produces.

Many people think that business is of purely instrumental value. In other words, business is a means to an end, not an end in and of itself.

However, we need to recognize that business is of both fundamental and instrumental value.

Living and working in business is, as we shall see, a way that we partner with God and live according to our created purpose. This gives it fundamental value. But business is also a means by which we produce and distribute goods and services allowing us to take care of one another and do other good works outside of the sphere of business. Thus business also has instrumental value. It is, unfortunate, however, that most people only see the instrumental value of work and business.

Through the centuries people's perspectives on work have varied. Work has been elevated (think Karl Marx) and disdained (think teenagers cleaning up after a party). Regardless, work was originally viewed as a divine action. This view of work as a spiritual activity has been present throughout church history and was prominently emphasized by groups such as the Benedictines and the Puritans.

The Bible opens in Genesis 1 with the creation account. As the Scriptures say, God worked for six days to form the heavens and earth and everything in it.[3] It is worth noting that there are many possible interpretations of the creation account in Genesis. Nevertheless, it would be difficult to remove the clear implications of work as a divine activity. Genesis 2:2 explicitly states that God finished His work and rested on the seventh day. This makes clear that the creation of the universe was to be perceived as work. At the end of Genesis 1, God creates humans in His image. In a very real sense this means, among other things, that humans were created to imitate God in certain respects, including work. After creating humans, God gives them the command to work (Genesis 1:26–28). Consider the flow of the passage: God worked; He created humans in his image; He directed the humans to go work. In the first two chapters of Genesis there are seven principles that should inform our view of work today:

1. Through work we are to be stewards of the earth (Genesis 1:28; 2:5–8, 15).
2. Using tools and making tools are an integral part of human existence (Genesis 2:15).

3. We are to be self-sustainers and producers, remembering God is the ultimate Provider (Genesis 1:28–30; 2:9).
4. We are to be appreciators of beauty (Genesis 2:9).
5. We are to work in partnership with one another (Genesis 2:18).
6. We are to work in partnership with our Creator (Genesis 2:19–20).
7. Work is fundamentally good, a source of joy, and makes rest enjoyable (Genesis 1:31–2:3).

In his critique of Adam Smith, considered by many the father of the modern economy, Karl Marx, considered by many the father of Communism, alludes to the fact that Smith inherited from the Bible the idea that work should be viewed as a curse.[4] This idea of work as a curse has been prevalent throughout the centuries and remnants of this way of thinking are still found in church pews everywhere. However, it should be reemphasized that God worked and passed the work baton to humans before there are any mentions of any type of curse in the biblical account. Work is therefore best understood as an intrinsic part of our human spiritual experience. It is not the result of a curse. In fact it is the exact opposite; it is a blessing, part of our role in the world and something that we can do to serve each other, God, and the rest of creation.

This is not to say that weariness and dreariness are not aspects of work in our present situation. It is natural at times that work will not seem so spiritual. While writing this I became aware that I had a flat tire and spent a couple of hours changing the tire, going to get it fixed, etc. This did not feel like a spiritual exercise, especially since I enjoy writing about other people doing such a thing more than actually doing it myself. However, in the middle of the endeavor I realized that what I was doing was spiritual, and this helped me adapt my attitude and appreciate the experience, even if it was not exactly the way I prefer to spend my mornings. Now this may not strike you as particularly spiritual. How does "wasting" a day repairing a tire qualify as spiritual? It is spiritual in the sense that I was partnering with God by fixing and repairing a part of creation that is beneficial for contemporary life on this planet. For work to be spiritual it does not need to be anymore dramatic than that.

The difficulty and unpleasantness associated with work, according to the Genesis account, can be attributed to the wrongdoings of humanity. In Genesis 3:17, in response to Adam's violation of His commands, God told him, "Cursed is the ground because of you; through painful toil you will eat of it all the days of your life." Thus there is a scriptural warrant for saying that work to a degree is cursed. But what is most important to notice is that work was first and foremost a divine activity and that God invited humans to imitate Him by working.

Work is truly a part of our essence. We are spiritual beings created by the Spiritual Being to do spiritual things and that includes work. In the beginning, work was a spiritual exercise. A lot has changed since the beginning. Adam and Eve failed to maintain God's moral standard, resulting in the Fall. The world's population has grown and professions have proliferated. Sin has expanded into all human endeavor, perhaps most obviously in business. Yet, despite ever-changing job descriptions and sin's multiplication, work and business have not lost their spiritual core.

Partnering with the Creator

One of the most notable things about the Genesis creation account, seen in all of Scripture actually, is that God desires to work through humans to carry out His mission in the world. Consider the creation of human beings. God created Adam and Eve in two distinct ways: Adam from dirt and Eve from Adam's rib. He was undoubtedly capable of creating more human beings in innumerable ways. However, instead of making human beings *ad nauseum* by Himself, He invited Adam, Eve, and their descendants to do so with Him. His first command was to "be fruitful and increase in number" (Genesis 1:28).

No person of faith in their right mind thinks that humans are creating humans by themselves. We contribute the easiest and most simple part of it (at least males do) and understand that God is doing the mysterious and miraculous part. As the Apostle Paul said, "So neither he who plants nor he who waters is anything, but only God, who makes things grow" (1 Corinthians 3:7). So it is with creating a child. We have our part, but God is the One who makes the child grow.

This has become increasingly more real to me as I have become a parent. Watching our children being formed in my wife's womb, through ultrasound technology, produced a tremendous sense of humility within me. I realized that I had done so little, yet God had allowed us to partner with Him in the extraordinary and awesome task of bringing a new child into the world. Though human beings have played their part in reproducing since the time of Adam and Eve, it is clear that God "from one man [has] made every nation of men, that they should inhabit the whole earth" (Acts 17:26). Thus we are partners with God or as Paul said, "We are God's fellow workers" (1 Corinthians 3:9).

This concept is not limited to childbearing but also extends to other forms of work. God created the entire universe without any human help. Paul makes clear, "[God] is not served by human hands, as if he needed anything, because he himself gives all men life and breath and everything else" (Acts 17:25). Yet clearly He created humans so that we could partner with Him in continuing His work in the world.

In Genesis 2, the idea of work as partnership with God becomes increasingly clear. In verses 19 and 20, God and Adam work together in the naming of all of the animals. God created the animals and brought them to Adam, and Adam was given the task of naming them. Thus work is fundamentally a way of partnering with God to carry out His mission in the world in service to one another and all of creation. It seems clear that God desires to work with and through humans and His creation to express His love to humans and creation; and for humans and creation to express their love for Him. This is the essence of spirituality. This is why He invited Adam to name the animals, and commissioned Adam and Eve to fill the earth and care for it.

Karl Barth in his *Church Dogmatics* advocated that only humans were created to be "a genuine counterpart" to God. The meaning and purpose of our creation is to be a partner with God. Barth notes that God "willed the existence of a being which in all its non-deity and therefore its differentiation can be a real partner." Barth also connects this concept of partnership with the idea that we are to imitate God, saying that we are a "creaturely repetition, as a copy and imitation, can be a bearer of this [divine] form of life."[5]

Doctors and nurses partner with God to provide health care and treatment to other people. Veterinarians partner with God to provide care for animals. Botanists similarly work with plants. Police and fire professionals partner with God to protect humans and property from harm. Professors partner with God to teach, educate, and train others. Scientists partner with God to explore the natural order in service to God, humanity, and creation. Pastors, preachers, and priests partner with God to explore His truths and communicate them in a meaningful way to people. Likewise, business is a way of partnering with God and imitating Him in service to humanity and creation through the development and distribution of goods and services.

By stating, in essence, that we partner with God to generate profits, I do not mean to imply that somehow God profits. God already owns everything (Haggai 2:8). As with all endeavors in which humans partner with God, the benefits are for us as God cannot gain what is already His. The benefit of the profits thus goes to humankind. Therefore, we should be careful that the profits from business are not hoarded but rather are dispersed. Through the dispersion of profits, humans partner with God to provide for other humans. This partnering with God and providing for one another should be seen as living faith.

As Miroslav Volf noted in a lecture at Yale Divinity School, "We make decisions in boardrooms, we flip hamburgers at McDonald's, we clean houses, we drive buses — and by doing that, we work with God and God works through us. No greater dignity could be assigned to our work."[6]

Creative God, Creative Creature

Human beings do not really create in the same way that God does. For God created the universe *ex nihilo* or out of nothing. In our partnership with God to sustain the created order, to preserve and care for it and for our fellow humans—those living now and those to come—it is, undoubtedly, necessary to be creative. Clearly God expected creativity from us since the beginning. Adam had to use tremendous ingenuity and creativity to name all of the animals. Furthermore, in Genesis 2:15, Adam was told by God to work the garden and take care of it. This strongly implies that Adam had to develop tools to use. This facet of creativity is another fundamental aspect of the spiritual nature of business and how business partners with God.

In order to thrive, business must be able to predict the needs of others as well create a combination of productive actions in order to meet those needs. This is how people are creative. We do not create something out of nothing like the Creator; rather we can (and must) be able to perceive our future needs and creatively develop and produce ways of meeting those needs. This creativity is not done in isolation from God. We cannot function apart from the help of our Creator. We are like Adam creatively giving names to animals in the garden, while our Creator stands by giving us the animals to name. Creativity is an act of partnership with God whereby He gives us the means and the process. However, we are not robots simply doing what we are programmed to do. We are fully engaged and participatory in the creative process and very much an integral part of the means and the end achievement.

We are now in a knowledge society and the labor theory of value as promoted by Marx does not work. Business succeeds today by working smart. "Intellectual capital"—ingenuity and creativity—is the primary component for success in contemporary business. God modeled and embodied creativity as He placed the moons and the stars in the sky and set trees and plants in the ground and put animals on the earth. Thus human creativity is an inherently spiritual activity. For it not only partners with the Creator in sustaining His creation but it also mirrors or imitates Him. Created in His image, we reflect His image (Genesis 1:26).

There are, of course, many different perspectives on God, but one thing that seems difficult to deny is that the One who brought us everything in existence is a creative genius. All the books of the world could not sufficiently discuss the diversity and creativity found in our universe.

The ingenuity of the Creator is not only seen in the amazing range of animals and the various forms that they take but also by looking closely at one animal in particular. For example, take the simple hermit crab. Once on a beach vacation, our two young children saw hermit crabs for the first time and became so excited about them that they asked to bring a couple home, which we did. I had never given much thought to hermit crabs, but now that they were sharing our home, I set about to learn a little bit about them.

I discovered that they shed their shells when they become too cramped and find a "second home." Interestingly, the hermit crab's body is asymmetrically twisted so that it fits into the shell. The legs are uniquely designed for its unusual way of life. Its two hind pairs are used for walking; the others grip the shell. Its huge right-hand claw, which is significantly larger than the left, is used as a protective door when it retreats inside its shell. When a suitable shell is not readily available, they have been known to inhabit joints of bamboo, coconut shells, and even discarded garbage.[7] That is just one small animal. The amazing list of descriptions could go on.

God is creative. As human beings created in His image, creativity is also a part of our design. Our creativity will never match the genius of the Creator. Nevertheless, in partnership with our Creator and in the spirit of human collaboration we can creatively sustain creation and lovingly support one another. Business is a means through which we creatively partner with God to do this.

In business, our principal resource is ourselves. In *Landmarks of Tomorrow*, Peter Drucker advocates this line of thought saying, "The ultimate resource in economic development is people. It is people, not capital or raw materials, that develop an economy."[8] As businessmen and women work creatively to meet the needs of others, they are living out a fundamental part of our created purpose.

As mentioned before, work is not synonymous with business. All of work should be seen as spiritual and done in partnership with God.

However, a business is an organizational entity that creates an environment so that the production and effectiveness of our work is increased, thereby better serving one another. This is the spiritual mission of business. Since the Fall, though, people have failed to live up to our Creator's ideals. Business, like all human activity, has been marred with egocentrism and exploitation. For the spiritual mission of business to be fulfilled, it must be conducted with hearts of compassion and lives focused on love. The goal, as we will see in the next chapter, is to produce *shalom*.

Questions for Reflection & Discussion

1. How can churches help bridge the gap between faith and business?

2. How have churches mishandled the topics of money and business?

3. How can particular professions partner with God?

4. How does creativity reflect God and improve business?

5. How should we distinguish between the fundamental and instrumental value of business?

chapter 3

SHALOM

The spiritual mission of business is not to establish a kingdom of wealth and power but to bring the kingdom of God into tangible reality. The kingdom of God can be most simply defined as *God's reign.* So, the kingdom is the manifestation of God's ideals, principles, values, and will. It can also be understood as a physical expression of a spiritual reality.

The kingdom of God is not an esoteric, abstract concept; rather it is observable and concrete. When we see expressions of love, generosity, and grace these can be said to be a glimpse of the kingdom of God. This is not to say that everything about the kingdom of God is observable and physical. The kingdom of God refers to God's reign over all things, both visible and invisible, both physical and spiritual, throughout all of creation. But it is, as Methodist missionary and theologian E. Stanley Jones pointed out, realism and not idealism.

Jesus came preaching the kingdom of God. It is His primary message as well as the message of Scripture. It is something real that has been happening for all eternity and since the beginning of time. Thus it has an historical quality. It is the unfolding story of God throughout creation. It is seen through the Old Testament, particularly in the concept of *shalom,* which is typically defined and translated as "peace." However, it carries a stronger connotation than peace. It is more of a worldview where all things function in harmony.

Like shalom, the kingdom of God is a holistic paradigm, meaning that it covers every area of life. It is not simply about church activities or

Sunday sermons, although these are definitely a part. It is focused on God's redemptive plan of reconciling all things unto Himself (Colossians 1:20).

God's enemies oppose His kingdom. They are attempting to establish their own kingdoms and seek through antagonistic and antithetical practices to bring harm to the kingdom of God. Human beings choose which kingdom they will promote. Though they may not be aware of the importance of their choices, they are responsible for them.

The kingdom of God is one of grace, mercy, love, justice, righteousness, and judgment. Though these may seem like mutually contradictory aspects, they are not. God in His wisdom and sovereignty rightfully balances these aspects and the tension involved in human responsibility and the results of our moral choices.

Many Christians think of the kingdom of God purely in future terms. However, there is biblical warrant for understanding the kingdom of God as being manifested on earth in the current age, at least in part. Christ prayed for the kingdom to come and God's will to be done on earth as it is in heaven (Matthew 6:10). Would it not be odd for Christ to pray for the kingdom to come if it were purely a heavenly reality? Failing to understand the present reality of the kingdom of God has caused many Christians to become withdrawn or inactive.

Business can be at the forefront of creating chaos or it can bring spiritual good into physical reality. The integration of economic and social systems transpiring in the world today is most commonly referred to by the term *globalization*. The reality of globalization means that we are more interdependent than ever before. Now, when we call a customer service line we are likely to be connected to someone in another country. But it is not just offshore call centers. It's everything. Businesses of all types are integrated around the world. Supply chains spread across continents and wire transfers unite financial institutions just as fiber-optic cables across the ocean floor enable us to communicate broadly and quickly.

Nearly every day I relate with people in several different countries. For the most part I use email, but I also frequently have video conference calls over the Internet. On some days I'll communicate directly with people in more than ten different countries. Most of it I'll do through the Internet, without any fees charged to me. We are living in interesting days, indeed.

As the world is becoming increasingly integrated, we are becoming more aware and knowledgeable of various illnesses, injustices, problems, and suffering around the world. The population in developing countries is growing exponentially. Sadly, suffering instead of success is accompanying this increase. Every day, almost 2,000 babies are infected with HIV, either during pregnancy, at birth, or through breast-feeding.[1] A sixth of the world's countries receive two-thirds of the world's income. For every $1 created through exports, $0.03 goes to low-income countries.[2] More than 2.8 billion people live on less than $2 a day, and 1.2 billion people live on $1 or less.[3]

Business can be a means of bringing justice to the poor and disenfranchised around the world. Or it can be a way to exploit them and/or the natural resources of their land. Jesus called us to love our neighbor (Matthew 22:37–39). In our new global reality, our neighbor can be rightfully understood as numerous people groups scattered around the globe.

This love for God and neighbor needs to be the foundational principle on which the missional entrepreneur stands. Christ said this love for God and neighbor was of utmost importance (Matthew 22:37–39). Paul said that love was the greatest attribute (1 Corinthians 13:13). John wrote, "Dear friends, let us love one another, for love comes from God. Everyone who loves has been born of God and knows God . . . If anyone says, 'I love God,' yet hates his brother, he is a liar. For anyone who does not love his brother, whom he has seen, cannot love God, whom he has not seen" (1 John 4:7, 20). We must emphasize the importance of love in all that we do, including business.

Business as mission reflects a desire for the kingdom of God to be manifested in a substantive way in the present age. When business fulfills its spiritual mission it can contribute significantly to creating economic shalom for many of the world's peoples.

Missional entrepreneurs can have an important and vital role in an age of economic globalization. They can serve as practical extensions of the church to relieve people's sufferings, and they can demonstrate physically the love of God by loving their neighbor. In doing this they can extend the kingdom of God, God's reign on earth, and spread the shalom of God around the world.

Shalom Comes to Southeast Asia

Joe Smith (pseudonym) was a successful entrepreneur who cashed out, but was antsy to get back in the business world. Over the years he had also developed a burden for poverty-stricken parts of the world and wondered if his business skills could bring shalom to people in underdeveloped areas.

Eventually, Joe and his wife, Marcy (pseudonym), moved to Southeast Asia, as missionaries with a traditional missions agency. Their agency gave them permission to use whatever means necessary (including business) to bring Christ's love to those people who needed it desperately.

Joe opened up a business with three distinct activities: digital publishing, digital mapping, and data entry. The goal in digital publishing is to put positive, helpful, and spiritual resources into the hands of people who had virtually no access to it. Mapping products are sold to various business interests but their primary purpose is to equip the local church to better understand where churches have been planted and needs for future churches. The data entry arm is the most profitable part of the business and, through the Internet, the company can perform data entry for companies all over the world at exceptionally inexpensive prices.

Each branch of the business is profitable and aims to serve Christians as well as non-Christians. However, Joe wanted to go a step further after becoming burdened for an oppressed minority in his country. Realizing that many of them were capable but just lacked training, he began to hire people from this group, who in the larger culture are often refused dignified work. Thankful for the opportunity, these individuals have proven to be hard workers, who often perform at a higher standard than the majority nationals. Originally, Joe's decision could have been considered a compassionate risk; however, it has turned out to be a good business decision due to their productivity.

Through intentional engagement, Joe has brought shalom to nationals (both majority and minority groups), valuable services to a wide variety of people in this impoverished company, and empowered the local church with tools and funds—all through a financially profitable business.

Building Community

As stated in the previous chapter, God partners with humans not only in work but also in the making of other human beings. This is one of the most fundamental parts of the creation narrative in Genesis. God observed Adam was alone and that this was not good (Genesis 2:18). Therefore, God also created Eve. He then called Adam and Eve to be fruitful and multiply. At our core, we are relational creatures designed to be in relationship with our Creator and with one another. Because of this, God directed Adam and Eve (and subsequent humans as well) to build a community. We are not only relational beings, but we are also community builders.

In a very real way, business functions as a community in a practical and spiritual sense. Businesses must learn to operate in and know how to organize a large-scale community because an isolated individual cannot accomplish the needed tasks. Business is work done with others and for others. Business requires multifaceted interaction.

Therefore, it has an amazing ability to reach into every corner of the earth. Even a simple, small business is a web of relationships connecting the business to customers, suppliers, landlords, product technicians, business partners, government agents, lawyers, investors, bankers, and the list goes on. If the business is larger, there will also be supervisors, employees, executives, stockholders, and analysts to interact with. I have worked in a variety of countries to establish legal entities (both business and nonprofit) and have been amazed at the number of people I have met and interacted with, just in the initial process of setting up the organization. Business is a hub of relationships, a network of human interaction.

This is an integral and fundamental aspect, not only of business, but also of our human existence. God created us to work in cooperation with other people for the sake of serving one another. Business is an avenue that we have to travel together. There is no way to do business without personal interaction. Companies are forms of communities and in many ways can function like a kind of extended family. They produce their own identity and live their own stories. They have their own beliefs and are shaped by their own values. Just as there are healthy, happy families as well as dysfunctional ones, so it is in business. But it is difficult to deny that business is a community activity.

This is seen in the fact that the most commonly used word in all of the literature on corporate human resources and organizational development is *community*. In *The Search for Meaning in the Workplace*, Naylor, Willimon, and Österberg define a community as a "partnership of free people committed to the care and nurturing of each other's mind, body, heart and soul through participatory means."[4] Who wouldn't want to join that kind of community? In my years at work, I have not always been able to enjoy such an idealistic environment. To create such a genuine community takes intentionality, integrity, and perseverance.

However, just because my (and perhaps your) experiences in work environments have not perfectly embodied the community just defined, this does not remove the fact that business is communal and that community is a spiritual aspect of business. It can be conducted in a way that is spiritually flawed or that is spiritually fulfilling. For the latter to occur, the most influential people of the community need to practice the fruit of the Spirit: love, joy, peace, patience, kindness, goodness, faithfulness, gentleness, and self-control (Galatians 5:22–23).[5]

Intergender Synergism

Human beings were not only created to interact relationally with one another, but also to interact relationally while working. This is seen in the Creation account. God created Eve to be Adam's helper (Genesis 2:18). One aspect of this is commonly overlooked, namely that men and women were designed to work together. An essential part of building community in the business world should be to create an environment where the genders can work in a mutually beneficial fashion, which I refer to as the principle of intergender synergism. From my observations, it seems some businesses are starting to do this quite well and are reaping benefits from it. God created men and women to work together. Therefore, it is by nature more effective and productive if we restore our working communities to reflect this aspect of the original creation.

Unfortunately, many times, the fact that Eve was created to be Adam's helper is taken to mean that Eve and therefore women are somehow inferior to men. However, if Adam was superior, why did he need Eve to help him? In a sense Eve was sent to "rescue" him from his situation. It is worth noting that the same word used in Genesis 2:18 to describe Eve as a helper is used to speak of God on several occasions in the Old Testament. This is a significant indication that helper should not be interpreted to imply subordination or inferiority.

For example, Eliezer saw God as a helper who rescued them, saying, "My father's God was my *helper*; he saved me from the sword of Pharaoh" (Exodus 18:4). Moses also saw God as a helper and rescuer, proclaiming to the nation of Israel, "Who is like you, a people saved by the LORD? He is your shield and *helper*" (Deuteronomy 33:29). Likewise, a psalmist saw God as one who helped those in need: "But you, O God, do see trouble and grief; you consider it to take it in hand. The victim commits himself to you; you are the *helper* of the fatherless" (Psalm 10:14). David succinctly said, "The LORD is with me; he is my *helper*" (Psalm 118:7). This should show quite conclusively that a lower position is not implied. The proper perspective seems to be one of communal partnership.

I believe Bible commentator Matthew Henry had it right when he said that God made woman from the side of man — not from the head so she would rule over him and not from his feet so he would trample on her. Many Bible translations say that Eve was taken from Adam's *rib*. However a more appropriate translation of the Hebrew word, *sela*, would probably be *side*, hence Henry's comment.[6]

In terms of work it is well worth pointing out that Adam and Eve were both given responsibility from God to care for His creation (Genesis 1:28). This is important for two reasons. First, this means that males are not inherently superior nor do they have more responsibility than females in terms of work, business, and caring for creation. Since work is spiritual it needs to be done in partnership with one another without limiting one gender. We need to reflect on the words of the Apostle Paul, "In the Lord, however, woman is not independent of man, nor is man independent of woman. For as woman came from man, so also man is born of woman. But everything comes from God" (1 Corinthians 11:11–12). We are not independent of each other, and we need each other. It seems to me that this world still has a very low view of women in general, when one considers the sex industry, the absence of effective maternity laws, and the amazingly few women who serve in leadership roles in large corporations and as heads of state. Clearly there is much work to be done and progress to be made around the world.

Second, when society does place legitimate restraints on business to prevent exploitation and discourage discrimination against minorities, including women, this provides a fruitful environment for true spiritual community. For example, businesses in the US, Canada, and the European Union, among other places, must demonstrate that they are not discriminating against women or other minorities. As a result of being "forced" to integrate women into the workplace, many businesses have discovered that women are just as talented and skilled as their male counterparts. This exposes such myths to the contrary. These myths have existed in faith communities despite the fact that the values of women in business are explicitly expressed in the Bible. A woman of virtue is one who "sees that her trading is profitable" (Proverbs 31:18).

Many businesses have recognized that female-male partnership is more fruitful, or in business terms, more profitable. Though they may not understand or articulate this, they have rediscovered the original design in the creative order—spiritual community. This is the divine purpose in human cooperation.

Businesses that actively seek to integrate women into their workforce see positive results. Spiritually speaking, this is because they are recapturing our created design. Practically speaking, it is because they are eliminating three factors that hinder productivity and are harmful to any business. First, restrictions on active female engagement, in certain areas or in general, are a source of frustration at best and oppression at worst to women who are uniquely gifted by God.

Second, such restrictions harm the organization because it does not benefit from the gifts of its female workers. Despite the fact that our society still seems to be lagging in terms of true equality for women, there are many women who have already demonstrated extraordinary talent and skill in positions of great importance in a variety of corporations. Consider Meg Whitman, who was CEO of Ebay for ten years. Business and organizations that do not intentionally integrate women into leadership miss out on the skills of someone like Meg Whitman.

Third, the organization misses the synergistic dynamic when women and men work together in a mutually supportive environment. This synergistic cooperation produces a win-win dynamic that is a reflection of the aforementioned original creative order and design of how females and males are to work together.

Providing for Humanity Through Profit

Recently, I spoke with a Christian entrepreneur who had devoted his life to developing and building up his business, which had grown and expanded through the years and was deemed quite a success. Near the end of his working career, he had been reflecting on his career. Through the years, he had hit some tough spots, faced difficult ethical situations, and had sometimes wondered if it had been worth it.

One day as he was struggling with the meaning and purpose of his life's work, he looked around at his company picnic and saw all of his employees, their spouses, and their children, talking, laughing, and playing. In that moment, it was as if scales fell from his eyes and he realized that, even if he had done everything else wrong, at least he had been used by God to provide a living wage to all of those people. This is one of the most beautiful and spiritual parts of business, to provide humanity with the means to survive, thrive, and enjoy God's good creation.

For many, one of the most controversial aspects of business is financial profit. This is because many people believe there is X amount of money and to make money is to essentially take it from one place and bring it to oneself. This leads to a condemnation of business because when they are *making* money, this is perceived as the functional equivalent of *taking* our money. They view the money supply as a pie and you take pieces from one group and give to another.

However, profit is not so simple. There are clearly many business plans (some legal and some not) that are essentially designed to take money from some people and bring it into the pockets of others. However, to sustain long-term profits, businesses know that they have to meet a real need and provide for their employees in a sustainable fashion. When a business has been profitable, it generally means that it has been effective and productive in organizing diverse resources to meet human needs. These corresponding human needs are not just that of the customer or the stockholder but also of the employee. Without meeting real needs and generating profit, businesses would not be able to provide for their employees. Businesses are about creating wealth or increasing the size of the pie.

In fact, business profits do not just benefit the owners, stockholders, and employees of the company, but rather all of society.

Just as it is nonsense to say that economic life is possible without profit, it is nonsense to believe that there could be any other yardstick for the success or failure of an economic action but profitability. Of course, it is always necessary for society to go in for a good many unprofitable activities in the social interest. But all such activities which are undertaken in spite of their economic unprofitability must be paid for out of the profits of some other branch of economic activity; otherwise, the total economy

shrinks. Profitability is simply another word for economic rationality. And what other rationality could there be to measure economic activity but economic rationality?
— Peter F. Drucker, *Concept of the Corporation*[7]

Of course, as mentioned above, many profit schemes are unethical and not beneficial to society. Likewise, there are many who pursue profits to such a degree that they employ unscrupulous means to do so. Numerous easy examples come to mind but I will refrain from mentioning them. It seems better not to focus on who is doing it wrong and who is doing it right, as it is to reflect for a moment on the essential spiritual nature of providing for humanity, which business can, does, and should do through the generation of profits.

Productivity is a hallmark of business and is a necessary component of human society. The fundamental goodness of productivity is seen when God put Adam in the Garden of Eden to "work it and take care of it" (Genesis 2:15). This was before the Fall and God wanted Adam to be productive in his work in the Garden. He also commanded Adam and Eve "to fill the earth and subdue it" (Genesis 1:28). To subdue in Hebrew is *kabash* and implies that Adam and Eve should make the resources of the earth useful. Productivity is definitely the goal of this command.

We can infer that Jesus also affirmed the fundamental goodness and inherent faith involved in productivity and profit when He told the parable of the minas (Luke 19:11–26). This parable describes three people who have been given minas (Greek coins worth about 100 days' wages) and who each reproduce them at a different rate. The one who realizes the greatest reproduction receives the greatest reward and the one with the least is rebuked. While there are many applications for this parable, it is best interpreted as teaching about the stewardship of all resources that God gives us. So, financial profit or using money to increase production would fall under this general application, especially considering Jesus used the example of finances in telling the parable.

When discussing financial profits and spiritual faith, one should not only emphasize the benefits of profits, but also the moral temptations that accompany it. We are all susceptible to the temptation of making immoral choices or unwise decisions when presented with the opportunity of increasing our financial intake. History has shown that people will do horrible things in order to profit financially. Slavery and various abuses of American Indians are two scars on the history of my birth country. Human trafficking and the related globally expanding sex industry are current evils done for the sake of financial gain. These horrors deserve focused attention and as spiritual beings, we should fight and counter them on behalf of the oppressed and persecuted. But we should not let these evils distort our view of the way that business can operate morally, ethically, and spiritually in the production of profits for the provision of humanity.

Think about how modern society functions. Every social entity needs business to provide for it. Every nonprofit organization, hospital, and church that receives donations benefits from business because those donations come from the profits of business.

There are many different types of organizations that form a society, such as faith and service organizations, educational, governmental, health care, and business institutions. We could undoubtedly list others. However, the point is that every category is dependent at some point on business for funding. Either business will fund its sector through donations or taxes, or the sector will devise its own income-generating business model to sustain and grow itself. But the bottom line remains: *business is the engine that financially supports and sustains every sector of society.*

Questions for Reflection & Discussion

1. How can business produce shalom?

2. What role can businesses play in alleviating human suffering?

3. How can businesses create and/or destroy community?

4. How can businesses help and/or hinder women and men to work productively together?

5. How important are the profits from business to society (providing for humanity's needs)?

chapter 4

SERVICE, PROFITS, AND SALARIES

Jesus said He "did not come to be served, but to serve" (Matthew 20:28). This act of serving is one of the greatest virtues of the Christian faith and is expressed in numerous parables, teachings, and commandments. Paul encouraged his readers to "serve one another in love" (Galatians 5:13). In the context of work, he told employees to "serve wholeheartedly, as if you were serving the Lord and not men" (Ephesians 6:7). Peter said we should use our gifts "to serve others" (1 Peter 4:10). He encouraged church leaders to be "not greedy for money, but eager to serve" (1 Peter 5:2). John reminded us that our ultimate purpose is to "serve God" (Revelation 1:6; 5:10).

Serving people is a foundational Christian teaching. Jesus taught what has been called the Golden Rule: "Do to others what you would have them do to you" (Matthew 7:12). Serving people, by treating them the way we desire to be treated, tends to produce reciprocal action. If you treat people right then they will tend to treat you right. Furthermore, there is an internal liberation that occurs when we serve others that strengthens us and makes us better equipped to deal with the challenges of life.

As previously defined, a business is an organization that creates and/or distributes goods and/or services and relies on financial profit for survival, success, and expansion capability. Although profit is a controversial aspect of business, it is also an indication that business is effectively distributing its goods and services. If society does not want or need these goods and services, then this is reflected in the related loss of profits to the business.

This causes the business to respond and adapt, either serving its people in a meaningful way or closing shop. Business cannot survive much less thrive if it is not serving people. Service is a way to imitate the Creator. As C. William Pollard, former CEO of ServiceMaster, writes in *Serving Two Masters? Reflections on God and Profit*, "We seek to honor God as an *end* goal and recognize that growing profitably is a *means* goal."[1]

Though society needs many different activities, including many that are not profit-oriented, the profit mechanism ensures that businesses are at least serving some people. Profit should not be the guiding rule of thumb for all organizations, but it is an effective tool in many cases for business. One of the weaknesses of many nonprofit and faith-based organizations is that they do not have internal feedback mechanisms to properly evaluate if they are truly serving their constituents. I have consulted with several nonprofit organizations and churches that had no idea if they were effectively serving their people. They had no built-in system to determine that. Many even rejected the idea that they should develop such a system, preferring to "trust God." But if we really want to serve people and serve them well, we need to have a means of determining whether or not we are achieving this goal.

However, it should be noted that just because a business is making a profit does not mean that it is truly serving people. It could be manipulating them, exploiting them, or providing them with a destructive product, like drugs, pornography, and the like. There is also the issue of the production of perceived needs through advertising. Unfortunately, many businesses attempt to make consumers believe they need a product that they really do not. This has been a criticism of many pharmaceutical companies. As one medical doctor told me, "The medicine with the most life-saving potential for people over 50 is aspirin. Look through all your news mags and pore through all the full-page ads for expensive drugs, but you will see none for aspirin. If pharmaceutical companies were interested in people's heath, they would put out big ads for aspirin, but since aspirin is cheaper than dirt, they don't try to sell it."

Obviously, businesses need money to survive but to fulfill their spiritual mission businesses should seek to serve the most people as effectively as possible. This means that when inexpensive means exist they should not falsely create the perception that a more expensive and less effective item is needed. This is a disservice to society.

However, for a legitimate business to make a profit, it must serve people. This is beneficial to society and can be an authentic spiritual act. Serving people aligns us once again with the way the Creator designed us to be. Functioning in accordance with our created design not only has personal benefits, but also benefits society and increases the effectiveness of human activity. Service is an inherently spiritual part of business. The benefits of a service orientation for business are widely acknowledged.

Of course, a pastor or theologian may be tempted to critique business in this regard saying that the acts of service are diminished because they are done in pursuit of profit. Clearly the heart's intent of a person's actions does have spiritual consequences. If a person habitually engages in seemingly righteous behavior for personal monetary gain, then that person needs to be corrected in order to live an authentic spiritual life. However, serving people to increase effectiveness and the productivity of a business should not be perceived as wrong. Rather it is authentically spiritual because it is a natural way that business aligns human activity with our original created design.

Rewarding Performance

In business, rewards are typically given based on productivity and performance. While this may not seem particularly spiritual, this too is a part of our created design and the idea of reward (or lack of reward/judgment) based on one's actions is reflected in the Scriptures. Thus the concept of rewarding good performance is a practice of business that reflects aspects of scriptural teaching. However, this is a facet of business that is easy to manipulate. Therefore, caution and wise guidance are necessary.

As mentioned previously God told Adam and Eve to work the land in order to gain their food (Genesis 2:15–16). This also demonstrates that inherent to our created design is the principle of reaping and sowing. We reap what we sow, and we deserve to receive what we put in. If Adam and Eve wanted to eat, then they had to produce the food. Their work performance automatically yielded an appropriate reward.

Paul also implied this when writing to the Thessalonians, "Make it your ambition to lead a quiet life, to mind your own business and to work with your hands, just as we told you, so that your daily life may win the respect of outsiders and so that you will not be dependent on anybody" (1 Thessalonians 4:11–12).

Paul told the people to work so that they would gain two things: credibility and independence. These things do not come without effort. The people had to work for them. Thus their work, and only their work, would yield an appropriate reward.

Jesus said, "The worker deserves his wages" (Luke 10:7). Furthermore, He also affirmed the responsibility to be productive, as well as the correlation of performance to rewards. The aforementioned parable of the minas (Luke 19:11–26) is applicable again here. The nobleman gave a mina (three months' wages) to each of ten employees. When the nobleman returned later, three of his employees reported to him. One had multiplied the mina ten times, and he was given responsibility over ten cities. The second had multiplied it five times and was given responsibility over five cities. The third hid it and did nothing with it out of fear of losing it. The nobleman questioned him as to why did he not at least deposit it so that he could collect interest. He then condemned him as unworthy.

Parables are a unique form of conveying a particular truth or insight. In this case, it does not appear that Jesus is speaking directly to the business world, but using the parable to teach a more general principle of stewardship and responsibility. However, the economic component cannot be denied for two reasons: It falls under the general principle of stewardship and Jesus used the concept of economics to teach the parable.

In this parable two important things are taught. First, the people received in return for what they produced. Second, they were responsible for producing something. Business, in general, follows this same trajectory. People who produce are thus rewarded, and people who do not produce, yet are fully capable of doing so, really have no good excuse. As stated in

Proverbs 10:4, "Lazy hands make a man poor, but diligent hands bring wealth." Such logic has a commonsense appeal resulting in such truisms like "You get out of it what you put into it." This is also taught on a moral or ethical level in Christianity (1 Corinthians 3:15; 2 Corinthians 5:10).

Of course, there are legitimate cases in which society and business should provide for people who are unable to work due to health concerns or some other appropriate allowance. It is important to note that in Christianity, salvation is a free gift: "For it is by grace you have been saved, through faith—and this not from yourselves, it is the gift of God—not by works, so that no one can boast" (Ephesians 2:8–9). Rewards, however, are earned: "If what he has built survives, he will receive his reward" (1 Corinthians 3:14).

Integral to much of scriptural teaching is the concept that rewards are distributed in accordance to one's performance. This shows that this is a part of our created design.

My fundamental point is this: In many situations it is justifiable and even spiritual to reward people on the basis of their productivity and performance. This is a natural occurrence in business; thus this is another way that business is inherently spiritual because it naturally aligns with our created design.

Of course, within this logic there is an ethical tension with saying that everyone deserves what they get. Financial disparity and the improper distribution of wealth have produced an unspiritual climate, economically speaking. This tension is one that is not only felt and perceived by spiritually sensitive people but also expressed in the Bible.

The Scriptures describe wealth in a juxtaposed manner. In some cases it is spoken of as a divine blessing. The crops of Isaac multiplied a hundredfold in one year "because the LORD blessed him" (Genesis 26:12). That was not the end of the blessing either as "his wealth continued to grow until he became very wealthy" (Genesis 26:13). Job is described as a man of tremendous wealth who was blessed by God (Job 1). God gave Solomon wealth as a result of his wise answers (1 Kings 3:9–13; 2 Chronicles 1:11).

People of wealth should be hesitant to perceive themselves as deserving. They are not the sole creator of their wealth.

> "You may say to yourself, 'My power and the strength of my hands have produced this wealth for me.' But remember the LORD your God, for it is he who gives you the ability to produce wealth, and so confirms his covenant, which he swore to your forefathers, as it is today."
>
> — Deuteronomy 8:17–18

All accumulated wealth carries enormous responsibility. This is the other side of the biblical account regarding wealth. People of wealth have the responsibility of fulfilling the spiritual virtue of providing for humanity. God doesn't give wealth to people so they can maintain a privileged position at the expense of others. Rather, it is given to talented people to expand their capacity to serve others. As Paul wrote, "Now it is required that those who have been given a trust must prove faithful" (1 Corinthians 4:2).

Profiteering from wrongdoing is not to be commended. Such greediness is the product of selfishness. This selfishness causes many spiritually inclined people to have generally negative views toward financial profit and issues of economic gain.

Unfortunately, the corrupt are sometimes rewarded for doing wrong and escape human judgment. But this carries natural consequences, as it is written, "Whoever loves money never has money enough; whoever loves wealth is never satisfied with his income. This too is meaningless" (Ecclesiastes 5:10). Wealth is hoarded "to the harm of its owner" (Ecclesiastes 5:13).

Jesus had an encounter with a wealthy individual who claimed to have followed all the commandments. He asked Jesus what he lacked to gain eternal life, and Jesus responded, "If you want to be perfect, go, sell your possessions and give to the poor, and you will have treasure in heaven. Then come, follow me" (Matthew 19:21). Unfortunately, the rich young man went away sad and did not follow through on the directives from Jesus. Paul followed this teaching and taught those who were wealthy "not to be arrogant nor to put their hope in wealth, which is so uncertain, but to put their hope in God" (1 Timothy 6:17). They should also "do good, be rich in good deeds, and be generous and willing to share" (1 Timothy 6:18). If they did this, Paul taught that they would "lay up treasure for themselves as a firm foundation for the coming age, so that they may take hold of the life that is truly life" (1 Timothy 6:19). According to the Bible, the responsibility of wealth is a difficult burden to carry.

Faith-based organizations and the government have the responsibility to advocate for the poor and to ensure that the poor are not taken advantage of or forgotten as businesses grow and prosper. Though businesses are justified in rewarding performance and productivity, they should do so in a way that serves their fellow creatures, particularly those in need.

The Thorny Issue of Executive Pay

One particular performance-reward issue in our current day is that of executive compensation. The Boston-based United for a Fair Economy and the Institute for Policy Studies in Washington, D.C., reported that the companies with the highest number of worker layoffs had CEOs who received larger pay increases than companies with fewer layoffs. There was a 44 percent median pay increase for the CEOs of the 50 companies with the largest numbers of layoffs. The report also exposed that executives are sheltering their retirement plans from the risks that everyone else is expected to shoulder. Thankfully, there are a few companies where the CEOs took pay cuts, like Cisco Systems, whose CEO took a 100 percent pay decrease in 2002.[2]

All of this rose to the surface again in early 2009 with the US government's economic bailout plan. After some banks laid off thousands of employees, they requested and received government money only to use a portion of that money to divvy out seven-digit executive bonuses.

The Scriptures teach clearly that we are to serve God with our income, "Honor the LORD with your wealth" (Proverbs 3:9). This is required because God says, "The silver is mine and the gold is mine" (Haggai 2:8). True wealth from God is received only when one has competed in accordance with the rules (2 Timothy 2:5). Wealth gained at the expense of others deserving of it is not true wealth—it is exploitation. As mentioned before, Jesus said the laborer deserves his wages (Luke 10:7). This builds on the Mosaic law that taught "'Do not hold back the wages of a hired man overnight" (Leviticus 19:13) and that the wealthy should not "take advantage of a hired man who is poor and needy" (Deuteronomy 24:14).

God does not give wealth so that one can live a lavish life and laugh at the misfortunes of others. James harshly rebukes those who seek wealth for purely personal gain.

> Now listen, you rich people, weep and wail because of the misery that is coming upon you. Your wealth has rotted, and moths have eaten your clothes. Your gold and silver are corroded. Their corrosion will testify against you and eat your flesh like fire. You have hoarded wealth in the last days. Look! The wages you failed to pay the workmen who mowed your fields are crying out against you. The cries of the harvesters have reached the ears of the Lord Almighty. You have lived on earth in luxury and self-indulgence. You have fattened yourselves in the day of slaughter.
>
> — James 5:1–5

This demonstrates the extraordinarily negative view espoused by the Scriptures toward those who accumulate wealth *at the expense of others.* Though the Bible sometimes portrays wealth as God's blessing, it also places a tremendous responsibility on those who possess wealth. Wealth that comes from God should be used to love others rather than exploit them.

Despite this clear condemnation of those who serve themselves rather than others with their wealth, we must ask ourselves: Is this the case in excessive executive compensation? The situation may not be so simple. Some claim that the extraordinary skills required to manage a large modern firm are extremely rare and the competition to attract top talent pushes up their market value. Thus high pay is fair and legitimately justified. So, the logic follows, executive compensation in an increasingly complex society should rise in accordance to its market value. Though this may appear logical and defensible, this response, in isolation of other aspects of the situation, is also too simplistic.

There are five primary reasons why business, in order to properly cultivate the spiritual principle of rewarding performance, should limit executive excesses. First, in many cases excessive executive compensation is actually a violation of the principle of rewarding performance. Often the executive is awarded high bonuses not on the basis of actual results, but for some other reason.

Kenneth Lehn, formerly chief economist of the Securities and Exchange Commission, did a doctoral dissertation analyzing how performance relates to the pay of professional baseball players. He found that their pay tends to be directly linked to performance. However, when given large, extended guaranteed contracts, players were more likely to report injuries, miss games, and perform at a lower level. In short, he found that a lack of incentives demotivates.

In contrast, Graef C. Crystal, an executive compensation consultant, argues that in the executive world there is not a direct correlation between pay and performance. He points out that "today's typical CEO is given a huge base salary, a guaranteed bonus, a slushy award of free stock that pays off even if the stock price falls by half, a pile of perks, and a lush Golden Parachute just in case he can't find his way."[3] This means that while major league baseball players and corporate executives are both highly paid, major league baseball players are actually paid more in accordance with actual performance than are executives. An example of this would be the aforementioned cases of executives who were highly compensated even though the company was running so poorly that they had to lay off thousands of employees. A company that cannot provide for its employees should not excessively compensate its executives. Reward compensation should be based on the overall performance of the business in light of all of the spiritual principles, not just one in isolation of others.

A second reason why it is justifiable to limit executive excess is that it is simply bad business. Jim Collins found while researching his book *Good to Great* that truly great companies are not run by executives who are paid in excessive fashion. As Peter Drucker puts it, Collins's book "disproves . . . the cult of the superhuman CEO."[4] Collins's team discovered that "[l]arger-than-life, celebrity leaders who ride in from the outside are *negatively* correlated with taking a company from good to great."[5] This means it is bad business to pay a large salary to a CEO to come in and transform a company. Collins' study essentially demonstrated that excessive executive compensation has largely negative effects on individual corporations. Therefore, the type of executive compensation that we see today is not really rewarding performance but is given under the false allusion that it will produce performance. That is a significant difference.

A third reason is that such excess inevitably leads to social tension. This is not just true in our times, but since the beginning of wealth accumulation. Consider that after Isaac became wealthy, the scriptural narrative records that "[h]e had so many flocks and herds and servants that the Philistines envied him. So all the wells that his father's servants had dug in the time of his father Abraham, the Philistines stopped up, filling them with earth" (Genesis 26:14–15). This is just one example among many and this can be readily observed in our current society.

I remember reading an article somewhere that said Bill Gates no longer goes out to eat because angry people so regularly confront him. Envy is a common human reaction to excessive wealth accumulation, even if the wealth has been honestly acquired. Not just envy but also anger is heightened if it is perceived that such accumulation has been done at the expense of others. Certainly a contemporary example would be when an executive lays off massive numbers of people in order to boost profits and thus reaps the benefits of an incentives-laced contract.

Though envy is a common human reaction, it is not a morally appropriate one. Envy is so destructive that in the final of the Ten Commandments it is forbidden seven times (Exodus 20:17). To eliminate envy, we cannot afford to simply prohibit it with platitudes but must also seek to remove the factors that foster it. This is why it is appropriate to reduce excessive executive compensation and to ensure that financial payment is not done at the expense of others deserving of it.

A fourth reason to resist excessive pay is that it creates an atmosphere conducive to corruption. As Paul taught, "People who want to get rich fall into temptation and a trap and into many foolish and harmful desires that plunge men into ruin and destruction. For the love of money is the root of all kinds of evil" (1 Timothy 6:9–10). When excessive amounts of money are on the line, lovers of money are drawn in like flies to a manure pile. I am not in any way trying to condemn all executives. Many are wholesome, spiritual people truly concerned about the well-being of their employees. They receive a vast amount of money, but do not profit at the expense of others. In fact, many are generous in providing for others from their resources. Nonetheless, wealth accumulation carries tremendous responsibility, and there is great temptation to use it in ways that do not benefit society or care for creation.

There are executives overly concerned about the money and who care little about the people they should be serving as leader. These people bring on themselves "many griefs" (1 Timothy 6:10). And in the process they are also capable of exorbitant corruption that harms those in their companies and society. To prevent this type of environment, excessive compensation packages should be restricted to ensure that an atmosphere of corruption is not fostered.

A fifth reason to resist excessive pay is to avoid the consolidation of power. Centralized power is frequently destructive because it puts the vast majority of people under the control of just a few people. This puts people at risk for oppression and exploitation. If just a few people have large amounts of power, then there is little that can be done if those people choose to do evil with their power. It is in the interests of an open society to diversify its resources among its people. We should look out for those who are not in position to do so themselves. Thus it is spiritual to restrict excessive executive compensation in order to prevent the consolidation of power that can be used to abuse and take advantage of others.

Leaving free market forces to themselves without proper ethical and rational restraints is not a proper system for the distribution of rewards. Performance-based rewards are an important and integral part of business and can be handled ethically and morally, but they should be distributed in light of other spiritual principles. Financially rewarding wrongdoing or profit at the expense of others violates human dignity and the created order. Thus rewards should not be doled out at the expense of the poor or others, but in order to create an economic system that seeks to bring them up.

In rewarding people on the basis of performance and productivity, business can align us with our created design. However, it is necessary to restrict excessive and unspiritual expressions of this principle in order to reduce the likelihood of envy, corruption, and exploitation. It is not in the created order to receive rewards at the expense of others nor is it beneficial to society. In the words of Jürgen Moltmann, "Work should be a creative and holistic achievement of the human community. If it does not fulfill this expectation, then it is dehumanizing and produces alienation and an inhumane society."[6] In order for us to create a spiritually humane society that brings people together and affirms the dignity of all people, all people should receive the opportunity to participate with others in the creation of business and share in the rewards it brings.

Stewarding Creation

In addition to carefully considering the generation and distribution of wealth, spiritually integrated businesses should take seriously their impact on God's creation. Though God blessed Adam and Eve and called them to rule over "everything in the earth" (Genesis 1:28), this should be understood within the context of the rest of the chapter. The first blessing from God in the Bible was for *nonhuman creation*. At the end of the fifth day, before God created human beings on the sixth day, God blessed the fish of the sea and the birds of the air, calling for their increase and multiplication (Genesis 1:22). This is just a mere six verses prior to Genesis 1:28, a verse that is sadly often interpreted as saying that humankind has dominion over the earth and can do whatever it wants with the earth's resources.

Therefore, it seems obvious that our call to work the earth in Genesis 1:28 gives us the responsibility to ensure the reality of the blessing that God gave to nonhuman creation prior to our creation. We are stewards of creation rather than owners of it. Through the years, businesses of all types have been callous in their treatment of God's creation and have acted as if there would be an eternal and constant supply of natural resources. The unreflective consumption and degradation of God's creation will result in harm to the generations that come after us. As Christians we are called to reflect on the whole Bible and God's purposes in it, as well as think of the impact our actions will have others, including our children and their children.

One of the chief problems of laissez-faire capitalism is that there is no safeguard to ensure a proper stewarding of the environment. This type of unregulated market creates a supply-and-demand approach that does not account for the impact meeting current demand may have on future supply. I was once at a business conference and an executive from a large chocolate company was demonstrating how his company had moved from country to country in Africa getting cocoa. He pointed out that overuse in each country had decreased each country's ability to produce. The problem they faced now was finding a new country in which to operate. For years they had rushed to meet *current demand* without considering that doing so would dramatically decrease *future supply.* Destroying God's creation for business is contrary to God's will, and it is ultimately bad business.

The Spiritual Good in Business

God declared His work very good and rested (Genesis 1:31–2:3). Work is therefore fundamentally good. Thus, business can be rightly viewed as inherently spiritual and fundamentally good. There are several ways that business can be spiritual. Five have been mentioned here:

- Business can help to build community.
- Business can provide for humanity.
- Business can serve people according to their needs.

- Business can rightly reward people based on performance.
- Business can generate opportunities to care for God's creation.

Figure 4.1

BUSINESS AS A WAY TO SERVE

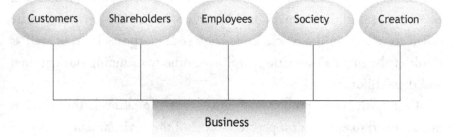

Business is not immune to temptation. To the degree that business succumbs to these temptations, it should be viewed as spiritually flawed. Business should hold itself to a higher standard that reflects its spiritual mission in the created order. However, considering the power that comes from the control of economic resources, it is also necessary for society and faith-based organizations to vigilantly ensure that business is conducted in accordance with its created purposes and design. Clergy, professors, and fellow business practitioners should work together in a mutually affirming way to help the business community fulfill its important and honorable spiritual tasks.

Questions for Reflection & Discussion

1. How can business uniquely serve others?

2. How can wealth be good?

3. How can wealth be destructive?

4. How should Christians in business approach executive compensation?

5. How should Christians in business approach environmental stewardship?

part 2

LEARNING

FROM THE

APOSTLE PAUL

chapter 5

PAUL'S CONTEXT

Even casual students of the Bible know that the Apostle Paul was a tentmaker. However, the BAM movement in general has not grappled with the full meaning or implications of Paul's work as a tentmaker. In this chapter, we examine the social contexts in which the Apostle Paul worked as a missionary and as a tentmaker. The goal is to glean some understanding of how and why he practiced the trade of tentmaking.

We will briefly examine some of the background of Paul's world, as well as his life. Then we will touch on the nature of his mission. After that we will explore his trade. We will attempt to draw some conclusions about exactly what he did, as well as how much Paul worked and earned.

Then in chapter 6 we will explore some of the reasons why Paul, as a matter of policy, worked the tentmaking trade throughout his missionary career. We will examine the nature of patronage in his context and why he desired to offer the gospel "free of charge." Then we will examine some of the distinctions between his apostolic calling and that of Peter. The point is to consider if unique callings and situations require different approaches.

Finally, in chapter 7, we will also explore how Paul could model the Christian lifestyle in the workshop, thus serving as an example for converts to follow. We will also see how, through his trade, he gained credibility for the gospel message. Furthermore, we will examine how he showed his followers that they too should earn a living by working with their hands. We will end this section by exploring the dynamics of how Paul could teach effectively in his workplace setting.

Paul's World

The world of the Apostle Paul was an interesting and fascinating one with many parallels to our contemporary world. Paul lived in an area that, due to the expansion of the Roman Empire, saw a convergence of cultures. It appears to have been a time of extraordinary human progress.

From 27 B.C. to around A.D. 180, the Roman Empire experienced something frequently referred to as the *Pax Romana,* which is Latin for "Roman peace." This is considered a period of relative peace and stability, although it is better understood in terms of Rome's forced pacification of what they considered imperial territory. There was armed resistance in Israel and the Roman Empire "imposed" the peace by force on occasion. However, this was a time of relative tranquility and Rome suffered from neither a major civil war nor a significant invasion.

There were several practical advantages to the Pax Romana. Public services were greatly increased. Aqueducts carried water. This allowed people to operate more effectively since they did not have to spend as much time per day retrieving water for survival. Roads allowed for relatively quick and safe travel to the various corners of the far-flung empire. It also created an environment where a single language was used over a wide area. Koine Greek, the language of the New Testament, was the *lingua franca* of the Mediterranean region at this time and was the first or second official language of the Roman Empire. Trade relations and capabilities were greatly expanded during this time.

The ease of travel, the ubiquitous nature of Greek, the relative peace, and the rise of public services all coalesced to create an environment conducive to the rise of Christianity. Paul, like many other missionaries at the time, was able to use the benefits of Pax Romana to his advantage. He traveled far and wide. He preached in synagogues, taught in lecture halls, and wrote letters, all in Koine Greek (though see Acts 21:40 and 22:2). This helped him spread the gospel farther and faster than otherwise would have been possible.

In many ways this is like our world today. Advances in travel and technology are allowing cultures to come together and interact like never before. Trade relations are spreading farther and wider. The English language has become something of a *lingua franca* of the developed world. The Roman Empire was a regional phenomenon similar to the convergence of cultures that is currently taking place on a worldwide scale, which is commonly referred to as globalization.

Nevertheless, we must not be misled by the significant similarities between Paul's world and ours. There are major differences as well. Once I was talking to an American who had just taken a trip to Germany. When I asked him what his thoughts were on the Germans, he surprised me by saying that they were exactly like Americans. I was a bit taken aback because, as an American who has lived in Germany, I was well aware of significant cultural differences. When I asked him to elaborate he said, "Well, they wear clothes, drive cars, and go to work, just like we do." He had focused on superficial similarities and had not taken the opportunity to explore the intricacies of the local culture. Likewise, any comparison of the world and work of Paul to our world and work today requires that we look in intricate detail at Paul's context so that we can rightly discern its implications for us today.

Paul's Life

It can be difficult to figure out who Paul was and what he was truly like. If one reads widely on Paul, an easy conclusion to draw would be that he is something of a riddle wrapped in a mystery inside an enigma. He has been described as a peacemaker and a divisive sectarian. Many people simply don't understand him, and even a few committed Christians admit to simply not liking him.

Though frequently called Paul of Tarsus, he did not grow up there. This is a reference to his place of birth. Acts 22:3 quotes Paul as saying, "I am a Jew, born in Tarsus in Cilicia, but brought up in this city [Jerusalem]. Under Gamaliel I was thoroughly trained in the law of our fathers and was just as zealous for God as any of you are today." Most likely Paul's preschool education, which would have been done under the guidance of his parents and other relatives, was also done in Jerusalem. Furthermore, being a Pharisee also suggests that his formal education was completed in Jerusalem. It is also possible that he learned his tentmaking skills in Jerusalem. However, it is more likely that he learned it from his parents since cilicium, a covering of goat's hair used in making tents, is from Cilicia.

First, Paul mentioned the fact that he is Jewish. He was somewhat proud of this aspect of his life and when prodded would not hesitate to assert it. He once wrote, "What anyone else dares to boast about—I am speaking as a fool—I also dare to boast about. Are they Hebrews? So am I. Are they Israelites? So am I. Are they Abraham's descendants? So am I" (2 Corinthians 11:21–22). He even argued that if anyone was confident in their Jewish standing, they could not outdo him. "If anyone else thinks he has reasons to put confidence in the flesh, I have more: circumcised on the eighth day, of the people of Israel, of the tribe of Benjamin, a Hebrew of Hebrews; in regard to the law, a Pharisee; as for zeal, persecuting the church; as for legalistic righteousness, faultless" (Philippians 3:4–6). This is rightly interpreted as mock boasting intended to shame others, as he is parodying sophistic self-praise. However, this does show the depth of his Jewish roots.

His Jewish faith and culture were driving forces for him before his conversion to Christianity. He wrote, "For you have heard of my previous way of life in Judaism, how intensely I persecuted the church of God and tried to destroy it. I was advancing in Judaism beyond many Jews of my own age and was extremely zealous for the traditions of my fathers" (Galatians 1:13–14). However, his conversion did not change or diminish his Jewishness; rather for Paul it enhanced it. He wrote, "I ask then: Did God reject his people? By no means! I am an Israelite myself, a descendant of Abraham, from the tribe of Benjamin" (Romans 11:1). He still believed that there was an advantage to being Jewish, "What advantage, then, is there in being a Jew, or what value is there in circumcision? Much in every way! First of all, they have been entrusted with the very words of God" (Romans 3:1–2).

Paul next mentioned his place of birth. Even though he was not raised there, the culture of Tarsus still would have had a formative influence in his life as his parents were Tarsian. Tarsus was a prestigious and honorable city in Paul's time. It was one of the top two or three university towns in the region and was the greatest metropolis.

At this juncture, it is also important to note that Paul was a Roman citizen (see Acts 16:37). Roman citizenship was originally granted only to freeborn natives of Rome. However, as the Empire expanded citizenship was conferred on approved people. It is not known if Paul was a Roman citizen by birth. But for a Jewish family to have citizenship, it is clear that someone in his family, presumably his father or possibly a grandfather or great-grandfather, did something extraordinary to obtain citizenship for the family. It has been suggested that his family provided tents for the Roman military. Such a service could have resulted in citizenship. Regardless of how his family obtained citizenship, it is clear that this put them among the social elite.[1]

The world at the time of Paul was experiencing a confluence of cultures, which also shaped Paul's identity. He was the product of the convergence of Jewish, Hellenistic Greek, and Roman cultural orientations. Just because he grew up in Jerusalem and was educated by family members in the Jewish tradition does not mean that he did not receive a formative Greco-Roman education. Gamaliel was one of the more broad-minded early Jewish teachers and F. F. Bruce maintains "it is quite probable that Paul acquired the rudiments of Greek learning in Gamaliel's school."[2] He was among the educational elite of the culture and his letter writing indicates that he was in the top one or two percent of the population. Though the Jewish faith and culture would have been the prominent influence on Paul's life, the role that the Greco-Roman culture had on forming Paul and his intellectual thought should not be underestimated.

Paul was the most prolific writer in the New Testament, due, in no small part, to the extraordinary education that he received. He wrote at least

13 books of the canonized New Testament and his education would have been obvious to those around him. In one verbal debate even his opponent referred to his "great learning" (Acts 26:24). In Acts 17:28, in order to build a bridge with a group of Greek philosophers, he quotes one of their poets. In 1 Corinthians 15:33, he probably quotes from a play of the fourth-century B.C. Greek playwright Menander entitled *Thais*. This shows that his knowledge and education far exceeded a narrow Jewish upbringing.

Paul had access to a broad education and was a man who could function comfortably and confidently in the various cultural factions of his world. His diverse background prepared him well for the far-flung missions he would undertake. Nonetheless, though his education helped him to write influential letters, he was otherwise unremarkable. Some people even said, "His letters are weighty and forceful, but in person he is unimpressive and his speaking amounts to nothing" (2 Corinthians 10:10). This is an acknowledgement that Paul was weak in terms of personal appearance and oral rhetorical sophistication, but strong in his written persuasiveness.

In a noncanonical book called the *Acts of Paul* there is a physical description of Paul and from it we are able to get an idea of what he looked like.[3] The book tells the story a man named Onesiphorus who was going to meet Paul and had been told by Titus what Paul looked like. The passage reads:

> And he saw Paul coming, a man of small stature, with a bald head and crooked legs, in a good state of body, with eyebrows meeting and nose somewhat hooked, full of friendliness; for now he appeared like a man, and now he had the face of an angel.[4]

Paul's name as we find it throughout his letters is actually Paulus. In Latin, Paulus can mean little or short. It is quite possible that his name was a reference to his height. The mentioning of the crooked nose and the meeting eyebrows were intentionally included as elements considered desirable in the culture. The meeting of eyebrows was a sign of beauty and the hooked nose most likely implied royalty or magnanimity.

It is possible that his head was bald (shaven?) as a part of a religious vow. This was something that Paul did from time to time. Before one trip he "had his hair cut off at Cenchrea because of a vow he had taken" (Acts 18:18). At a later time he says that his colleagues needed to shave their heads, "Take these men, join in their purification rites and pay their expenses, so that they can have their heads shaved" (Acts 21:24). A large forehead was a symbol of wisdom.

What are we to make of the crooked legs yet "in a good state of body"? It appears that in antiquity that slightly bowed legs showed firmness and stability and was not to imply an impediment. A face full of friendliness, like an angel, is no doubt an external indication of the internal work of the Holy Spirit in Paul's life.

Some scholars consider the physical description of Paul to be positive and probably a reference as well to his character.[5] Despite this seemingly positive description of Paul, it is interesting that there is no reference to his eyes. This is especially intriguing since the eyes were often considered the most valuable of all organs and were windows on the soul.

It seems highly probable that the author of the description would have only omitted the eyes if it would have reflected negatively on Paul. In his letter to the Galatians, Paul wrote, "As you know, it was because of an illness that I first preached the gospel to you. Even though my illness was a trial to you, you did not treat me with contempt or scorn. Instead, you welcomed me as if I were an angel of God" (Galatians 4:13–14). Here he refers to an illness that could have prompted contempt or scorn. This implies that it was an illness with a visible manifestation.

He is thankful they did not reject him for his physical weakness and in fact says to them, "You would have torn out your eyes and given them to me" (Galatians 4:15). This is not a reference to some gruesome act of homage but probably indicates their sincere desire that Paul had functioning eyes. Furthermore, near the end of the letter, Paul writes, "See what large letters I use as I write to you with my own hand" (Galatians 6:11). Obviously, Paul used a scribe for the majority of the letter and decided to write with his own hand at the end. Why else would he write with "large" letters if he did not have a problem with his eyes? Additional evidence that Paul possibly had an eye problem would include:

- He regularly used scribes for his letters (Romans 16:22; 1 Corinthians 1:1; 2 Thessalonians 3:17).
- Paul always traveled with companions, including Luke, a physician.
- According to Acts 9 and 22, Paul was blinded at conversion, so recurring problems might not be out of the question.

Taking all of this into consideration it seems highly probable that Paul had an eye disease that not only impaired his ability to see but also detrimentally altered his physical appearance. In Paul's case this was a real impediment, since presence was considered a very important part of public speaking (and some would argue still is, especially with the advent of television). For instance, Paul's physical ailments seem to have bothered the Corinthians. Their thinking was likely influenced by writers like Quintilian, a first-century Roman rhetorician, who wrote that good delivery "is hampered by incurable speech impediments . . . physical uncouthness may be such that no art can remedy it."[6] These criticisms, however, did not deter Paul. He was so focused on his objective of glorifying God that any complaints did not thwart him. In the Corinthian case he simply responded by citing Jeremiah 9:24, "Let him who boasts boast in the Lord" (2 Corinthians 10:17).

Paul recognized that his credibility could not come from his physical prowess or speaking ability. Rather his credibility came from his character. What better way for people to see his character day in and day out than by working alongside them? This is surely one of the primary reasons why Paul chose to work in tentmaking.

Paul's Mission

In his mission, Paul was committed to the conversion of households (1 Corinthians 1:16). He went to places like Corinth, Ephesus, Philippi, and

Pisidian Antioch where his Jewish heritage and Roman citizenship helped him plug into social networks. These cities also provided a context for him to profitably operate his tentmaking business so that he could offer the gospel free of charge.

His strategy was also to spiritually influence the urban centers. He went to cities that lay on major Roman roads such as Ephesus, Philippi, Thessalonica, and Corinth. He was a tireless traveler, but he did stay in locations for extended periods of time. He was in Ephesus for years as one passage makes clear, "He took the disciples with him and had discussions daily in the lecture hall of Tyrannus. This went on for two years, so that all the Jews and Greeks who lived in the province of Asia heard the word of the Lord" (Acts 19:9–10).

He wanted to plant churches in new locations, frontiers for the gospel. "It has always been my ambition to preach the gospel where Christ was not known" (Romans 15:20). But he was not a fly-by-night missionary who would dump tracts and be on his way. He would stay as long as the situation warranted, "But I will stay on at Ephesus until Pentecost, because a great door for effective work has opened to me, and there are many who oppose me" (1 Corinthians 16:8–9). However, he didn't want to linger and was looking to move on as soon as he could, "Our hope is that, as your faith continues to grow, our area of activity among you will greatly expand, so that we can preach the gospel in the regions beyond you. For we do not want to boast about work already done in another man's territory" (2 Corinthians 10:15–16). On other occasions he would have preferred to stay longer but was chased out of town. In one situation colleagues had to lower him over the city wall in a basket in the dead of night (Acts 9:25).

Staying for extended periods of time in a single location enabled him to set up his trade and propel him into various social networks. On some occasions his trade would have coalesced well with what was going on in the surrounding community. An example of this is the biennial Isthmian Games that took place in Corinth in A.D. 49 and 51. This means that they occurred at least once while Paul was likely there. As Ben Witherington points out, "These games provided a great deal of short-term work and sales of, for instance, tents."[7] Paul's trade would have met a real need and allowed him to interact with travelers from all over the region.

Paul's mission was definitely a mission to all people. Paul was willing to do whatever it took to reach as many people as possible with the truth that had transformed his life. He clearly stated such to the Corinthians:

> Though I am free and belong to no man, I make myself a slave to everyone, to win as many as possible. To the Jews I became like a Jew, to win the Jews. To those under the law I became like one under the law (though I myself am not under the law), so as to win those under the law. To those not having the law I became like one not having the law (though I am not free from God's law but am under Christ's law), so as to win those not having the law. To the weak I became weak, to win the weak. I have become all things to all men so that by all possible means I might save some. I do all this for the sake of the gospel, that I may share in its blessings.
>
> — 1 Corinthians 9:19–23

Paul had a ministry to the Jews but was also "an apostle to the Gentiles" (Galatians 2:8). He clearly had a ministry to the well-educated. He wrote widely in order to promote his mission, which shows that at least some of his converts were literate and able to read his letters to the rest of the congregants. It is even clear that they were able to write back to him, since Paul wrote in response to "the matters you wrote about" (1 Corinthians 7:1). Paul also ministered to slaves, women, prison guards, high officials, and surely common people of various backgrounds. Paul appears to have intentionally designed his mission to reach a cross section of society.

Questions for Reflection & Discussion

1. How did the *Pax Romana* create a positive environment for business activities and for spreading the gospel?

2. How is *Pax Romana* similar to globalization today?

3. What apparent weaknesses did Paul have as a communicator?

4. How could Paul compensate for these weaknesses?

5. What distinctives of Paul's mission might have led him to work as a tentmaker?

Questions for Reflection & Discussion

chapter 6

PAUL'S TRADE

What was tentmaking exactly? Scholars propose that the original term could have meant anything from saddle maker to one who works with goat haircloth. It would be nice to know precisely what Paul did. However, given our current evidence it is imprudent to declare with absolute certainty exactly what he did. Most likely he did some of all of it.

The New Testament accounts do not provide enough information to satisfy our intellectual curiosities on a number of issues. The nature of Paul's trade is definitely one of those matters where it would be nice to have some more scriptural information, but alas, we do not have it. Therefore, it is necessary to go to other sources in hopes that they will shed accurate light on the nature of Paul's work.

Trade associations were common in Paul's day, and there is evidence of a corporation of tentmakers in Rome. These trade associations were found in nearly every city, including locations with populations that would not seem to support a respectable membership. These associations typically had more than a hundred members but could range in size from a dozen to a couple thousand. On rare occasion these guilds organized themselves to push the government in the direction of their interests.[1]

However, these organizations focused more on the pursuit of honor rather than economic gain, helping people in lowly trades acquire some sense of social standing. They also supplied a way to build and develop relationships. The names of many communicate this social aspect: "The Friends and Construction-Workers," "Mates and Marble-Workers," "The

Comrade Smiths," and "Brother Builders."[2] In these associations the members shared their lives and their meals together. These associations would have helped Paul make a quicker adjustment to a new city, meet people, and develop a social network, which he could seek to influence with the gospel of Christ.

The Social Status of Artisans

It has been generally assumed that in antiquity artisans were people of low social status. However, grave inscriptions from that period frequently express people's pride in their work. One grave inscription mentions a Jewish linen merchant, named Isaac, who, like Paul, was from Tarsus. He was also "an elder in the community," meaning that he was a person of high status.[3]

Paul was probably a textbook case of what sociologists now call *status inconsistency*, a term used when a person's social positions have both positive and negative influences on her or his social status. For example, in many countries teachers have a positive societal image coming from respect and prestige for the position. This increases their status. But, teachers also frequently earn relatively little money, which simultaneously lowers their status. Status inconsistency is a situation in which a person, for whatever reason, simultaneously occupies two or more statuses of different rank. Despite his respected education, Paul was frequently treated like a person at the absolute bottom of the societal totem pole (2 Corinthians 11:23–27).

How Much Did Paul Work and Why?

In 1 Corinthians 9:6, Paul states that he and Barnabas were supporting themselves on their journey to Cyprus and Galatia. In 2 Corinthians 11:9, while in Philippi, Paul says that he would continue to work so as not to be a "burden" to the Corinthians. In both of his letters to the churches in Thessalonica, he says that he and his companions worked "night and day" to avoid burdening them (1 Thessalonians 2:9; 2 Thessalonians 3:8). In

2 Thessalonians 3:8 Paul even says that they did not eat food without paying for it. In Acts 19:9–10, it is mentioned that Paul ministered in the lecture hall of Tyrannus for two years (during the long midday breaks).

In *Paul: Apostle of the Heart Set Free*, F. F. Bruce observes, "It says much for the staying-power of Paul's hearers as well as of Paul himself if they frequented the lecture-hall daily during the heat of the day for two years. Paul for his part seems to have spent the early morning, and possibly the evening, in manual labour: 'these hands', he later reminds the elders of the Ephesian church, 'ministered to my necessities, and to those who were with me.'"[4]

In 1 Corinthians 9:5–9, Paul quite strongly defends the right of preachers and missionaries to be financially supported by the church. As a result, many people have concluded that he simply made tents when money was scarce. However, Paul's references to self-support and the fact that three times in the same chapter he says that he did not receive financial support strongly suggest he worked as a matter of habit rather than as an exception (1 Corinthians 9:12,15,18).

Paul was a tireless missionary par excellence who established churches in four provinces of the Roman Empire (Galatia, Macedonia, Achaia, and Asia) in a 14-year period (A.D. 48–62) Even in a casual reading of Paul, it is obvious he traveled greatly and took every opportunity possible to preach and teach in public places, reason with local intellectuals, and seek out responsive people. It seems he did everything he possibly could to promote the advance of the gospel and that he would have little time for such seemingly worldly activities like making tents.

In conversations with clergy and laity alike, people frequently point out to me that the reference to Paul working as a tentmaker in Acts 18:3 is followed shortly by an implication that Silas and Timothy arrived with financial gifts from Macedonia so that Paul could devote himself fully to the work of the Lord. The underlying assumption is that Paul worked because he had to in order to survive. When there was the option of surviving without working as a tentmaker, then Paul would do it. The presumption is that his work as a tentmaker was a *distraction* to his work as a missionary rather than an *enhancement* to it.

However, a closer look at Paul shows that he most likely worked at his trade a tremendous amount. He worked for extended periods in Corinth and Ephesus but also for shorter ones as in Thessalonica. It is my contention that Paul worked more often than is commonly assumed and that his reasons for it were numerous, not just to sustain himself on occasion. Rather, he worked a trade for a myriad of reasons, primarily because it was the best option for the advancement of his cause.

Acts 18:3 is written in the context of Paul's stay in Corinth and says that Paul worked as a tentmaker with Aquila and Priscilla. In 18:4 it says that he reasoned with the Greeks and Jews in the synagogue on the Sabbath. In 18:5 there is a mention of Silas and Timothy coming from Macedonia, presumably bringing financial support. This is based on 2 Corinthians 11:9 where Paul writes, "And when I was with you and needed something, I was not a burden to anyone, for the brothers who came from Macedonia supplied what I needed. I have kept myself from being a burden to you in any way, and will continue to do so."

Therefore, traditionally, people have assumed that the brothers from Macedonia in 2 Corinthians 11:9 are referring to Silas and Timothy and their arrival in Acts 18:5. After their arrival, the passage says that Paul "devoted himself exclusively to preaching." This seems to imply that Paul would put aside his trade when he had the means to do so in order to follow his primary passion of preaching the gospel. However, this may not be so straightforward.

First, the passage does not explicitly state that Paul stopped working as a tentmaker. The traditional interpretation that Paul ceased working in order to exclusively preach the gospel does not consider how probable it is that he was able to conduct his missionary task in his workplace setting. In Corinth, it seems clear from the Corinthians' perspectives of him, as well as his rebuttal in 1 Corinthians 9, that he worked as a matter of policy while in Corinth. Therefore, it seems like quite a stretch to interpret this verse as saying that Paul completely ceased his trade for the rest of his time in Corinth.

Ronald Hock in *The Social Context of Paul's Ministry: Tentmaking and Apostleship* argues that the Macedonian aid simply "filled Paul's needs in addition to his work. . . . Paul continued to work, even when he received occasional support."[5] It is possible that Paul had found a way to be simultaneously occupied with the Word and work.

Second, even if Paul did stop working, the passage does not specify for how long he stopped. It is possible that any work stoppage would have been temporary. Any stoppage would have lasted for just one verse. In verse 6 of Acts 18, it says, "But when the Jews opposed Paul and became abusive, he shook out his clothes in protest and said to them, 'Your blood be on your own heads! I am clear of my responsibility. From now on I will go to the Gentiles.'"

A very likely scenario is that when Silas and Timothy arrived with gifts from Macedonia, Paul stopped working temporarily in order to be able to spend more time preaching to the Jews in the synagogue. This would have been in keeping with a "first to the Jew" missionary strategy (Romans 1:16). However, when they reacted strongly in opposition to him, Paul returned to focusing on Gentiles, as well as to his tentmaking trade, which created a context for him to connect with them.

Third, the passage actually seems to imply that Paul most likely was able to spread the gospel message in his workplace setting. This could have taken the form of conversations with just a handful of people. Consider Paul's relationship with Priscilla and Aquila. The text says that they had arrived from Rome after "Claudius had ordered all of the Jews to leave Rome" (Acts 18:2). Upon arriving in Corinth, Priscilla and Aquila became acquainted with Paul and soon began to work together. It is very possible that it was their trade that brought them together in the first place. They were probably members of the same trade association. At the time these trade associations provided the opportunity for fellowship and support for those new to an area.

Priscilla and Aquila are Roman names, not Jewish names, but this was not uncommon at the time. They were probably people of relatively high wealth as they were able to move about and established a sizeable household in three different cities. Even though they had a low occupation, they were independent and by ancient standards operated on a fairly large scale. Interestingly, Priscilla is usually mentioned before Aquila which was uncommon for the time (Acts 18:18, 26; Romans 16:3; 2 Timothy 4:19). Most likely this reflects her having higher social status than her husband, or greater prominence in the church, or both.

It is possible that Priscilla and Aquila were converts of Paul, but this is unlikely. It appears from Suetonius's *The Life of Claudius* that Claudius expelled the Jews because of religious dissension surrounding someone named Chrestus, which is likely a reference to Christ, as *Chrestus* and *Christus* were two spellings of the same name. If the debate was over Christ then this means that Priscilla and Aquila were probably Christians already when they arrived in Corinth after their expulsion.

Paul, Priscilla, and Aquila would have spent a significant amount of time together as business partners. Clearly, they all became quite close. In the first letter to the Corinthians, Priscilla and Aquila send along their greetings from Ephesus to the church there (1 Corinthians 16:19). Paul sends special greetings to them (Romans 16:3; 2 Timothy 4:19). Paul even says that they "risked their lives" for him (Romans 16:4) Their work time together would not only have helped them to forge a strong and lifelong friendship, but Paul also would have taught them more about their mutual faith in the risen Christ. Their level of learning is shown as the story progresses. In Acts 18:18 when Paul leaves Corinth to sail to Syria, Priscilla and Aquila accompany him. In 18:19 they arrive in Ephesus and Paul leaves them to travel to other regions.

In 18:24–26, we read of a man named Apollos, a learned man, knowledgeable of the Scriptures, and a follower of the Lord. Yet he only knew of the baptism of John, therefore he was in need of some correction and further teaching. But Paul, the master teacher, had already left everybody and gone in another direction. What could be done?

Well, it was quite simple. Priscilla and Aquila were so thoroughly immersed in the Scriptures from their time working with Paul that they were now capable of explaining to Apollos "the way of God more

PAUL'S TRADE ▲ 97

adequately" (Acts 18:26). Apollos then went on to be a "great help" to believers in Achaia (Acts 18:27) and turned into a powerful apologist for the gospel (Acts 18:28). Naturally, it is possible that Paul also lived with Priscilla and Aquila and undoubtedly spent time with them in settings outside of work. However, the reference to their common trade in Acts 18:3 seems to imply that this was the basis of their relationship.

From Acts 18, there is no reason to believe that Paul considered teaching the Word and working as a tentmaker as mutually exclusive. He was likely able to do them simultaneously. The passage also illustrates the dynamics of Paul's teaching method. He instructed all with whom he came in contact and taught them in such a way that they became teachers and taught others as well to become teachers. For Paul taught Priscilla and Aquila, and they taught Apollos, and he in turn helped other believers and defended the gospel.

The amount of time Paul spent at work and the importance of tentmaking to his missionary strategy have not been adequately addressed. Most people falsely assume that his work was inconsequential and something he jettisoned when he got a chance. However, the whole of the biblical account suggests that his tentmaking work was an important part of his life and something he used to gain an advantage in spreading the gospel message.

Gifts: Acceptable or Not?

Nevertheless, just as it is clear that Paul worked hard, it is also obvious that he accepted financial donations in many cases. For example, he writes the church in Philippi:

> Yet it was good of you to share in my troubles. Moreover, as you Philippians know, in the early days of your acquaintance with the gospel, when I set out from Macedonia, not one church shared with me in the matter of giving and receiving, except you only; for even when I was in Thessalonica, you sent me aid again and again when I was in need. Not that I am looking for a gift, but I am looking for what may be credited to your

account. I have received full payment and even more; I am amply supplied, now that I have received from Epaphroditus the gifts you sent. They are a fragrant offering, an acceptable sacrifice, pleasing to God. And my God will meet all your needs according to his glorious riches in Christ Jesus.

— Philippians 4:14–19

Even though Paul rightly expresses gratitude for their graciousness, he does make it clear that he was not "looking for a gift." Gift seeking was clearly not Paul's *modus operandi*. However, the gift would have encouraged Paul as it would have shown him that "the gospel had taken root in the community, and consequently, that his mission had been successful."[6] This giving and receiving indicates a relationship of equality and parity and that the gift is an act of reciprocity for the work Paul had already done among them.

While Paul did accept gifts, there are three good reasons to believe that these gifts did not always replace his tentmaking income but rather complemented it and provided for him during times when he was unable to ply his trade. First, Paul's language does not imply "salary." In *The Social Context of Paul's Ministry* Hock points out that Paul's choice of terms is along the lines of *provisions* or *gifts* rather than salary. Second, Hock also notes, "The length of time between gifts (see esp. Phil. 4:10) speaks against the interpretation of these gifts being regular enough even to function as a salary."[7]

Third, and this is important for understanding Paul—his workshop provided him with excellent opportunities to connect with people, establish a social network, and teach the truth of the gospel. In summary, it seems likely that Ronald Hock's assertion that Paul continued to work even when he received occasional support is generally valid. This does not deny that in certain situations, such as in Philippi, Paul probably chose not to work.

Therefore, it seems worthwhile to address why Paul would accept gifts at all. It seems that he would so in the cases listed below.

• *To carry funds to people in need*

Paul would have not shied away from soliciting donations in order to carry the funds to people in poverty. He said he was "eager" to "remember the poor" (Galatians 2:10). In order to avoid patron-client relationships, he steadfastly refused to accept any funds from the Corinthian congregation. He repeatedly asserted that he did not use his rights to financial remuneration (1 Corinthians 9:12,15,18). Nevertheless, he still commanded them to gather a financial collection.

> "Now about the collection for God's people: Do what I told the Galatian churches to do. On the first day of every week, each one of you should set aside a sum of money in keeping with his income, saving it up, so that when I come no collections will have to be made. Then, when I arrive, I will give letters of introduction to the men you approve and send them with your gift to Jerusalem."
>
> — 1 Corinthians 16:1–3

Obviously, he had given a similar command to the Galatian church. He also mentions that the churches from Macedonia and Achaia were "pleased to make a contribution for the poor among the saints in Jerusalem" (Romans 15:26). Later Paul makes it clear that the funds found their destination, "After an absence of several years, I came to Jerusalem to bring my people gifts for the poor and to present offerings" (Acts 24:17). When it came to helping people in need, Paul actively pursued provisions. When it came to pursuing provisions, Paul would not hesitate to do so in order help those in need.

• *To have funds for travel expenses, commonly referred to as "sending them on the way"*

The Book of Romans ends with Paul commending to them a woman named Phoebe. She was a prominent member of the church in Cenchreae, the port city of Corinth. Most likely she delivered the letter to the Rome-based church. Paul says that she "has been a great help to many people, including me" and asks the Romans "to give her any help she may need from you" (Romans 16:2). It is possible that Paul sent her to Rome to collect funds for his planned missionary trip to Spain. This seems plausible since just before commending Phoebe, Paul writes, "I have been longing for many years to see you, I plan to do so when I go to Spain. I hope to visit you while passing through and to have you assist me on my journey there, after I have enjoyed your company for a while" (Romans 15:23–24). While Paul's work could have covered his living expenses, some ministry expenses, and expenses for some of his team, most likely he and his team still would have needed financial assistance to travel long distances. This is most likely a situation where Paul would have solicited donations.

- *To give him the means to set himself up in a new location*

In addition to needing funds to travel great distances, it is quite possible that Paul would still need support once he arrived. Paul was a pioneer and most likely he wasn't always able to set up shop and conduct business within days of arrival. Therefore, it would be necessary to have gifts to support these periods of time. This, however, should not be construed as implying he would not work if he didn't have to. Generally speaking, after orienting himself, Paul is likely to have started his trade as soon as possible.

- *To cover expenses when stays were so brief he did not have the time to conduct business*

It seems that some of Paul's stays were as brief as a few weeks. In these instances it is highly probable that he would have neither the time nor the inclination to conduct his business. Therefore, it is appropriate to assume that he used financial gifts during these times to pay for his transitory living expenses. It is possible that Paul went through some financially straining times. His constant movement would have made running an economically profitable business quite a challenge. Even though he undoubtedly had times that were financially better than others, the accumulation of wealth was not a consideration for him and his lifestyle choices clearly required simple living and serious frugality. As he wrote the Corinthian church,

"So I will very gladly spend for you everything I have and expend myself as well. If I love you more, will you love me less?" (2 Corinthians 12:15).

• *To cover some general ministry expenses*

In certain situations Paul would have had ministry expenses in addition to his personal living expenses. In Ephesus, readers learn, "[Paul] took the disciples with him and had discussions daily in the lecture hall of Tyrannus. This went on for two years, so that all the Jews and Greeks who lived in the province of Asia heard the word of the Lord" (Acts 19:9–10). Renting the hall would have been expensive. There are numerous ways this expense could have been paid for. One possibility is that Paul could have paid for it himself out of excess earnings from his trade. Perhaps Priscilla and Aquila also helped to defray some of the costs. A second possibility is that the Tyrannus mentioned in the passage was a convert and could have donated the use of the lecture hall or rented it to them at a substantially reduced rate. A third possibility is that Paul accepted financial gifts from another congregation to cover at least some of the expenses. This is another case where it easy to see how Paul could possibly use gifts in such a way that would not have precluded his continued work.

• *When offered genuine hospitality (no strings attached)*

He surely would have accepted true hospitality from brothers and sisters, thus cutting down on certain expenses. Frequently, Paul and his friends accepted the gift of housing and stayed with many people, such as Lydia, seller of purple fabric, in Philippi (Acts 16:15), Jason in Thessalonica (Acts 17:5–9), Priscilla and Aquila in Corinth (Acts 18:2–3), Titius Justus (Acts 18:7), Philemon (indicated in the book named after him), and Gaius (Romans 16).

• *To minister in locations other than the marketplace when the situation called for it*

It is quite possible that, at times, Paul would have used gifts in order to minister in a location other than the marketplace. Perhaps, as mentioned before, while in Corinth, he used the gifts from the Macedonian church to preach daily in the synagogue. Though this would not have lasted for an extended period in Corinth, it is altogether possible that he also did this temporarily in other situations.

• *To have provisions during imprisonment*
He would have accepted gifts when he was in prison and could not earn a living. The church in Philippi sent Epaphroditus to carry gifts to Paul when he was under house arrest (Philippians 2:25). Paul was clearly thankful for the gifts (Philippians 4:10–18) and this would have been an obvious situation where gifts would have met a dire need for him.

Finally, it seems most likely that Paul only accepted gifts from a location other than the one he was working in at the time. Drawing on examples mentioned above, he may have solicited money from the Roman church in order to go to Spain (Romans 15:24). He collected funds from the Corinthians to take to the poor in Jerusalem (1 Corinthians 16:1–3). He accepted funds from the church in Philippi while in Thessalonica (Philippians 4:15). Possibly, he accepted funds from Macedonia on a temporary basis while in Corinth (Acts 18:5). Therefore it seems clear that Paul would accept gifts but only when those gifts came from a location separate from where he or his team would use the funds.

Regardless of how much Paul worked, we should not imagine Paul as simply spending all of his time in the workshop. Rather, he traveled a lot, spent time in the synagogue, and enjoyed fellowship in the houses of seekers and converts. There were times and situations where Paul temporarily stopped working and either lived off of financial gifts from other congregations or from saved reserves from his own work. It seems clear that Paul worked a significant amount of the time. Or as F. F. Bruce put it, "Paul, as a matter of policy, earned his living in this way during his missionary career."[8]

Was Paul Rich?

Generally speaking it is assumed that Paul did not earn much money as a tentmaker and lived a difficult life trying to make ends meet. Though it appears true that Paul sometimes needed extra aid from others to cover some of his expenses, it seems quite possible that Paul could have earned a substantial amount of revenue at times. Undoubtedly, Paul experienced tremendous hardships, but it seems likely that his work revenues were dispersed along an income continuum, sometimes just getting by and other times earning a significant income.

As mentioned earlier, many have assumed that Paul worked only when his cash reserves were spent and he was going to default on rent or start to starve. However, a closer look at the situation makes clear this is not correct. Paul said, "You yourselves know that these hands of mine have supplied my own needs and the needs of my companions" (Acts 20:34). This implies that Paul was not simply "making ends meet" but was actually able to produce a substantial income, providing for himself and his teammates.

It seems quite possible that Paul did not work to supply merely his own expenses. Consider that Barnabas was a partner in ministry and work with him (1 Corinthians 9:6). Barnabas previously was a landowner and gave his land to meet the needs of other Christians. Luke recounts this: "Joseph, a Levite from Cyprus, whom the apostles called Barnabas (which means Son of Encouragement), sold a field he owned and brought the money and put it at the apostles' feet" (Acts 4:36–37). As Barnabas used his financial resources to provide for others, so too Paul would have been motivated along those lines.

Paul also said, "I know what it is to be in need, and I know what it is to have plenty. I have learned the secret of being content in any and every situation, whether well fed or hungry, whether living in plenty or in want" (Philippians 4:12). Therefore, sometimes he had a little, yet in other situations he had a lot. It seems highly probable that at times Paul had the financial means to provide well for himself and other people.

It is not clear where this money came from. Was it from working as a tentmaker? Did it come from other church collections? Most likely it was a combination of resources. Acts 20 shows that even after all of the missionary journeys he had just completed, probably providing for other colleagues along the way as well (Acts 20:33–35), he was still able to cover other people's expenses.

Did he continue working through all of his trips to have this much money? Did God prosper him so much in the few times he did work that he had an overwhelming abundance? Or was it an inheritance or gifts from some other source?

Later in his life Paul had to have been a man of considerable resources. He was able to sustain a long and expensive judicial process, he traveled with fellow missionaries, and he gained a favorable hearing from regional administrators. We do not know the specifics of how Paul had the means to do all that we know he did. It seems highly probable that it came from a variety of sources, including donations from congregations. However it also appears that Paul's work could have generated enough income to cover his personal expenses, as well as the expenses of some of his colleagues at times.

Regardless of how much Paul earned, his decision to work a trade was a tremendous sacrifice. As a Pharisee, he was probably married, but he bypassed Christian marriage and children to dedicate himself to the cause.[9] He could have suffered various physical maladies and hardships as a result of his trade. Furthermore, whatever excess Paul had he presumably gave to his teammates or to the poor or spent it in some way to further the cause of spreading the gospel as far and as wide as possible. Therefore, to say that Paul at times earned more than previously considered does not highlight a lack of sacrifice but rather draws attention to how much he really was sacrificing.

The Influence of His Trade on His Writings

• *Military Metaphors*

As mentioned before, it is possible that Paul's family attained Roman citizenship through the making of tents for the Roman military. This would make it probable that Paul also took on other assignments in different locations to supply various needs for the military. The metaphor he uses in Ephesians 6—likening a warrior's uniform to armor for spiritual warfare—may have come to him while working on military uniforms or tents. Possibly his meditations and teachings in this working context could have led him to develop this spiritual metaphor.

• *Sports Metaphors*

Likewise Paul's sports metaphors may have formed in his mind during the time he spent working and providing tents to crowds at sporting events. Similar to the above example of the military uniforms, Paul's meditations and even teachings in the context of the games could have led to his use of sports metaphors and analogies. As mentioned before, Paul was in Corinth at the time of the biennial Isthmian Games. The quadrennial Imperial and Caesarean Games also took place in Corinth.

These major sporting events would have been an excellent opportunity for Paul to meet a legitimate need, generate revenue for the mission, and interact with people from all over the region. It would have also been a time when he and others were thinking about sporting activities. Paul, undoubtedly, would have taken advantage of this and used the opportunity to not only talk sports but to use sports metaphors to communicate spiritual truth.

It is interesting that at the end of 1 Corinthians 9, a chapter in which Paul vigorously defends his decision to work as a tentmaker, he concludes with the use of athletic imagery. Perhaps Paul was remembering his times at work during the games in Corinth.

> Do you not know that in a race all the runners run, but only one gets the prize? Run in such a way as to get the prize. Everyone who competes in the games goes into strict training. They do it to get a crown that will not last; but we do it to get a crown that will last forever. Therefore I do not run like a man running aimlessly; I do not fight like a man beating the air. No, I beat my body and make it my slave so that after I have preached to others, I myself will not be disqualified for the prize.
>
> — 1 Corinthians 9:24–27

• *Slavery Metaphors*

Paul's slavery metaphors likewise may originate from the fact that he worked frequently alongside slaves. Though it is highly possible that Paul worked with slaves, his ethical guidance regarding slavery was very progressive in his cultural context.[10] Working in this context may have led to his metaphor of being a slave to righteousness juxtaposed against being a slave to sin (Romans 6:17). He also said that we were free in Christ and not slaves to legalism (Galatians 2:4). He gives guidance to slaves in his letters to the churches in Corinth (1 Corinthians 7), Ephesus (Ephesians 6), Colosse (Colossians 3–4), as well as in letters to Titus (Titus 2), Philemon (Philemon), and Timothy (1 Timothy 1, 5). Paul taught that there was "neither slave nor free" (Galatians 3:28) in Christ and that "we are not children of the slave woman, but of the free woman" (Galatians 4:31) and described slave traders as ungodly, unholy, and contrary to sound doctrine (1 Timothy 1:9–10). His ability to speak to the situation probably arose from his actually spending quality time with those in slavery, quite possibly in a workshop. His concern would have led to his desire to offer spiritual liberation in Christ (speaking in relevant, specific metaphors) and his admonition for slaves to obtain their earthly freedom if possible (1 Corinthians 7:21).

After understanding how much Paul worked, one naturally comes to the question of why. Why would Paul work as a tentmaker? As we shall see in the next chapter(s), there are many reasons.

Questions for Reflection & Discussion

1. What is the relevance of considering how much time Paul spent working as a tentmaker?

2. What is the relevance of considering how much Paul earned as a tentmaker?

3. How would Paul's workshop be conducive to promoting the gospel? What parallels exist in today's world?

4. Why did Paul at times likely choose not to work as a tentmaker?

5. How can workplace metaphors be used today to express God's truth?

chapter 7

PAUL'S CHOICE

So what if Paul worked as a tentmaker much of the time and at times earned significant money doing so? What is the relevance to us today? In order to make sense of Paul's trade work and to make application to our world today, it is necessary to understand precisely why he made tents. As we shall see, Paul had numerous reasons. Not all of these will be applicable to every BAM practitioner today. However, I think you will find Paul's likely reasoning compelling enough to view business as an effective means to live out the gospel.

The Pro Bono Preacher

Paul wanted to preach the gospel for free, and he wanted to be free to follow God without being controlled by others. The issue of freedom was very important to Paul. He sought personal freedom in paradoxical ways. He gave up his rights to payment to work a physically arduous trade in order to retain the freedom to preach the gospel without external control and free of charge.

The paradoxical theme of slavery and freedom runs through Paul's thought. In the Book of Romans, he wrote, "You have been set free from sin and have become slaves to righteousness" (Romans 6:18). He also asserted that the antithesis was also a paradox: "When you were slaves to sin, you were free from the control of righteousness" (Romans 6:20). He asserted that Christians had not ceased being slaves but had simply changed masters: "But now . . . you have been set free from sin and have become slaves to God" (Romans 6:22). When writing to people both slave and free, he taught them that neither was completely free nor a total slave: "For he who was a slave when he was called by the Lord is the Lord's freedman; similarly, he who was a free man when he was called is Christ's slave" (1 Corinthians 7:22). For Paul, true freedom came only from God: "Where the Spirit of the Lord is, there is freedom" (2 Corinthians 3:17).

In terms of charging for his services, Paul definitely believed he was free to do so. Many of the people in the Corinthian community critiqued Paul as an inadequate apostle since he did not earn his living from preaching the gospel. Paul argued vociferously that he was an apostle and had the right to charge for his service and could do so easily.

> Am I not free? Am I not an apostle? Have I not seen Jesus our Lord? Are you not the result of my work in the Lord? Even though I may not be an apostle to others, surely I am to you! For you are the seal of my apostleship in the Lord. This is my defense to those who sit in judgment on me.
>
> — 1 Corinthians 9:1–3

Paul goes on to point out that no one serves in the military at his own expense and that other apostles do not work for a living. He said that since he had "sown spiritual seed" among them that it was not "too much if we reap a material harvest" (1 Corinthians 9:11). He noted that God taught in the Old Testament that the worker deserves to be paid, quoting Deuteronomy 25:4, "Do not muzzle an ox while it is treading out the grain." He stated clearly that this applied to him and his team: "Yes, this was written for us, because when the plowman plows and the thresher threshes, they ought to do so in the hope of sharing in the harvest" (1 Corinthians 9:10). He even added that Jesus, the Lord "has commanded that those who preach the gospel should receive their living from the gospel" (1 Corinthians 9:14). In his epistle to the Galatians he said that their teachers deserved to be compensated: "Anyone who receives instruction in the word must share all good things with his instructor" (Galatians 6:6).

Despite this clear argument that it was well within his rights to collect funds for the preaching of the gospel, he clearly at times "did not use this right" (1 Corinthians 9:12).

Why on earth would he build such a strong case to be paid then not act on it? As we shall see, there were a multiplicity of factors but one of the clearest and most obvious was simply that Paul wanted to be able to preach the gospel free of charge. He said, "What then is my reward? Just this: that in preaching the gospel I may offer it free of charge, and so not make use of my rights in preaching it" (1 Corinthians 9:18). In a later letter to the Corinthian congregation, he reiterated his purpose for working, asking rhetorically, "Was it a sin for me to lower myself in order to elevate you by preaching the gospel of God to you free of charge?" (2 Corinthians 11:7).

Paul saw his decision to work as something like a decision to go into slavery in order to maintain the freedom of preaching the gospel for free. As he culminated his argument on working a trade for financial remuneration he wrote, "Though I am free and belong to no man, I make myself a slave to everyone, to win as many as possible" (1 Corinthians 9:19).

Patronage in Corinth

One of the big issues underlying Paul's decision to work as a tentmaker and preach pro bono was that of patronage. E. A. Judge writes that, at this time, "The Christians were dominated by a socially pretentious section of the population of the big cities."[1] One of the complications of the Corinthian situation was that many were "already suffering from a self-made-person-escapes-humble-origins syndrome."[2]

Paul says that not many of the Corinthians were wise, influential, or of noble birth (1 Corinthians 1:26). But there were undoubtedly a few wealthy and it seems that they probably, as a result of their wealth, had a disproportionate influence over the others. The wealthy were the ones who hosted church gatherings in their homes (1 Corinthians 16:15,19). These homes could hold up to 50 people. Two passages, Romans 16:23

and 1 Corinthians 14:23, describe "the whole church coming together," which seems to imply gatherings of the church of an entire city in a single location. This would have only been possible if there were wealthy and hospitable members with large houses.

The Corinthian congregation was a diverse lot. Many appear to have been fairly poor. 1 Corinthians 1:28 communicates that there were many of lowly status. Domestic slaves were also in the congregation (1 Corinthians 7:21–23). Despite the presence of poverty in the congregation, 1 Corinthians 16:2–3 proves that they had the means to collect financial donations in order to help the poor in Jerusalem. The Corinthian congregation had members who fit along a socioeconomic continuum, which appears to have been typical of the churches that Paul planted. This would have created a certain complexity that a homogenous community would not have had.

Unfortunately, a type of dysfunctional relationship between the wealthy and the poor was hindering spiritual maturity in the congregation. Paul rebuked them for this.

> For as you eat, each of you goes ahead without waiting for anybody else. One remains hungry; another gets drunk. Don't you have homes to eat and drink in? Or do you despise the church of God and humiliate those who have nothing? What shall I say to you? Shall I praise you for this? Certainly not!
>
> — 1 Corinthians 11:21–22

This type of phenomena in the congregation showed that their behavior was more reflective of Greco-Roman society than of the Christian faith. The wealthy in Corinth were still more concerned with maintaining their power rather than helping the poor near and far.

In order to accept patronage, Paul would have had to give up a substantial amount of personal liberty, which he felt was necessary in order to accomplish his God-given task of planting new churches in previously untouched territories. Essentially he would have had to do what he was told by his patron. This is something he was unwilling to do, especially given the obvious spiritual immaturity of the wealthy in this particular congregation.

In Corinth, Paul rebuffs attempts by the social elite to offer their patronage.[3] The situation is amplified because he works a "lowly trade." He wants to offer the gospel free of charge and asserts his "right" to refuse patronage. Paul used tentmaking in Corinth and other places because it was useful to the gospel. Patronage would have isolated him from the outside world and caused him to be consumed by the social network of patrons and clients. He preferred to have ready access to average people who would frequent the market.

Another problem related to patronage is that it tends to create an atmosphere conducive to greed and/or compromise. In seminary, a professor told me that he once had an offer to serve as a theological consultant to a wealthy businessman. The man would pay the professor a monthly stipend for the right to call him up and pose a question whenever he so desired. The professor wanted to accept this job as he could have used the funds. However, he refused and instead offered his services for free to the would-be benefactor. He explained his reason for refusing by simply stating he was too weak to do it: He knew that he would be unable to say whatever he truly believed once money was integrated in the process. There are many accounts in the Old Testament of professed prophets who simply said what their benefactors wanted them to say.

An additional key issue is that Paul seemingly needed to be self-sufficient in order to minister most effectively. This desire for self-sufficiency is a common aspect of modern missions. William Carey, the great pioneer missionary to India, eventually severed his relationship with his missions society because he was frustrated with the level of control they attempted to exert over his ministry. I have witnessed this same scenario repeated quite often in various parts of the world 200 years later. The majority of missional entrepreneurs with whom I have worked and communicated have indicated that a motivating factor in achieving economic profitability is to put themselves in position to be self-governing and self-sustaining. Many leaders are frequently irritated and annoyed, as Carey was, by interventions and interruptions to their work by far-off agency executives.

Similarly many missionaries also indicate a growing frustration with the need to constantly appeal to people back home for funds, characteristically described as "feeling like a beggar." While missionaries deserve to be supported and a system of checks and balances is often warranted, these aspects often feel restraining to entrepreneurial missionaries who live among the needy and long for the ability to respond quickly and effectively to them.

The Far Reach of Finances

Financial arrangements are always complicated, which is one of the reasons why developed nations have established elaborate judicial systems. There is a tremendous need to ensure that people are handling money fairly and ethically and that there is a system of recourse when disputes arise. This applies to the business world, the church world, and the missionary world. In the classic *Missionary Methods: St. Paul's or Ours?* Roland Allen wrote, "The primary importance of missionary finance lies in the fact that financial arrangements very seriously affect the relations between the missionary and those whom he approaches."[4] This was true 1900 years earlier when Paul was traveling about, and it is true in our time as well.

As one who has lived overseas and been involved in numerous intercultural church situations, I have experienced the various tensions involved with financial compensation. When I lived in Russia as part of a faith-based, educational nonprofit organization, I earned a mere $300 per month and lived in a 600-square-foot apartment. Nevertheless, people questioned why I had so much money and pointed out that I, a 22-year-old at the time, had the earning power of a manager in a Russian company.

Several years later, my wife and I moved to Santiago, Chile, with a missions organization. We earned a combined $1,000 a month and lived in a 70-year-old house. The house was smaller than an average US house and was in such dilapidated condition that the roof collapsed shortly after we moved out. Nevertheless, Chilean confidants told us that our standard of living was a matter of debate among the Christian community since we earned our living from the church. This debate occurred even though the money was not coming from the local church, rather from our US church network.

The situation today regarding missionary financing is complex and varied. It seems clear that missionary support was a thorny issue and a basis for criticism in Paul's day as well. He was aware of this and wanted to avoid problems as much as he could. By working as a tentmaker, he deflected some of the criticism that could have come his way had he relied purely on the church for his financial compensation.

Just an Average Guy

Paul sought to build real-world relationships. He wanted to develop relationships with people because he knew that this is how the message is spread. He used all of the connections available in the vast network of business relationships to promote and spread the gospel.

Paul said, "I have become all things to all men, so that by all possible means I might save some" (1 Corinthians 9:22). This quote concludes his explanation and justification of why he did not work as a donor-supported minister. This shows that Paul did not do this because he had to or because he wanted to—rather this was Paul's strategy! According to the obvious flow of this passage, this is Paul's climactic reason for working rather than taking support. He worked in order to become all things to all people.

Christians need to follow Paul's example and identify with the people to whom they are ministering. There are many ways to do this, but there is definitely a need to identify with them in a business context as well. It is worth pointing out that Paul's business enabled him to identify with a group of people with whom he would not normally identify. Paul was a Jew and a Roman citizen of high education so he could easily identify with those from similar backgrounds. His work as a tentmaker was a deliberate strategy that enabled him to identify with another, primarily different, group of people. By participating in trade associations and guilds he would have become enmeshed in their social networks. He avoided the patronage system for many reasons, but undoubtedly one reason was that he did not want to be consumed and confined by one particular social network.

Nonetheless, even though Paul didn't want to be a client to high-status people, Paul still managed to find a way to interact with them, convert them, and plug them into ministry. Many prominent people were church leaders of the early Christian movement. They were "people with households." Examples would be Philemon and Stephanus. The houses could fit up to 50 people for church fellowship gatherings. Many of the people clearly had disposable income.

Many tend to assume that Paul would have preferred to preach every day rather than work as a tentmaker. However, when one removes this preconceived bias from the reading it becomes clear that this is not true. First, Paul explicitly makes the claim that he purposefully chose to work as a tentmaker and neither people nor circumstances forced him to work as such (1 Corinthians 9). Second, careful reading and analysis show that he worked more often than is commonly assumed. Third, an awareness of evangelistic and relational network dynamics shows the effectiveness of his strategy.

Cultivating Credibility

In his theoretical work, Aristotle elaborated on a concept that he called *ethos*, which we would probably refer to as credibility. He calls this "the most important mode of persuasion." Aristotle taught that the presentation of the speaker's character causes the audience to "believe the speaker."[5] For Aristotle ethos was much more than simply a technical rhetorical device. As George Kennedy writes, "Aristotle does not use the term in the technical sense of 'rhetorical ethos,' the technique or effect of the presentation character in a discourse." For him, it meant character, especially moral character and is regarded as "an attribute of persons, not of a speech."[6] For Aristotle, credibility is so important that "an opportunity to present a witness of one's character should not be missed."[7] The purpose of this credibility building was aimed at "gaining the audience's goodwill."[8]

It should be noted that Aristotle's use of ethos built on the foundation developed by his mentor, Plato. For Plato, ethos defines the space where language and truth meet and are made incarnate within the individual. Plato's definition is based on "the moral, and ultimately, theological inseparability of the speaker-agent from the speech act." Plato continually restated in uncompromising fashion this formulation: "truth must be incarnate within the individual, and a person's language must express (or, first, discover) this truth." Plato taught that the aspect of character was inseparable from speech and actions. Following the example of his mentor, Aristotle later put even greater emphasis on the necessity of character.[9]

As mentioned before, Paul worked as a tentmaker in order to identify with people. By doing so, he also gained credibility. He showed that he cared more about his message than his money. Therefore, he would not appear as someone altering his message in order to increase his financial intake, being in it "for the money." He was able to silence this accusation from his critics. Paul was keenly aware of this possible basis for criticism and avoided it by not receiving his income from the church.

He also gained credibility by providing a visible manifestation of his true, inner character. By working in a normal job, Paul was able to naturally model or bear witness to a Christian lifestyle to the people around him. They could see that his speech and actions were inseparable. As we all know, it is easy to demonstrate a holy life within the confines of church, but much more difficult in the world. Paul was able to do just that. This move not only gained him credibility but also helped him to avoid the criticism of being out of touch with people's real lives.[10]

So what does the credibility that Paul gained on the job have to do with the Aristotelian rhetorical theory of ethos? It is possible that a variety of influences led Paul to develop a theory of communication that did not rely simply on rhetoric, but emphasized actions more than mere words. Paul likely would have been familiar with the Platonic and Aristotelian concepts of ethos, the gaining of credibility through the appearance of sound moral character.

It is very possible that Paul was well informed of and even shaped by Aristotelian thought. For instance, Quintilian, writing in the first century A.D., still cited Aristotle's assessment that ethos is the most important mode of persuasion.[11] Rhetorical schools of Greek thought were common in Jewish areas when Paul was a boy, and he may have attended one. Other Jews did, and one of the most famous communicators of the century before Paul was Caecilius of Calacte, also a Jew. Paul quotes Greek poets, and some scholars see influence of Greek communication theories in his writings.[12]

Paul intuitively knew that communication is not just about rhetoric. He knew that speech and actions should be inseparable. In other words, the perceived character qualities needed to be real. Furthermore, by the time Paul started his church-planting ministry he would have been deeply impacted by the incarnational mission of Christ. Paul would have reflected on its deep meaning and the impact it had on the people who understood it. This would have influenced his strategy development.

Therefore, we can say that Paul, whether consciously or not, practically applied Aristotelian communication theory. He did this because of his intuitive sense that there was more to communication than simply talking, and the impact of his reflections on the incarnation of Christ led him to develop a strategy for ministry that brought these truths together. Paul understood that just as faith without works is dead, so are words without supporting action. The point is this: Paul worked as a tentmaker to gain credibility by demonstrating his character and thus allowing him to effectively communicate the gospel message.[13]

Paul was not necessarily a very good orator. He pointed out that he was not "a trained speaker" (2 Corinthians 11:6) and that his message did not come "with wise and persuasive words" (1 Corinthians 2:4). As mentioned in the previous chapter, Paul most likely suffered from an eye illness and an unsightly appearance. This would have hampered his standing among many people. Therefore, he sought to strengthen his communication package by enhancing his credibility in other ways. Rhetoric is about persuasion. Paul's trade was part of a comprehensive persuasion strategy.

Credibility building does not mean that we do not have to use words. Rather it means that we have credibility when we use them and use them we must. Speaking is like legs to a marathoner. Credibility is like the heart, lungs, mental strength, and physical endurance. To run a marathon you need the complete package and so it is with being an effective communicator of the gospel. Paul understood this and his trade helped him to compensate for his weaknesses and to expand and improve his total communication package.

Living Out the Lifestyle

Modeling was another aspect of Paul's tentmaking strategy. He was not afraid to tell his followers to "become like me" (Galatians 4:12). Being an example for his converts to follow was clearly part of Paul's strategy. By working in a normal job, Paul was able to naturally model or bear witness to a Christian lifestyle to the people around him. The people with whom Paul worked would not have considered his work abnormal since most people had to work. Paul would not have had the opportunity to demonstrate his character in this way if he had gone the patron-client route.

As we all know, it is easy to demonstrate a holy life within the confines of church, but much more difficult in the world. Paul was able to do just that. This kept Paul free from being criticized for living a holy life in the synagogue but not in the marketplace. It also showed that his message was relevant to everyday life. Paul stated quite clearly that this was part of his strategy when he wrote, "Join with others in following my example, brothers, and take note of those who live according to the pattern we gave you" (Philippians 3:17).

In modeling a Christian lifestyle to the people around him, Paul was able to demonstrate how a Christian can handle temptations to sin in the workplace. One of the struggles I had when I served as a "full-time minister" was that I felt like I did not have opportunities to practice what I preached before the people to whom I was ministering. I had no opportunity to treat a customer fairly, to practice financial integrity in a business setting, or to demonstrate how to handle difficult ethical situations that are commonplace in the contemporary corporate environment. Paul did not have this difficulty.

The Corinthians had huge ethical problems, "Instead, you yourselves cheat and do wrong, and you do this to your brothers" (1 Corinthians 6:8). Since Paul worked among people, he was able to show what it meant to not cheat customers. When ethical dilemmas presented themselves, Paul could show how a mature Christian should handle it. Obviously many of Paul's other disciples also struggled with the temptations common to business. To the Ephesians he wrote: "He who has been stealing must steal no longer, but must work, doing something useful with his own hands, that he may have something to share with those in need" (Ephesians 4:28). He was not limited to just telling his disciples what to do, leaving them shaking their heads and muttering, "Easier said than done." Rather he showed them and helped them see that it could, in fact, be done.

By modeling a Christian lifestyle at work he not only showed how a Christian should respond to temptation but also demonstrated that authentic faith is an integral aspect of daily life. In his epistle to the church in Thessalonica, Paul admonishes the church not to focus on their persecution and mistreatment but on being credible witnesses for the gospel.

> Make it your ambition to lead a quiet life, to mind your own business and to work with your hands, just as we told you, so that your daily life may win the respect of outsiders and so that you will not be dependent on anybody.
>
> — 1 Thessalonians 4:11–12

Paul clearly instructs those people of the church of Thessalonica who were not working to work. He was not telling them to do something that he was not doing. Earlier in the letter he had already reminded them that "we worked night and day in order not to be a burden to anyone while we preached the gospel of God to you" (1 Thessalonians 2:9) and he had commended them as being "imitators of us" (1 Thessalonians 1:6). As Ben Witherington wrote, "In the end, Paul modeled how working with one's hands could actually aid missions and evangelism rather than impede them."[14]

These short passages in 1 Thessalonians are quite revealing of Paul's way of thinking. There are several aspects that deserve our attention. First, Paul makes it clear that his love for them is the driving factor for his exhortations. In 1 Thessalonians 2 and 4, before addressing the issue of work, Paul discusses love. He wrote, "We loved you so much that we were delighted to share with you not only the gospel of God but our lives as well, because you had become so dear to us" (1 Thessalonians 2:8) Then he explains how they worked constantly during their stay. Before telling them that they needed to "work with their own hands" Paul took the opportunity to gently remind them of the importance of love. He wrote, "Now about brotherly love we do not need to write to you, for you yourselves have been taught by God to love each other" (1 Thessalonians 4:9). Paul was not a civic official who was trying to put people to work so he could tax them. He was also not a controlling religious leader who wanted his converts to work so that they could give him more money. Rather he exhorts them to work only because he loves them and desires the best for them.

Second, Paul worked not only to avoid burdening them, but also so his work could serve as a model for them. He calls them to work for precisely the same reason he says he worked, namely that through work they would not be dependent on anybody. This is reiteration of the earlier theme of freedom from external forces. This, as we may remember, was a large reason why Paul refused patronage. The primary point here is that Paul's working was able to serve as a model for his disciples.

Third, work is again connected to the earning of respect or credibility. Paul wanted their daily lives to win the respect of outsiders. All too often Christians are left with the vague understanding that our faith is only of importance on the weekend. Paul wanted people to see that faith was important to daily life and that work was of value to their faith.

Fourth, there is Paul's interesting admonition to "make it your ambition to live a quiet life and to mind your own business" (1 Thessalonians 4:11). What does this mean? What is Paul asking them to do exactly? The ironic paradox of joining ambition with living a quiet life should first be acknowledged. The term *ambition* is seldom associated with living quietly and sticking to one's affairs. It more often conjures up images of becoming a high-powered tycoon in the societal spotlight. The statement was also loaded with irony when Paul wrote it. As mentioned earlier, this is in the context of persecution and Paul found it best to work on quietly building up the community through love, affirmation, and work. Through the development of such a Christian community they would then be credible and effective witnesses to the outside world.

Paul's concern that they live "a quiet life" should not be equated with withdrawal from the world. Paul was clearly not calling the Thessalonians to pack up and leave. While Paul elsewhere cautions against the spiritually harmful influences of the world (Romans 12:2), he models a life of active engagement with it and calls other Christians to do the same.

Paul modeled the Christian lifestyle in highly competitive unethical environments, which are similar to the world today. Scholars point out that Corinth was a city of unscrupulous business people who would do anything and everything to get ahead. Their competitiveness and ruthlessness is seen in the fact that Corinth was the first Greek city to have Roman gladiatorial contests. It was said to be a city where public boasting and self-promotion had become an art form. Paul's humble manner and willingness to lower himself would have starkly contrasted with the first-century "Joneses" who were doing all they could to "win" and look good in front of their peers.

Not Afraid to Work Hard

Paul showed what it meant to work for a living and he demonstrated to his followers that he was willing and able to work hard. He said, "In everything I did, I showed you that by this kind of hard work we must help the weak, remembering the words the Lord Jesus himself said: 'It is more blessed to give than to receive'" (Acts 20:35).

Instilling the need to work properly is also a necessity in many parts of the world. The minister who is not otherwise employed can have difficulties teaching on this subject and conveying its importance. Paul was also able to demonstrate a quality work ethic.

Laziness did not develop with the television, but has been around for a while. Paul had to admonish his readers not to be idle. Furthermore, he was able to back it up by pointing to his example.

> In the name of the Lord Jesus Christ, we command you, brothers, to keep away from every brother who is idle and does not live according to the teaching you received from us. For you yourselves know how you ought to follow our example. We were not idle when we were with you, nor did we eat anyone's food without paying for it. On the contrary, we worked night and day, laboring and toiling so that we would not be a burden to any of you. We did this, not because we do not have the right to such help, but in order to make ourselves a model for you to follow.
>
> — 2 Thessalonians 3:6–9

Paul was able to speak strongly and boldly, because he was doing what he was calling on others to do. A lack of work ethic in many countries of the world today has led to poverty, an inability to produce, and a socioeconomic quagmire that is not broken with mere speeches.

As a missionary in Russia, I was able to see how 70 years of communism had produced a lackadaisical work ethic that in turn led to an economy that could barely sustain its people at a minimal standard of living. The breakdown of the Russian economy was so severe that many workers would go months without receiving wages. This resulted in the oft-quoted Russian joke, "We pretend to work; they pretend to pay us." Of course, this is not limited to Russia, but is seen all over the two-thirds world. These poor, developing countries often need immediate and emergency humanitarian help. But to establish a long-term solution they need to have a self-sustaining and vibrant economy. This can only be developed when workers have a strong work ethic. A solid work ethic is vital for economic development and creates a more productive, just system. Paul did not merely preach this work ethic but practiced it as well.

Teaching and Modeling the Truth

Paul took every opportunity to teach God's truth to people. There was no question that Paul was strategic in whom he sought out. For instance, he would go to the synagogue and explain to the Jews how Jesus fulfilled the Law. Paul was not just a preacher in the synagogue though—he would have also communicated gospel truth in his tentmaking workshop.

From Paul's practical experience ministering in his workplace setting, he was equipped to pass on practical tips and applicable advice. To the Colossians, he said, "Be wise in the way you act toward outsiders; make the most of every opportunity. Let your conversation be always full of grace, seasoned with salt, so that you may know how to answer everyone" (Colossians 4:5–6). He knew what it was like to be around the same people everyday in the workplace, therefore he understood the importance of managing the relationships properly. He encouraged them to be wise and sensitive to their listeners. From his experiences working in other locations he had probably seen how a Christian lifestyle in speech frequently led to questions. Therefore, he told them to watch their conversation and be ready to answer.

The importance of Paul's workshop evangelism has been noted before. T. G. Soares wrote that Paul's relationship with Priscilla and Aquila "may very well suggest the constant personal evangelism that Paul must have carried on during his hours of labor with the various fellow-workers with whom he was thrown into companionship."[15] The likelihood is great when one considers the quiet nature of a leatherworking shop and that many philosophers at the time were known to conduct teachings sessions in their workplace.

The Acts 18 story of Priscilla and Aquila is probably the best example of how Paul ministered to fellow tradespeople and communicated the fullness of the truth of God to them. When Priscilla and Aquila met Paul they were probably already Christians. However, undoubtedly Paul took them deeper in the faith. It is very possible that Paul taught them how to blend workplace excellence and effective evangelism. They became tentmaking missionaries themselves, traveling on to Ephesus no doubt still practicing their trade and teaching the Way to people like Apollos.

Paul modeled teaching in the context of daily life, which made spiritual instruction seem natural and flowing rather than forced and uncomfortable as it is commonly perceived. Due to this style, Paul created a positive feedback cycle that enabled exponential growth. His converts became teachers and their converts became teachers and the positive feedback cycle continued. While Paul clearly sought to turn converts into missionaries, he did not necessarily call them to pack up and go. Rather he encouraged them to live out their faith wherever they were.

Paul did not have to continually exhort his students to be evangelists. He simply modeled and taught in such a way that evangelism seemed a normal and natural part of being a fully devoted follower of Christ. Too often being an evangelist is thought of as a specific and unique calling of God on an elected remnant of especially devout people. Paul's life and teaching exclaim the opposite: everyone should be a missionary in his daily life, just where he is.

Idols in the Workplace

An interesting aspect of Paul's life and teaching related to the workplace that deserves consideration is how he related to idolatry. To the Corinthians he was quite strong in his message saying, "My dear friends, flee from idolatry" (1 Corinthians 10:14). Yet when it came to food sacrificed to idols he allowed them some room for flexibility.

> So then, about eating food sacrificed to idols: We know that an idol is nothing at all in the world and that there is no God but one. For even if there are so-called gods, whether in heaven or on earth (as indeed there are many 'gods' and many 'lords'), yet for us there is but one God, the Father, from whom all things came and for whom we live; and there is but one Lord, Jesus Christ, through whom all things came and through whom we live. But not everyone knows this. Some people are still so accustomed to idols that when they eat such food they think of it as having been sacrificed to an idol,

and since their conscience is weak, it is defiled. But food does not bring us near to God; we are no worse if we do not eat, and no better if we do.

— 1 Corinthians 8:4–8

So Paul wanted his converts to flee idolatry, but was tolerant of people eating food sacrificed to idols if their consciences allowed for it, noting that food in and of itself does not take us away or bring us closer to God. Why is this relevant? It is interesting because we do not have any indication that Paul told his converts to quit working in workshops where pagan rites were performed. It seems 1 Corinthians 8 makes it possible for his converts to continue to work at their trades as members of guilds or societies that were anti-Christian in many regards. Many of the early Christians were from the working class, and a large number of them undoubtedly faced this situation.

There are a few reasons why Paul would not have directed converts to leave their jobs. First, as working class people they needed income. Therefore, had Paul encouraged them to leave those jobs he could have put them in a difficult situation financially. Second, as seen throughout Paul's letters, he values work and desires for his converts to continue working for its own sake. Nevertheless, Paul could have encouraged them to withdraw from the pagan guilds and form their own new "Christian" guilds and work societies.

This would have been undesirable, however, for one primary reason: namely that it would have removed recent Christian converts from the social network in which they were enmeshed and the one they should most influence with their newfound faith in Christ. Paul facilitated the growth of the church by teaching people in a natural fashion and in such a way that they were able to reproduce his teaching method. He then kept his converts in their regular jobs so that they could then follow his example and be a spiritual influence in their workplace and aid in the rapid spread of the gospel.

This does not mean that idol worship would not have been strongly condemned by Paul. There were Christians who quit the military and other professions when pagan worship was *required*. However, it seems that Paul allowed some Christians to stay in some professions that would have normally been related to idol worship, with the condition that they did not participate in idol worship.

There is a tendency in many church settings to emphasize "full-time" Christian ministers over the laity. This has led to three problems. First, vocational ministers are frequently overburdened trying to do everything. Second, the laity are not engaging the people around them like they could, because they believe the vocational minister is paid to do that. This results in the vocational minister running around trying to be creative and make contact with people in order to evangelize them. These are the same people that the laity naturally see on an everyday basis.

Third, church and personal growth is slowed tremendously when new people come to Christ and are then removed from their natural environment before being empowered in ministry. Too often today new converts are encouraged to separate from the very people they are most likely to influence—those with whom they regularly eat, work, and recreate. Perhaps the new Christian is encouraged to go to seminary or Bible college in order to learn more about his faith. Maybe he is encouraged to find a "full-time ministry position" and "leave the business world behind." Often her job is viewed as a "distraction" to ministry or perceived as "too secular."

In some cases it is undoubtedly wise and warranted for the Christian to make major life changes and pursue new endeavors. However, I have seen many people leave their jobs to pursue ministry only to find a ministry job and discover it is difficult to establish contact with the very people to whom they want to minister. These are the same people with whom they previously had frequent and natural contact. Paul encouraged his followers to be salt and light exactly where they were. He spawned a rapid, indigenous church planting movement across the Roman Empire (Romans 15:19–23). He did not do this alone, but rather in conjunction with empowered converts who followed his example of teaching God's truth naturally in their daily lives.

Reaching the Upper Crust

Business functions as a hub of relationships. To be involved in economic enterprise is to belong to a vast social network. I am continually impressed with the number of people with whom even a small, routine business can bring me into contact. Some of these people are entrepreneurs looking to expand their business by engaging in business with a new business. Others are government inspectors, ensuring that laws are followed and the proper processes are conducted. Still others are clients who need the service in question. Then there are the fellow employees. Any business activity functions in the context of relationships.

Paul not only established relationships with business partners and potential clients, but most likely with all of the people that his entrepreneurial activities brought along his path of life. One person who would have crossed his path would be the city's *aedile*. The aedile would have been a prominent person whose job was to maintain the public streets, buildings, and marketplaces and collect revenues from such places. The position could be called something like a city administrator today.

In Corinth, at the time of Paul, there was an aedile named Erastus. We know this from Romans 16:23 where Paul mentions Erastus, the city's director of public works (aedile). It is very possible that Erastus's task of collecting revenues from local businesses is what initially put him in contact with Paul. Erastus probably would have stopped by Paul's shops for the appropriate payment. Paul may have invited him in for a cup of tea, started up a conversation, and explained something of his apostolic mission. Being intrigued, Erastus could have followed up with other visits for discussion and been plugged into the burgeoning Christian fellowship in Corinth. Not only would Erastus have benefited spiritually from the meeting, it is quite possible that he proved very helpful to Paul and the local church. He may have even helped Paul get established selling tents at the aforementioned Isthmian Games.[16]

Paul sought to spiritually influence the entirety of the vast web of business relationships that his trade put him in. He found himself in relationships with the working class, even slaves. He also interacted with business partners like Priscilla and Aquila, who were most likely people of means and status. And in all business relationships there is an outer sphere of people with whom the businessperson has less contact but must interact with periodically. These people would also have a wide range of political and social importance. Paul desired to reach them all and reach many he did, even high-status city administrators like Erastus. This is part of the genius of Paul's business-missions strategy.

Conclusion

Paul clearly had reasons for why he chose to continue his tentmaking trade. Those reasons are far more sophisticated than a simple need for money. His approach helped him model a lifestyle to his followers that they could emulate, put him in relationship with a vast web of people, and helped him to show everyone that the Christian faith is a way of life and not simply a set of beliefs.

Questions for Reflection & Discussion

1. Why was Paul a tentmaker?

2. How can finances create complex personal relationships?

3. How could have Aristotle's theory of credibility influenced Paul?

4. What are the present implications for the workplace of Paul's teaching on eating food sacrificed to idols?

5. How can business be a vehicle to influence people of various social strata?

part 3

MOTIVATIONS
AND
MIND-SET

chapter 8

CURRENT AND HISTORICAL TRENDS AND PARALLELS

Business as mission (BAM) is an emerging missionary practice. The way(s) in which it is practiced and understood today is a fairly recent phenomenon. However, there is historical precedence for BAM, and there are several contemporary developments in the larger business community that relate to and/or parallel BAM. Thus, providing an historical context and an examination of these related trends for BAM is warranted.

BAM Forerunners

The term *business as mission* was first coined in 1999 by a small group of leaders meeting at the Oxford Center for Mission Studies in the United Kingdom.[1] But the history of BAM goes back much further than the turn of the last century. Historians Heinz Suter and Marco Gmür note that trade has been a means for spreading the gospel throughout 2,000 years of church history, often as an intentional strategy. They write, "History furnishes hard evidence that business, trade and solid Christian professionalism have been used of God in order to transmit the Gospel message along the regions of the silk routes, probably starting from as early as the day of Pentecost (Acts 2:9) . . . and continuing up until the fifteenth century."[2]

The Nestorians

The Nestorians were a group of Eastern Christians who had a passion for sharing their faith and supported themselves by their business as they planted churches across Asia in the first millennium after Christ. While their missionary strategy probably involved clerical and lay strategies—meaning that they made distinctions between priests and lay people—it is highly probable that both clergy and laity would have financially supported themselves through business.

Historian Samuel Moffett notes that Nestorian missionaries accompanied Arab embassies to China in order to take advantage of "Arab sea and trade routes to the Far East that were far superior to the long and arduous hardships of the Old Silk Road." Due to Nestorian missionaries' extensive experience in China, Muslim Arabs employed them as interpreters and advisers.[3]

William Carey

William Carey, considered by many to be the father of modern missions, engaged in numerous income-generating work projects, including spending six years as a manager of an indigo plant, and he infused into India a work ethic that is historically considered as revolutionary. Dwight Baker notes that the organizational structures of businesses influenced Carey, and he patterned the formation of missions agencies after commercial joint-stock companies.[4]

Basel Mission Trading Company

Basel Mission Trading Company, started in 1815 as the Basel Mission Society, is another historical precedent. The first president, C. G. Blumhardt, developed a model whereby the missionary would not only be trained in theology but also in a trade, as "craftsmen-theologians."

This ministry philosophy turned into a fruitful reality. The craftsmen-theologians went far and wide and founded a number of profitable, high-quality businesses. One of their missionaries even invented khaki cloth as a way to tolerate the withering and burning sun in India. This company grew dramatically in terms of economic production and profits. However, "profits shall not be the main goal of the company" was a guiding principle.[5]

Their primary goal was to be salt and light and provide living examples of authentic Christianity through business.

The Moravians

The Moravians, one of the first Protestant denominations with roots going back to the fifteenth-century reformer John Hus, expected their missionaries to be able to support themselves through business enterprise. Count Zinzendorf, an eighteenth-century leader of the Moravians, did not want to combine missions with colonization, so he had the missionaries work independently. He would send them out in pairs, and they would earn an income as they traveled. The goal was not to save money for the sending church but to teach the people the dignity of labor.

The Puritans

In 1904, Max Weber became quite famous in the world of economics writing about the Protestant work ethic among the Puritans. Through the years economists have discussed Weber's perspective but have largely ignored the relationship of business to missions for the Puritans. Steven Pointer and Michael Cooper assert that the relationship between business and missions for the Puritans in the seventeenth-century Bay Colony was a thoroughly intimate and integrated one at all levels. They point out that the planting of churches and evangelistic outreach to the Native Americans was of central concern to the Puritans and work was seen "as much a spiritual expression as it was an economic function."[6]

Chinese in Malaysia

The little known story of Chinese Christians in Malaysia is a worthy example of BAM. For them, Christian belief and economic progress were, from the beginning, in tight connection. For these Chinese economic and evangelical pioneers, economic progress and mission functioned interdependently in all pioneering missions work. According to Karl Rennstich, who worked among them, the relationship of their business to their evangelical missions helped clarify that their religion did not come from their culture and their jobs were not separate from their spiritual lives. Even generations after their arrival in Malaysia, their work ethic remains tightly connected to their understanding of faith, God, and missions.[7]

These historical accounts demonstrate that missionaries through the years have used business as a means in spreading the gospel.

Contemporary Phenomenon

In recent years the amount of attention given to business in missions activities has grown exponentially. There are several factors producing this increased interest:

- *Globalization.* The world is more interdependent than ever before. We trade more and communicate more quickly and more often with each other. Business is the engine that is driving globalization, and this has not gone unnoticed by Christians in business and Christians in missions.

- *Access.* Many of the least evangelized parts of the world are particularly hostile to Christianity but surprisingly open for business. Although, I argue that access alone is an insufficient reason to engage in BAM, it is undoubtedly a significant driver to the movement.

- *Empowerment of the laity.* In the last 25 years there has been a shift from "high church" structures with an emphasis on ordination, clergy leadership, etc., to a more lay-based approach. This trend is noticeable even in historically high church denominations.

- *Increased awareness of poverty and human suffering.* We have more technological and travel capabilities today than ever before. This has opened the eyes of many people to the world's suffering, and they have looked to business as a possible solution.

- *Increased social consciousness in business.* Historically, free market capitalism has defined the goal of business as the maximization of financial returns for shareholders. However, this definition is being expanded as businesses and business schools start to emphasize the social responsibility and potential of business. This has caused many

Christians to see business in a more favorable light, especially in regard to Christian missions.

Figure 8.1

CONTEMPORARY BAM

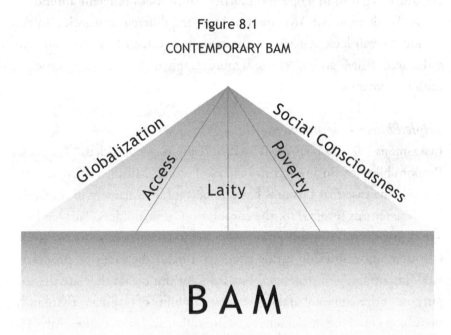

As a result of these factors, BAM has become a global phenomenon. It is not always recognized as BAM per se but the intentionality of using BAM as a vehicle for God's will is there. I have traveled in more 70 countries and have observed that BAM is not a "white man's solution" nor is it a Western phenomenon or concept. It is embraced and developed by people everywhere, whether they are South Africans working in Nigeria, Indians in Kuwait, or Thai businesspeople in Bangkok. BAM is being done by Christians who care deeply about God and His mission, enjoy business, and see it as an instrument for the will of God.

Current Cultural Influences

Because it is global in scope and practice, BAM looks different around the world. Work done as BAM could fit in several different categories. In this section we will look at some of the current trends in business that have influenced BAM and/or created more emphasis on socially conscious business activities.

Triple Bottom Line Business

In a famous 1970 essay in *The New York Times Magazine* titled, "The Social Responsibility of Business Is to Increase Profits," Milton Friedman tried to build the case that business has one bottom line, namely to maximize financial returns (profits) for the corporation's shareholders. This has been a dominant view in business literature and in business schools, including Christian universities. In earlier chapters, I made the case that profits are vital, important, and necessary. But I do not think that they are the sole purpose or the sum total of the social responsibility of business. Thankfully, there is an emerging movement in business that also sees it differently. The catch phrase of this new direction is "the triple bottom line," which means that business should not simply be measured by its quarterly profits but also by its long-term economic, social, and environmental performance. The shorthand for this is "people, planet, and profit." This triple bottom line is sometimes referred to as corporate social responsibility (CSR).

Part of the financial reasoning behind the triple bottom line is that a push for short-term gain can cause long-term pain. In other words, many businesses do not do well in the long run because of decisions they make to increase profits for the near future. Part of the triple bottom line rationale is that business should incorporate social and environmental metrics in order to ensure that their strategies are sustainable.

In terms of a social bottom line, businesses put extra concern into their labor relations, community involvement, and overall social impact. For years these issues had been seen in isolation from one another and subservient to the greater purpose of maximizing profits. Today, more and more business leaders from Fortune 500 CEOs to upstart entrepreneurs understand that these issues are interconnected and pivotal to long-term success.

Related to the social bottom line is the environmental bottom line. Environmental sustainability is generally defined as providing resources for this generation without doing harm to future generations. For many people, like myself, this seems like common sense and should be our minimal goal. Nevertheless, for years businesses did not think that they had to concern themselves with their overall environmental impact. Thankfully, that is changing and in today's world a business that does not seriously consider its environmental impact will face many challenges.

Corporate Philanthropy

Another component of corporate social responsibility is philanthropy. Many businesses and large corporations have philanthropic partners and see it as part of their mission to give back to communities. The Ronald McDonald House Charities is a famous example. It is a 501(c)(3) nonprofit organization, but was officially established in 1984 in memory of McDonald's founder Roy Kroc and McDonald's is their largest corporate sponsor. Its mission is to create, find, and support programs that directly improve the health and well-being of children.

Philanthropic endeavors have been a part of the corporate landscape for years. The first Ronald McDonald House opened in 1974 for example. But it would be hard to argue that there has not been a dramatic increase in philanthropic donations and conversations in recent years such that these are more integrated into normal business processes than ever before. Many people criticize corporate philanthropy as a marketing strategy or a means to divert attention from a company's negative social impact (unhealthy burgers for instance). This is undoubtedly true in many cases and watchdog groups should ensure that a company is actually doing what it says (not empty marketing), while companies ensure that their internal processes and products are themselves socially responsible.

But the tremendous social impact of philanthropic endeavors should not be missed. In 2005, our then two-year-old daughter was admitted to the hospital for poison ingestion. Thankfully, we lived near a hospital that specialized in such treatment. But during our time at the hospital we got to know several families who travelled a long way to get to our hospital. If it had not been for the Ronald McDonald House next to the hospital, these families never could have afforded to be with their child every day. That experience helped me see corporate philanthropy in a whole new light.

Collaborative Social Responsibility

A developing trend in business is to go one step beyond philanthropic donations to actively collaborating with nonprofit organizations in order to create synergy for greater positive social impact. These public-private partnerships try to utilize the best of both of these seemingly independent worlds to contribute to the common good.

The Global Alliance for Vaccines and Immunization (GAVI) is an example. GAVI is a public-private partnership formed to stimulate stagnating global immunization rates and reduce expanding disparities in access to vaccinations among industrialized and developing countries. The GAVI partners include: national governments, the vaccine industry, NGOs, foundations, research and public health institutions, the United Nations Children's Fund (UNICEF), the World Bank Group, and the World Health Organization (WHO).

The innovation of this public-private partnership is that it defines clearly what the problem is (lack of immunizations and vaccinations in developing countries), and affirms that real change can happen when all partners, even those with vested financial interests, work together.

Another example of collaborative social change is between Pepsi Cola and the Center for Community Transformation (CCT) in the Philippines. CCT is a Christian development organization based in Manila. CCT works in some of the poorest slums in the Philippines, where water quality issues abound; most people simply do not have access to potable water.

Pepsi donated a state-of-the-art water purification plant, and CCT installed it in the heart of a Manila slum. The first time I saw it, I was completely confused by how something so technologically advanced ended up in the middle of an area of such poverty. This slum has some of the cleanest water in Philippines. One worker proudly said to me, "Even babies can drink this water!"

CCT contracts with microentrepreneurial partners who "deal the water" in the community and have employed homeless people to deliver the water on bicycles with side carts. They sell five-gallon containers of water for 25 cents and use the wastewater to run a laundry facility. As a result of combining Pepsi's valued equipment and expertise with CCT's vision, ingenuity, and street smarts, poor people in Manila (even babies) are drinking pure and healthy water.

Ethical Business

Business has long been seen as a dog-eat-dog, win-at-all-costs type of world, reflected in phrases like "It's just business." This is supposedly an acceptable reason for mistreating or dealing harshly with another person. This long accepted axiom, however, is also starting to change. Many businesspeople and organizations have gone beyond paying lip service to doing the right thing, ensuring that business is done according to sound ethical practices.

Younger business professionals are starting to lead the charge for real change in this area. Some may dismiss this as youthful exuberance or a passing fancy but business professors at the most elite universities would challenge those ideas. For example, at Columbia Business School, all students must pledge to an honor code: "As a lifelong member of the Columbia Business School community, I adhere to the principles of truth, integrity, and respect. I will not lie, cheat, steal, or tolerate those who do." The code has been in place since 2007 and developed after a series of conversations between students and faculty.[8]

At Harvard Business School, long criticized by others as advocating a profit-at-all-costs mentality, hundreds of students signed an MBA Oath in early 2009. The oath encourages MBA graduates everywhere to be focused on socially responsible value creation. The oath begins with these overarching statements: "As a manager, my purpose is to serve the greater good by bringing people and resources together to create value that no single individual can create alone. Therefore I will seek a course that enhances the value my enterprise can create for society over the long term." The oath continues by calling for honesty, integrity, and responsibility in the context of triple bottom line business.[9]

Developments like this show that ethical business is a broader social trend, which means business is being viewed and approached differently than ever before. This is a unique opportunity for Christians to engage in these conversations and demonstrate through our actions that business has an important social and spiritual mission.

Fair Trade

Another recent development in global business is the rise of fair trade. Fair trade is naturally a play on *free trade*, or no restraints to international trade. Fair trade aims to ensure that everyone along the supply chain, particularly poor laborers in developing countries at the beginning of the supply chain, are treated appropriately and paid just wages. History has demonstrated that power tends to corrupt. Large multinational companies have, at times, exploited powerless and vulnerable people and extracted natural resources from poor countries in inconceivable ways. Fair trade opposes that. Fundamentally, fair trade is a strategy for poverty alleviation and sustainable development.

The Fair Trade Federation (FTF) certifies companies in a wide variety of industries such as clothing, coffee, food, furniture, home décor, housewares, jewelry, tea, toys, and personal accessories. Their Web site states, "[FTF] Members demonstrate that trade can be a positive force for improving living standards, health, education, the distribution of power, and the environment in the communities with which they work."[10] Companies can be certified as they adhere to requirements centered around nine foundational fair trade principles. These are:

1. Create opportunities for economically and socially marginalized producers.
2. Develop transparent and accountable relationships.
3. Build capacity.

4. Promote fair trade.
5. Pay promptly and fairly.
6. Support safe and empowering working conditions.
7. Ensure the rights of children.
8. Cultivate environmental stewardship.
9. Respect cultural identity.[11]

While people may disagree over the best ways to uphold these nine principles, it would be hard to argue against the ideal of upholding all of these principles. Fair trade conforms to the biblical concepts of human dignity, the stewardship of God's creation, and the unique spiritual mission of business. As a result, BAM practitioners can learn a lot from the fair trade movement and can be active participants in fair trade activities, seeking to make a difference for the kingdom of God.

Green Business

An environmental revolution is upon us. Everywhere you turn there are newspaper headlines, magazine articles, and online blogs about the greening of the world. Business has likewise been influenced by this developing environmental consciousness. Today, businesses are expected to account for their environmental impact, attempt to offset it, and ideally generate innovative and proactive solutions.

There are several streams to green business. The first is the reduction stream. Businesses are seeking to reduce their environmental impact. Walmart has required that all of their suppliers use less packing materials, which reduces waste and allows Walmart to put more products on its shelves.[12] Many shoe and clothing companies are intentionally reducing the size of boxes and materials used for shipping their products. Packaging companies are now researching and developing new technology and seeking innovative solutions to eliminate unnecessary packaging, thus lowering their environmental impact. BAM practitioners should likewise learn from these new environmental techniques and seek to incorporate them in their businesses.

A second stream is the offset stream. Many types of business, such as fossil fuel-based businesses like coal and oil, are considered dirty, but also necessary, at least in the short term. Therefore, the green plan for these types of businesses is to offset their negative environmental impact. This can be done in a variety of ways. These companies can invest money in research into cleaner alternatives or technology innovations that reduce the impact.

Another approach is that the company can donate funds to charities that work to correct their mishandlings. For example, a jewelry company may "offset" the environmental impact of its mining by funding positions at an environmental nonprofit organization that restores mining areas.

Many companies also buy carbon credits to offset their negative environmental impact whether it results from traveling or paper usage. Generally, these companies buy carbon credits from an investment fund or a carbon development company that has combined carbon credits (like tree planting, etc.) from individual projects. The quality of the credits is determined by the validation process and sophistication of the fund or development company that acted as the sponsor to the carbon project.

A third stream in green business is the innovation stream. These are creative, generally entrepreneurial ventures that push the envelope of technology and develop new and unique strategies to build an environmentally sustainable and friendly society. These companies are looking to do everything from developing and installing solar-powered street lights to making biodegradable coffee mugs. Many prominent venture capital funds have started to invest purely in innovative environmental start-ups convinced that this is the future of business.

The cumulative effect of these three streams and the increasing environmental emphasis in society is that green business is here to stay. It is yet another way that business is shifting from its traditional "profit at all costs" approach to a more socially responsible mind-set. As discussed previously, BAM practitioners should be environmentally sensitive and progressive, because God is the Creator and He has called us to be stewards of His good creation. The green business trend also encourages us to be environmentally friendly, aware, and proactive because it fits the contemporary business model.

Social Entrepreneurship

Social entrepreneurship is a newly developing field that can be defined succinctly as seeking to solve social problems using a business model. Such businesses are legally incorporated as for-profit companies but intentionally structured to serve an explicit social purpose. Put another way, the end goal of these businesses is the resolution of the social problem; the money generated through the business is simply a means to that end. Business schools around the world, including socially conscious Christian schools, now teach social entrepreneurship and promote it through social business model contests.

Social business ventures can include a wide variety of income-generating businesses, such as microfinance institutions that operate banks in the developing world to generate income and cover costs but have the distinct mission of alleviating poverty. One example would be my former employer, HOPE International.[13] Another example is Easy Office,[14] a for-profit social business venture that provides affordable finance, accounting, and bookkeeping services tailored to nonprofits nationwide. Its goal is to help nonprofits reduce costs and focus their energies on their distinct missions. Unlike the historical definitions of business, these companies are driven by a social cause and simply use the business as a means to that social goal.

J. Gregory Dees, faculty director of the Center for the Advancement of Social Entrepreneurship at Duke University's Fuqua School of Business, writes:

> The social mission [in these ventures] is explicit and central. This obviously affects how social entrepreneurs perceive and assess opportunities. Mission-related impact becomes the central criterion, not wealth creation. Wealth is just a means to an end for social entrepreneurs. With business entrepreneurs, wealth creation is a way of measuring value creation.[15]

Jim Collins similarly writes, "In business, money is both an input (a resource for achieving greatness) *and* an output (a measure of greatness). In the social sectors, money is *only* an input, and not a measure of greatness."[16] But this focus on the social mission can sometimes cause confusion for the social entrepreneur. Many profit-oriented social ventures become so focused on the social mission that they do not actually generate profits and instead lose a lot of money. William Foster and Jeffrey Bradach write of one organization that wanted to employ local youth by creating and selling bottles of salad dressing. They sold the bottles of salad dressing for $3.50 and believed that they were making a profit; however, a closer analysis revealed that the cost of making each bottle was $10.33. The venture was losing money badly.[17]

J. Gregory Dees and Beth Anderson list some of the potential benefits of for-profit social ventures as the promotion of efficiency and innovation, the leveraging of scarce public and philanthropic resources, and the ability to respond quickly to demand. However, in order for these for-profit social ventures to be successful, they have to confront many inherent challenges. Included among the challenges mentioned by Dees and Anderson are:

- "Differences in metrics and measurability affect management decision-making and external credibility . . . .
- Combining objectives from two different fields makes it difficult to build an integrated organization . . . .
- Competitive markets may drive out inefficient social preferences . . . .
- Investor expectations may undermine social value creation."[18]

Increasingly, BAM practitioners are looking at social ills and constructing business strategies to combat them. In Thailand, for example, there are several businesses operated by Christian missionaries with the explicit mission of providing alternative and dignified employment to women and girls enslaved by the sex industry. Other companies exist to create jobs for oppressed tribal minorities who are denied access to education and employment opportunities. Moving forward, BAM practitioners who are uniquely focused on social problems would be wise to acquaint themselves with the ongoing discussions of the broader social entrepreneurship community.

Conclusion

BAM has historical precedence. There is a continuous history from the Apostle Paul to today of Christ followers on a mission to restore the kingdom of God using business as a means to that end. The Nestorians, William Carey, the Basel Mission Trading Company, the Moravians, the Puritans, and many other groups, such as Chinese immigrant Christians in Malaysia, illustrate the tireless work of Christians in business with missional purposes.

We are living in exciting and changing times. Trends in the Christian world, particularly a focus on innovation in missions and the empowerment of the laity, have resulted in intensified efforts towards BAM. Additionally, the broader world is experiencing tremendous upheavals and integration through the process of globalization, which has produced several trends reflecting a new social consciousness. These trends, such as the triple bottom line and corporate social responsibility, corporate philanthropy, collaborative social responsibility, ethical business, fair trade, green business, and social entrepreneurship give Christians a unique opportunity to learn from and engage the broader world and to have a positive influence.

Questions for Reflection & Discussion

1. What are the implications of a consistent use of business in missions from the time of Paul to present day?

2. How can globalization work for or against God's mission in the world?

3. How should Christians respond to global poverty?

4. How can Christians make a contribution to global conversations on social consciousness in business?

5. How can the church continue to improve its understanding of the role of the laity?

chapter 9

EXAMINING MOTIVES

In chapter 8 we examined some of the contemporary trends in missions and the broader business world that have produced a rare confluence of attitudes spurring on the BAM movement. Now we turn to the individual missional entrepreneur. What motivates him or her to become involved?

Within the BAM movement, there are essentially two different groups of people: traditional missionaries who choose the BAM approach, and business professionals who want to work in business and be involved in missions. As one would assume the two groups have different motivations.

Unique Motivations of Traditional Missionaries

From my interviews with several hundred BAM practitioners there are five primary reasons why many missionaries are attracted to BAM. Undoubtedly there are many others but these are the most frequently cited.

Access

For some missionaries, a primary motive for BAM is simply to obtain a visa for residence in the desired country. There are many countries where it is impossible to get a visa as a foreign missionary. There are countries where church activities are greatly limited, sometimes through government force and regulation and in other places purely through social pressure. There are many places in the world where evangelism is illegal, and churches must meet in secret (referred to as underground churches). Many tend to think purely in terms of Islamic and communist countries, but Christian missionary activity is restricted in many ways around the world.

Many of these same countries have actually liberalized or opened up their trade agreements, becoming amazingly proactive in seeking direct foreign investment. They are actively engaging in the economic globalization processes of the larger world. The end result is that there are large parts of the world that are considered "closed" to missionaries, but are clearly "open" for business. Many missions agencies and missions strategists today refrain from calling these countries closed, preferring to call them "creative access" or "restricted access" countries. For many missionaries BAM essentially offers a creative way to access these countries.

However, some missionaries go into BAM for the purposes of obtaining a business visa even when religious worker visas are available. In Thailand, foreigners can obtain religious activities visas. One missions agency informed me that they have extras and have tried, to no avail, to give them to missionaries in other agencies. Nevertheless, many missionaries still prefer not to use these types of visas. They prefer a visa that matches the legitimacy and persona that they feel a business gives them.

Legitimacy

As mentioned above, another motive for choosing BAM is legitimacy, or at least perceived legitimacy. By operating a business, some missionaries believe they automatically gain respect and credibility in the surrounding community. In many parts of the world, missionaries feel that identifying themselves as such creates suspicion and reduces their ability to have a positive influence. The legitimacy they gain through BAM is appreciated at even the most basic levels, such as interaction with one's neighbors. Many cite that this legitimacy also creates opportunities to influence societal elites who oversee large companies or government offices.

Living in a foreign country can be uncomfortable on a number of fronts. The food is different; the language is different; the values and activities are different. Seemingly simple tasks can become frustrating day-long adventures. As a result it feels like an added burden to many missionaries to carry the societal stigma of being recognized as a religious worker affiliated with a minority and often despised faith.

In addition to this cultural-adjustment reason for seeking legitimacy, many missionaries believe that some governments that grant religious worker visas closely monitor those to whom they are given. In the opinion of some missionaries, these governments grant such visas merely as a way to look good to the international community and to more easily monitor the activities of those with the visas. Therefore, some missionaries choose to obtain a business visa to avoid government monitoring.

Persona

The third reason is closely related to the second. Many missionaries acknowledge that operating a business gives them a persona. They now have a "story" about who they are. As one worker told me, "We don't want to say, 'Hey, we're here to convert you.' Being a businessperson helps us to be a 'real person' in the community."

For years a private joke between my wife and me was how easily we could identify missionaries in creative access countries simply by paying attention to how they responded when asked what they were doing in a country. We would ask a simple question, and they would stutter or stumble over their words, or mutter something almost incoherent, or tell a long, rambling story that just could not be true. A few times, I shared that we were missionaries in hopes of alleviating their fears and creating an atmosphere for conversation. However, I quickly learned this didn't work either. My forthrightness labeled me as a loudmouth ready to announce my missionary status to the whole world (or expose theirs), and they would generally excuse themselves quickly.

This may seem quite strange to the average Christian churchgoer who sends missionaries to the end of the world, and who might ask, *"What in the world are they worried about?"* But the concerns of these missionaries are generally sincere, and in many countries there are good reasons to be very cautious in identifying oneself as a missionary. The solution of many missionaries in these situations is to start a business so they can have a solid, defendable answer when someone asks what they're doing in the country.

Relationship Contacts

A fourth reason frequently cited by missionaries is that the business enables them to make contact with other local residents. Many missionaries have tremendous difficulty forming genuine relationships with locals if they do not have a natural avenue for developing those relationships. If they live in a country where there is a Christian church, they will tend to establish relationships with local Christians and have a lot of challenges forming relationships with local non-Christians. Many of these missionaries view themselves as evangelists and church planters and do not aspire to work purely within the local Christian church. As a result they look for ways to get out into the community and get to know other people.

With a business platform they are in constant and normal contact with people they would never get to know through a church or other organized ministry. They are able to develop relationships with employees, clients, suppliers, government officials, bankers, shippers, and other businesspeople. As one missionary said to me, "The strength [of BAM] is that you engage people in day-to-day life."

Relationship Development

In addition to developing contacts with people in the broader community, many missionaries desire to develop deeper relationships with a core group of people. They choose to operate a business because this gives them an opportunity to be around a select group of people for up to 40 (or even more) hours per week.

BAM practitioners operating from this motivation tend to see deep, personal relationships as a necessary prerequisite for producing any type of life or faith change. They are generally critical of fly-by-night evangelistic approaches, such as open air preaching and the like, which are sometimes done with no relational context.

They also tend to see other evangelistic approaches, like developing relationships through leisure activities, as ineffective because it is quite difficult to really get to know one another. These BAM practitioners frequently see evangelism as a core or primary purpose of their personal mission and believe that deep, personal relationships are the most effective way to produce evangelistic fruit.

Figure 9.1

MOTIVATIONS FOR BAM FOR MISSIONARIES

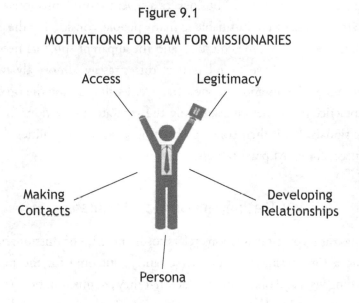

Evaluation

All five of these motives are worthwhile. However, I contend that they are not enough in themselves to justify the energy and expense of BAM. Mind-set makes the difference between those who do business purely as a means for relationship development and those who do business as mission. The former almost exclusively emphasize church planting and evangelism, and the latter emphasize an integrated view of spiritual business.

Missionaries who pursue BAM for only relationship development reasons usually find themselves greatly frustrated. They frequently see evangelism as their primary or perhaps only objective in missions yet they complain that they do not have the time and energy to follow up on their contacts because of the business work. The visa, legitimacy, persona, contacts, and relationship development are benefits of the business but they don't really view the business as that important. Nevertheless, business manages to squeeze out time for what they consider real "ministry."

Many, though by no means all, of these missionaries have ended up closing their business, or never even opened a real one in the first place, but continue to operate a "shell" business as a cover for other missions activities. This strategy may seem justifiable to many people, considering the difficulty in gaining access to some countries and the apparent spiritual needs there. However, what I have found is that this strategy almost always causes significant problems and is a poor practice. I will examine the problems of this practice below before examining the separate motivations of business professionals. I will then conclude by proposing some qualities that make for successful BAM practitioners.

The Problems with Fake Businesses

Business as a cover for missions refers to the practice of missionaries establishing a legal business in another country, but only for the purpose of obtaining visas and obscuring the fact that they are missionaries. These businesses do not actually engage in business at all. There are several problems with this such as: financial deduction, credibility dilution, integrity erosion, and suspicion creation.

Financial Deduction
One of the most obvious difficulties with these shell businesses is that they lose money. If there is no business, then why are there expenses? Generally, there are several unavoidable expenses. The business must legally establish itself as an entity in the country. This requires some legal guidance and sometimes additional application guidance from a consultant. Then there are the actual application and permit fees. These permits frequently require annual payments. The business must also frequently submit annual reports.

In many countries, a physical office space must be maintained, separate from a home residence, resulting in rental fees.

Many countries also require foreign owned and operated businesses to hire at least one local employee. Many of these cover businesses hire one person and give them busy work. As will be noted later, many of these businesses face constant visa trouble since they are not really operating. Frequently, this requires extra expenses to remedy through legal action or even more expensive options, such as leaving the country and living in a temporary location for a period of time. All in all, it can cost a lot of money to start and run a nonexistent business.

Since these businesses are not operating, there is no way to recoup any of this financial loss. So, in order to cover these losses, the owners are forced to raise additional monies from loyal and sometimes ill-informed donors in their home countries. Many of these donors would probably be quite frustrated if they realized how their hard-earned money and generous donations were consumed on the missions field.

Credibility Dilution

Over time people begin to realize that something is not what it seems at the local nonoperating business. Many missionaries confide in local Christians or other foreigners that their business does not really exist and is simply a cover. In several countries national Christians have asked me how it is that Joe Missionary can tell everyone that he is running a business when he is not. These Christians are sincerely confused and do not understand why someone they look up to so casually lives a lie. The end result, in many cases, is a dramatic dilution in the credibility of the missionary.

An unfortunate by-product is that many local Christians begin thinking that preserving their credibility is not inherently important. Then slowly but surely the credibility of many Christians is corroded. The cumulative effect of all of this is naturally destructive to any sort of influence the missionary and local Christians may aspire to have among non-Christians.

Integrity Erosion

Not only can the credibility of the missionaries and the surrounding local Christians be adversely affected, there also can be an erosion of their integrity. The cover business is, at its core, a deception. Obviously, many missionaries believe such deception is justified due to the greater cause of proclaiming the name of Christ in a difficult-to-access region. But what can happen is that the missionary becomes careless about truth telling in general. A certain elasticity develops regarding what is considered honest. Sadly, I've known many missionaries who have grown accustomed to telling boldfaced lies on a daily basis.

Most Christians would not assert that the ends justify the means. They know and understand that we should not commit a wrong in order to arrive at a desired end. You can't rob a bank and justify it by giving the proceeds to the church. Naturally, most people would not engage in such obvious wrongdoing. This end-justifies-the-means mentality on the missions field seems harmless, but I believe it can slowly erode the conscience of well-intended missionaries. Over time they drift to a place they never imagined they would go.

I have known several missionaries in such situations who have lost their marriages and ministries because their moral character simply evaporated over time. Obviously, each case is unique, and all of these situations are complex and influenced by a variety of factors. Nevertheless, I cannot dismiss the occasions I have observed a connection between deceptive BAM and eventual immoral behaviors.

Suspicion Creation

Imagine that a foreign family moved in next door to your family. They are from a distant country, but seem to be doing quite well financially. You introduce yourself, and they are quite vague on many points. They do tell you where they came from and that they have come here to open a coffee shop. Confused, you point out that there are several coffee shops nearby and ask why they would cross land and sea just to open a coffee shop. They just smile and nod.

You see several other families coming to their house on a frequent basis. One day you catch a couple of them and start a conversation. They are tense and nervous; they don't speak English very well. They explain they are in language school, which they are attending full-time for one year before they go to work with the other family in the coffee shop. You ask what job they'll have there. They'll be baristas.

Over time you notice that the first family is at home a lot. They do not really seem to be working extensively on the business. But no one seems concerned, and they appear to be well provided for financially. When you ask about the business, you notice at times they appear confused; other times they mutter something about setbacks.

They have to be getting money from somewhere somehow, but where, how, and why, you don't know. You mention it to your friends, who are all convinced that your neighbors must be terrorists since they do come from a country that is at odds politically with yours. One day the police come by and start asking pointed questions about the behaviors of your foreign neighbors.

What would you think in this situation? I think most of us would become extremely suspicious and quite concerned. Oddly enough, this is happening all over the world as Christian missionaries use business as a cover to conceal their missionary identity. Locals can figure out that something is off, but they do not know what it is.

Many missionaries assume that if the locals get suspicious, the locals will assume that the missionaries are missionaries. However, this is probably not the case. As I did my PhD research in Thailand, I conducted general interviews with a lawyer, a customs official, and the spouse of a police officer on global business. I asked them about the presence of many foreigners in the country. Interestingly, they pointed to two chief concerns they had with people who could not prove their purpose for being in the country: pedophilia and drug trafficking. These are two things most missionaries do not want to be associated with. Yet, for the local Thais, these concerns about foreigners are well founded. During my time in Thailand there were high-profile arrests of Westerners guilty of these two aforementioned crimes.

Creating suspicion through fake businesses has three very clear negative impacts: locals view the missionaries negatively; foreigners (including those doing legitimate businesses) encounter increased government inspections; and foreigners (including those doing legitimate businesses) encounter constant visa trouble.

1. *Negative perception.* If people are suspicious of a person's presence in a country and the suspicions center on drug trafficking and child molestation, then that person is not going to be viewed very positively. And what does that do to his/her witness for Christ and potential to influence others? It's effectively ruined. To make matters worse, many missionaries are unaware of these types of suspicions, so if they sense something is wrong, they frequently assume people know they are missionaries. They then seek to shield their missionary status by holding back on any sort of religious conversation that could in fact allay people's fears regarding, say, drug trafficking and pedophilia.

2. *Increased inspections.* Government officials are aware that shell companies exist for a wide variety of corrupt reasons, including money laundering, drug trafficking, extortion, human trafficking, and the like. As a result most governments are always on the lookout for fake companies. When something is suspicious, they will investigate. When they find the company is a front, they cannot always determine the reason why. Generally the government will simply kick out the people directly involved. But the presence of one fake company will often provoke the country to intensify its investigations to the extent that *all* foreigners in business are affected by the increased inspections.

In other countries, expatriates tend to be more aware of what other foreigners are doing and who they are. Thus, foreigners will be able to identify a family running a fake business as missionaries before the locals will. In Thailand I interviewed foreigners involved in business, including missionaries and non-Christians, and they all complained that fake missionary businesses caused them chronic problems because the government was always trying to make sure that they were not also operating a fake business. Not only does this incur extra time and financial expenditures for legitimate businesses, but it also corrodes the witness to observing and affected non-Christian business owners.

3. *Constant visa trouble.* Around the time that the Thai government made the high-profile drug- and pedophilia-related arrests, one missionary group was exposed for running a fake company. The missionaries involved were forced to leave. They talked as if they were martyrs suffering because they were doing the work of the Lord. However, the government obviously was concerned that they were up to something far more sinister than trying to get people to go to church.

The group of missionaries had to live in a neighboring and expensive country for six months. This of course created an enormous financial burden on their families and their missions agency.

Just as they face increased government inspections, fake businesses are always forced to justify their presence in a country, are plagued by constant visa problems, and are in jeopardy of being kicked out.

After uncovering a fake business, governments are apt to change visa regulations, which can cause problems for all foreigners, including those who are running legitimate businesses. Visa hassles drain precious energy and money from missional entrepreneurs who really need it. It is a real tragedy that fellow Christians frequently are the root cause of these visa hassles.

Alternative Responses

If business as a cover for missions is untenable, then what are the alternatives for gaining creative access to countries closed to traditional missions? Instead of designing and devising deceptive cover businesses, missionaries should dedicate themselves to finding legitimate employment. This will enable them to gain credibility, live with integrity, and have a valid reason for why they are there. They can live with authentic legitimacy. When looking objectively at the choice between running a fake business or finding other employment, it seems quite obvious which is best. In the fog of missionary activities in creative access countries, this clarity can be easily lost.

Operating a legitimate business is an exhausting and generally expensive exercise. People who are fully committed to business, who are willing and able to face the inevitable stresses and who have the skills or access to the skills necessary to make it happen are the only people who should seek to launch an entrepreneurial endeavor. It is definitely not for everyone. There are many other legitimate options for missionaries that will enable them to live in a creative access country with complete integrity. These options include but are not limited to:

- teaching English at any level.
- teaching a particular specialty in an elementary school, high school, technical school, or university.
- enrolling in a university study program.
- becoming a part of a community development project.
- providing a professional service (medical, engineering, etc.) if one has the skills and background.
- living in a nearby country and traveling regularly as a tourist to the desired country.
- becoming involved with evangelistic radio and television broadcasting from nearby countries.

Many other alternatives are possible. These options do present challenges of their own, but can be fulfilling and successful with prayerful intentionality and planning. The commitment to complete integrity is worth it.

Unique Motivations of Business Professionals

Business professionals tend to have different motivations from BAM practitioners with traditional missionary backgrounds. One of the reasons they have distinct motivations is because they define missions differently. There are, of course, exceptions, but most BAM practitioners from business backgrounds are more apt to point to the functions of the business and its unique social contribution as elements of missions, particularly of their personal mission.

While I have interviewed several missionaries from traditional backgrounds who acknowledge that business is an honorable profession and part of God's mission, they will tend to be somewhat schizophrenic in the way they discuss missions when not directly answering a question about business. For example, when I ask many missionaries what they think about business, they will note its positive attributes and say it has a place in the outworking of God's mission. But the more they discuss their view of missions the more the contributions of business fade away. They frequently begin articulating a dichotomy of business and missions that makes it clear that missions is about evangelism and church planting exclusively. Therefore, they will have motivations for BAM and use strategies that serve that definition of missions.

Business professionals, on the other hand, are more consistent in their definition, meaning that what they say when talking about business is close to what they'll say when talking about missions. They tend to see the two fields as integrated and not separate. As a result they have some different motivations for missions.

Business professionals will tend to cite access, legitimacy, persona, contacts, and relationship development as benefits of BAM but not as motivations for BAM, as traditional missionaries will do. Rather, business professionals tend to cite the following as their motivation: engaging their passions; using their skills; creating jobs; confronting unjust social structures; and influencing social elites.

Engaging Their Passions

Most BAM practitioners with a business background are excited by BAM because they are able to continue the type of work they enjoy doing. While many missionaries are self-starting pioneers, not all of them like the tasks of business, such as business plan development, hiring employees, managing employees, monitoring payroll, etc. Business professionals, on the other hand, frequently go into business because they were innately drawn to these activities and actually enjoy them.

One BAM practitioner said to me, "I'm in business because I love it. I just moved to [this country] because I sensed this is where God wanted me to be in business." They do not tend to see their business as a distraction to other worthy activities but generally see the business as a worthy activity.

Using Their Skills

Similarly, business professionals are pleased to be able to use their skills. Many have spent years in undergraduate and graduate education learning about business as well as years and even decades in the business world learning through the school of hard knocks. They feel comfortable in a business setting and are glad to have a place to use their skills.

Many of them feel unqualified to do things that are traditionally done by vocational ministers, such as counseling, preaching sermons, administering the sacraments, or presiding over special ceremonies. Since many feel unqualified, they also feel uncomfortable doing those things.

One BAM practitioner said to me, "I could never preach a sermon. That would scare me to death. I really respect those guys who do that. I know I never could." Business is a place where these men and women feel comfortable because they are familiar with the territory, it's in line with their skills and background, and it allows them to focus on their interests.

Creating Jobs

Many business-background BAM practitioners are tuned into economic realities and have a desire to create jobs for the un- or underemployed. Remarkably, when I interviewed business-background missional entrepreneurs and asked why they started their business, they almost invariably mentioned the creation of jobs.

They are also quick to cite that this benefits other missions activities. One pointed out to me, "Since we are adding value to society by creating jobs, bringing in capital, and enhancing people's lives, we are able to do other things, like evangelize, disciple, and be open about our faith from a position of strength."

Confronting Unjust Social Structures

Missional entrepreneurs from business backgrounds are often motivated to combat unjust social structures. They see business as an important weapon against injustice. Many seek to combat social evils, like the exploitative sex industry, by providing dignified employment alternatives to at-risk women and girls. Others seek to provide employment opportunities to physically or mentally challenged or otherwise disadvantaged peoples. Some are motivated to create positive work environments for oppressed and ostracized minority social groups. While the issue and the particular approach may change, what is central to many of these missional entrepreneurs is that they see business as a means of creating a new and more just way of life for many people who have been denied it.

Figure 9.2

MOTIVATIONS FOR BAM FOR PROFESSIONALS

Influencing Social Elites

Missional entrepreneurs from business backgrounds are frequently motivated to reach society's elite. They view business as a way to gain access to and earn credibility with influential people in society, like company executives and government leaders. Frequently, they are able to develop relationships with and impact people who can influence thousands, even millions of others.

BAM practitioners from traditional missionary backgrounds often also see influencing the elite as a possible benefit to BAM. However, for some business-background BAMers, this potential is a primary motivation. Because they respect business they believe that business can gain respect for them, their work, and the message they bring.

Finding Perspective

It is important to note that just as some traditional missionaries ignore, underestimate, or de-emphasize the business side of BAM, businesspersons frequently have a tendency to do the same for aspects of missions that are not directly business related. In other words, if a missional entrepreneur is not very intentional and focused on the business, the business will fail. But also, if missional entrepreneurs are not intentional and focused on building relationships and sharing Christ, then they will not be as effective a witness as possible. This tension is very real, and the temptations to ignore one or the other are also real.

To be truly effective, missional entrepreneurs must balance the tensions in developing relationships. For example, I know several missional entrepreneurs who kept poor performing employees because they believed that relationship development superseded the business needs. However, keeping such employees almost invariably causes an unfortunate ripple effect through the companies. Other employees see that they can get by with poor performance if they feign being good friends with the manager. This causes a downward spiral in business quality.

I also worked with one BAM enterprise that intentionally maintained the same suppliers because the entrepreneurs wanted to continue to develop that relationship. However, this had an adverse effect. The suppliers sensed weakness in the managers and lost respect for them while simultaneously increasing their prices. Eventually, the entrepreneurs had to find new suppliers and realized that being astute in having multiple suppliers actually gained them more respect from their suppliers and other business owners, while also decreasing their costs.

On the other side, I once worked with a missional entrepreneur who was selling his business to a national businessman. As we worked through the process the missional entrepreneur continued to talk about how this was his dream come true; he had built a successful business and was transitioning it to a national's control. As I asked questions I realized that the new owner was not a Christian and was quite antagonistic to the gospel. The missional entrepreneur had not discussed his faith very much with this national because of the antagonism he felt. In fact, very few people even knew the missional entrepreneur was a Christian, much less a person who been commissioned by a missions agency to plant churches. This missional entrepreneur made the unfortunate mistake of nearly equating his business with a church and thought that building up a business and passing it on to national control was the extent of his mission. Due to his lack of intentionality in sharing Christ, there was virtually no spiritual fruit and the business continues to this day under the control of someone seemingly opposed to the gospel.

What Makes a Great Missional Entrepreneur

To navigate these tensions and to thrive in BAM, missional entrepreneurs need to value both relationship development (evangelism) and the integrity of running a quality business enterprise. They cannot sacrifice the business for the sake of relationships. But neither can they sacrifice intentionally influencing others with the gospel of Christ for the sake of the business. Being intentional on both fronts is required for a missional entrepreneur to succeed holistically.

Figure 9.3

BUSINESS WEB OF RELATIONSHIPS

The missional entrepreneurs that I have researched come from varied backgrounds. Some are traditional missionaries who decided that running a business was a more effective means to attain their missional goals. Others are businesspeople who wanted to be involved in missions, and business was the most practical avenue for them to pursue. However, doing business in missions is not for everybody. Those who are committed to it and effective at it view business as an important component of a just society, understand the influence of economics in people's lives, and believe that their purpose is to serve God and their neighbor through their business. They have the skills necessary to run a business, are diligent in obtaining the skills, and/or find good people to do the things they cannot do. They view their workplace as the location and the means to have an effective ministry and believe that a good business is a ministry in its own right.

However, not all missionaries operating businesses have these perspectives. Many express frustration that they do not "have time for ministry" because it takes so much time and energy to run the business. They consider the business good for getting them into the country, but do not really consider the valuable social contribution the business can make. Further, they do not view that valuable social contribution as a part of their mission. Some missionaries have simply stumbled into working in or running a business. Others became enamored with the BAM concept without being fully aware of the implications of running a business in a developing country for missional purposes.

The bottom line is many traditional missionaries are more qualified and gifted to be pastors, evangelists, or full-time church planters. That is reflective of who they are, and it is who they really want to be. These missionaries should not pursue operating businesses; it will be a drain to them, their missions agency, and probably many people's finances. Many missionaries explained to me that their missions agency was pushing them to be innovative and pursue entrepreneurial strategies. In these cases, the missions agency needs to understand that it requires a special mix of gifting, commitment, and unique context to make missional business ventures work effectively. Not just anyone can do it or should do it.

Conclusion

Motivation is a complex issue. People do things for many different reasons. But after interviewing hundreds of BAM practitioners from various backgrounds, the motivations in this chapter emerged as most prominent. As we will see in the next chapters, a person's motivations for going into BAM are deeply rooted in his or her understanding of missions. They impact the strategies employed and ultimately influence the type of results the BAM company will produce.

Questions for Reflection & Discussion

1. Assess the motivations of many traditional missionaries for going into BAM.

2. What do you think about using business as a cover in missions?

3. What additional alternatives do missionaries have in order to live and work in a creative access country?

4. Assess the motivations of business professionals for going into BAM.

5. What qualities would make a good missional entrepreneur?

chapter 10

TWO JOURNEYS IN BAM

Robert and Susan Kolbowitz[1]

International Christian Agency (ICA) missionaries Robert (Bob) and Susan Kolbowitz had always been drawn to other cultures. As collegiate ministers at a secular university in the midwestern US, they tried to constantly expose students to international missions. They counted it a success that 28 students from their college ministry had spent a summer overseas doing missions work. Following what they took to be the Lord's call, Bob and Susan decided to attend seminary and to use that time to determine if God was leading them to be overseas missionaries.

During the final year of work on his master of divinity degree at a large evangelical seminary, Bob went to Chiang Mai, Thailand, on a reconnaissance trip with Dwight Foster, the missions pastor at his home church. Dwight and Bob met with several missionaries from their denomination. They both were overwhelmed by how few Thai Christians there were. They were also frustrated as they realized that the vast majority of missionaries in the city were focusing on other countries and people groups in the region and were to a large extent ignoring the plight of the Thai.

During their trip they also met some other young missionaries from a different agency. This missionary couple had also been college ministers, but now they were engaged in business as mission (BAM). Bob and Dwight were not really familiar with the concept but understood quite quickly that the "traditional" approach of other missionaries was not effectively reaching the Thai Buddhist people. What they felt was needed was innovation, a new way, a way to blend into the culture without sticking out as a foreign missionary. Being a businessperson seemed like the perfect means. Fascinated with BAM, Bob returned home to Susan and announced he had caught a vision for doing BAM in Chiang Mai. He said he sensed God leading the family to move there after graduation. Susan, finally glad to know what the future held and excited to hear about this new approach to missions, was quickly on board.

Ron and Dawn Marshall

Ron Marshall grew up as a missionary child in a rural part of the Central African Republic. His parents were missionaries with Bible Mission Agency (BMA), and this was really the only world he ever knew. Though his siblings aspired to engage in other types of work and were anxious to be "typical Americans," Ron always sensed he was supposed to be a missionary. While attending Bible college in the US Ron met Dawn. The two quickly fell in love and married.

Dawn had only traveled out of her state a handful of times and was quite nervous about living in the jungle after hearing Ron's crazy stories. Nevertheless, she decided that if it was meant to be, she was willing to go. Ron always imagined himself on the missions field, but he decided to spend the first few years of marriage in the US. Though he grew up in a very undeveloped part of the world and his undergraduate education was in theology, Ron had an intuitive sense about business and quickly became a successful tire salesman at a locally owned auto shop. Impressed, the owner continued to give Ron raises, bonuses, and promotions. But Ron's heart was never in it. He always wanted "to get back out there."

One night Ron told Dawn he really wanted to go back to the missions field. She smiled and said, "I've been wondering when you were going to admit that. Let's go!"

A few months prior, they had heard a missionary couple give a presentation at church. The couple talked about their work among a tribal group in northern Thailand. Ron and Dawn had never really thought of

Thailand as a missionary destination. The presentation, however, really touched Dawn's heart, so they decided that was the destination to which God was leading them.

The Kolbowitz Family in Chiang Mai

Bob and Susan arrived in Chiang Mai and quickly started researching what type of business would help them integrate into the community. Alarmed at the lack of evangelism occurring among the Thai, they were anxious to get going. They visited with several missionaries from other missions agencies and analyzed their approaches.

"Some of them are so slow in their approach and mentality," Bob remarked to Susan, "This is why the gospel is not taking root."

After visiting Craig and Cheryl Ramsey, a missionary couple who owned and operated a local coffee shop, Bob and Susan believed they had found their model. Young Thai business professionals constantly popped in and out of the coffee shop and the Ramseys greeted each one. "They know everybody in town!" exclaimed Susan.

Intrigued, Bob visited Craig another time to get more information. Craig noted that running the coffee shop had been a lot more complex than he imagined.

"Sometimes we cannot even get sugar," Craig told Bob. "Inventory is hard to manage. I thought a coffee shop would be easy, but I feel like I don't do anything other than just try to maintain the status quo. Furthermore, the market is starting to get crowded here. Starbucks is expanding around the city, and it's just hard to compete with coffee shops like that."

Bob was a little concerned by the amount of time Craig was spending on the business. *"Isn't Craig here for ministry?"* he thought.

That evening Bob talked it over with Susan. "I think Craig has lost his priorities. He seems disorganized. We can do this better than they can," he said.

Convinced that the Lord had shown them the way, Bob and Susan wrote a formal ministry plan for ICA. The ICA board had said they wanted to see innovation in missions and were pleased by the BAM model that Bob and Susan had developed. The plan seemed like a reasonable one that would help them integrate into the culture but "wouldn't take too much time away from ministry" or cause them to lose focus on "the salvation of souls." ICA quickly approved the plan and approached a Christian businessman who had said he would financially support board-approved ministry plans that use business. The businessman supplied $50,000 for them to get the coffee shop "up and going."

The Marshall Family in Chiang Mai

Ron and Dawn arrived in Chiang Mai and quickly set about learning the Thai language. They both found language learning arduous. Though Ron was trilingual, he had learned the other languages as a child. Dawn had never learned a second language, except for two years studying Spanish in high school. Despite these challenges they were convinced that learning the language was an absolute necessity. Ron remembered how he had translated for missionaries as a child and remarked to Dawn: "They never had an impact on anyone."

Ron and Dawn started attending a local Thai church and quickly made Thai friends. Not a weekend went by that they weren't visited by a handful of Thai Christians. Slowly Thailand became home to them. The language, though always a challenge, became easier. Their Thai Christian friends were a strong basis of support.

As their time in language school came to an end, Ron and Dawn prayed about what their next steps should be. They spoke with the leaders of the local association of Thai churches about possible needs. Though the Marshalls loved the Thai Christians, they were a bit frustrated that so many of them perceived money as the primary need. They wanted to help, but felt uncomfortable about just supplying money. They wanted to do something.

At this time, Ron's former boss at the tire store called. He told Ron that he was looking to send a lot of work, such as data entry and inventory monitoring, offshore in order to lower expenses and asked Ron if he could help. From his experience at the tire store he knew this type of work, and he was confident he could teach some of the local Thais how to do it. Ron asked his boss for a rough estimate of how much he was looking to invest and some time to check out his options. Quickly, Ron realized that he not only could do this, but he could do it profitably from the outset. Though he never considered himself a businessperson or considered business as a part of his mission, he realized that the local Christians needed money and this would help that cause.

The Kolbowitzes Get Started

Bob and Susan got their coffee shop up and going in no time. Several smart and charming young Thais applied as baristas and helpers, and Bob hired them quickly. To maintain priorities Bob took a long lunch every day to be with family. However, this became increasingly more difficult. When he returned everything seemed to be in disarray. The staff seemed to do absolutely nothing while he was gone. He started to work long hours feeling he could never leave the shop unattended. *"Are they stealing from me?"* he wondered. He couldn't figure out why virtually no money would come through when he was gone.

Susan began to complain that she felt lonely as Bob was at the coffee shop all day, and she was home with their young kids. Since they were focused on reaching the unreached, they intentionally stayed away from Thai Christian churches, believing that interaction there would lead to requests for work that they simply didn't have time for. Furthermore, they might be labeled as "missionaries" by the local Thais and not recognized as the true entrepreneurs they wanted to be considered.

Since Susan did not speak the Thai language very well, she felt increasingly isolated from the culture. After much thought, fights, and prayer, Bob and Susan asked the ICA to send some more missionaries. Considering their BAM initiative as innovative and a future direction for the entire missions agency, ICA rerouted two missionary couples who were going to a nearby Southeast Asian country. They also sent two recent college graduates on short-term assignments for further support.

Immediately, everything got better. Susan enjoyed passing the days with the new missionary wives. Bob was glad to have extra help at the coffee shop. Frankly, it was good to have a little bit of America in the coffee shop. The long days of trying to communicate with people who did not speak English well were getting difficult.

But business was not prospering. The staff was very unreliable. Frequently, workers would simply stop showing up for work without telling anyone they were quitting. Bob tried to befriend the employees but frequently felt betrayed. He sensed they were talking negatively about him, but he didn't know what to do. He felt he was a good boss. He did not micromanage; he did not try to control them. Nevertheless things were just not going well.

Bob knew they were going to need another injection of capital to pay bills. He had taken out a line of credit simply to make payroll a couple of times. He was trying hard to pay off this debt, but with the high employee turnover it seemed he was either hiring or training all the time. Worse, he did not have time for ministry; he was consumed with the business. Several customers openly asked him if he was a missionary, a charge he would vehemently deny. They could not afford for everyone to know or perceive them as missionaries in this Buddhist kingdom. One of their prime motivations for doing BAM was to be regarded by locals as business entrepreneurs.

The Marshalls Get Started

Ron and Dawn were very excited about this new opportunity to help the Thai Christians move toward self-sufficiency by generating local income. They immediately hired five young ladies who had been attending their church after moving to Chiang Mai from a tribal village. These young ladies had no money at all. Ron knew part of the reason the Thai church requested donations from foreigners was due to the fact that many of its members were unemployed. Perhaps they could help the Thai church financially by employing church members. Uncomfortable with using donations as handouts to churches, Ron and Dawn felt really good about giving a hand up to individual church members.

Though Ron had never previously considered doing business on the missions field, he reflected on how much he learned when he worked at the tire store and how useful that was becoming. One night he exclaimed to Dawn, "I can't believe I never thought of this before, but I think this business could be a real blessing to Thailand. We can give jobs to people who need it. They can then take care of their families and give money to the churches. This will help the church's financial situation and reduce the dependency on foreign donations. After we get going maybe we can find a way to employ some non-Christians so we can witness to them. It seems to me that it takes a long time for people to become Christians around here. The office could be a place for them to learn gradually over an extended period of time."

Ron wanted the company to function like a family and he cared for the employees like a father. He was kind and thoughtful yet also provided leadership and direction. He sensed they needed regular interaction and realized that talking with all the employees on a regular basis not only improved performance but also generated opportunities to discuss spiritual issues. This didn't change when they added several new Buddhist employees.

Over time the Buddhist employees began to ask questions and initiate conversations. Initially the questions seemed to be a matter of curiosity, but eventually Ron could tell that a few were sincerely seeking. Ron sensed that they needed something more than he and the other Christian employees could provide during spontaneous conversations. But he also knew that being from strong Buddhist families, these employees would not want to go to church and risk offending their relatives.

One night while going over this with Dawn, she remarked, "Why don't you get Pastor Prabhu to come in and do devotions for them?"

Pastor Prabhu was an Indian immigrant and a dynamic pastor of the growing congregation that the Marshalls attended. Ron decided to start a weekly Bible time with all of the employees. Originally he considered doing it during the lunch hour and providing free lunch. However, he decided to have it every Tuesday morning for the first hour of work. He noted that the Thai hierarchical orientation would enable him to have an obligatory Bible study without it being counterproductive.

"In America it would anger everyone so much that it would never be effective. But we're not in America," he said to Dawn when she questioned the approach.

The Kolbowitzes Reach Their End

Frustrated, Bob stomped in the door, "I cannot figure these Thai people out!"

After being in Chiang Mai for seven years, Bob was becoming increasingly frustrated with his employees. "They are so unreliable! They never do any task I give them and they just quit coming to work. I didn't know it would be so hard to find employees who speak English."

The company was hemorrhaging money; Susan was stressed and there was constant friction with his missionary colleagues. *I never knew Thailand would be so hard,* Bob thought to himself.

The other two missionary families were returning to the US. One family left for medical reasons; the other because "the business is a major distraction to ministry." Bob still believed that it was important not to be seen as missionaries in Thailand, but was starting to doubt if anything would ever work. Two months earlier they had hired a Thai Christian, Nuananong, who was aware of their missionary purposes and had graduated from an American university.

Nuananong came to Bob one day and said, "Bob, I know you do not want anyone to think that you guys are missionaries, but the employees say that everyone knows. They also wonder why you have never talked to them about it."

Bob was frustrated. He had thought that some of them might know, but he was not aware that it had become a topic of conversation. Bob and Susan were very depressed that after seven years, they had only seen one Buddhist convert to Christianity.

"We came here to see people become Christians and it's not happening. Maybe we should just go back home," Susan sighed to Bob one night. "Maybe we should," said Bob looking off into space.

But Bob was not ready to go just yet. He was determined to keep trying. However, he knew now that his missionary cover was being blown; he would have to be even more careful about presenting himself as a Christian. One day at work, he angrily confronted an employee who had not completed a task that he had given her a month earlier. She left for lunch and never came back. Completely frustrated he went to Nuananong and asked him to explain how his people could do such things.

"I do not think she understood the task you gave her," replied Nuananong, "I think that maybe she thought you did not care about her since you never explained to her how to do the task."

"What? Are you saying this is my fault?" retorted Bob. Nuananong looked away nervously and did not say anything. "I do not want to micromanage people, Nuananong. They need to be able to do things on their own. That is part of being mature. Everyone here is just very immature."

Later that night he went over the incident with Susan. "Maybe she lost face when you yelled at her?" suggested Susan.

"Face. This whole face thing is just too much. These people need to get over it. America is a successful country because we are not worried about face. They need to learn not to worry about it," replied Bob with a strong tone of irritation in his voice.

"Well, maybe the American way works in America but it does not seem to be working here," cautioned Susan.

"That's exactly the problem," exclaimed Bob. "They need to adapt to the American way. You do not see American companies clamoring to learn the Thai way of doing things, do you?"

"Well, honey, I don't know. Maybe we're all just different," muttered Susan.

The next day Bob was in the office early to look over the accounting books and clean up some of the frequent mistakes. Nuananong came in looking downcast. He told Bob that he was moving to Bangkok. "I've always wanted to live in the big city and I think it is time for me to do it."

Bob could not believe it. He had come to rely on Nuananong to make sense of what was going on and to function as a bridge to the Thai staff. He sensed that Nuananong was not telling him the complete story, but he had seen so many employees come and go that he just nodded and wished him the best. After Nuananong left the office, Bob started thinking back on all the employees who had come and gone. Even all of his missionary colleagues had gone back home. He looked at the finances and he could not see how he could make it work. Most painfully, he pondered how after seven years they had only seen one Buddhist convert to Christianity.

"If I'd known it was going to be so hard, I never would have started this," he said to himself. That night he went home and told Susan that they needed to move back home, saying "It is just not working." She agreed. He closed the shop the following day.

The Marshalls Going Strong

Business was booming. Ron's old boss had told several other business associates about what Ron was doing for his company. Opportunities were coming from everywhere. Ron looked back at the seven years they had been in business and could not help but smile. They had grown to 45 employees and were making significant profits every quarter. Ron had come to Thailand as a "faith missionary" raising support to cover his personal expenses. The business was now generating a sufficient income to pay him a decent salary, but he decided against it. He continued to receive monies from friends and family in the US. All of the profits were either reinvested into the company or donated to six locally run ministries that the company fully supported.

Ron liked to tell the story of an employee's friend who came to visit one day and became so enamored with the culture of the company that she stayed until Ron gave her a job. Proudly, Ron pointed out to employees and visitors alike that no one had ever left the company. Every employee had worked there since the day they were hired. But what made him most happy was not the flourishing business—it was the impact it had on people's lives. Twelve employees had become Christians through the years. Three of the earliest hires, in fact, had become Christians after six years with the company.

Ministries had expanded and grown as a result of the finances the company had provided. Mothers and fathers were able to send their kids to school and feed them as a result of consistent employment. Three of the women were former prostitutes whose first job off the street was with Ron's company. Lives had been changed. Though they never said so to Ron, the employees considered him a father and the company a growing family.

One night in reflection, Ron said to Dawn, "I would have never imagined that the Lord would have used business to bring such blessing to these people. This opportunity just fell in our laps as if from heaven!"

Making Sense of the Contrasting Stories

Contrary to the opinions of some missionaries, effectiveness in business as mission is neither random nor determined purely by external factors. The two models described above, though presented a bit one-sidedly for emphasis, do accurately reflect common patterns that emerged during my research in Chiang Mai, Thailand. In Chiang Mai there are approaches that work and ones that do not work. Admittedly, many BAM entrepreneurs and enterprises there mix the various approaches, motivations, and attitudes, and thus experience moderate or mixed results. However, I was amazed at how many companies could easily be fit into one of the two broad categories described in this chapter. In other words, they strongly matched either the Kolbowitzes' coffee shop or the Marshalls' offshoring operation in both business and ministry results, even down to some of the smaller details. In the following chapter I will further explore some of the practical reasons for the divergent realities and present more detailed findings from my research.

Questions for Reflection & Discussion

1. Which of these two families seems more representative of a "missionary" to you?

2. Why did employees never stay with the Kolbowitzes and why did the Marshalls never lose an employee?

3. Why do you think the Kolbowitzes had only seen one conversion and the Marshalls had seen several?

4. Why did the Kolbowitzes' coffee shop lose money and the Marshalls' business profit significantly?

5. Why did the Kolbowitzes return frustrated to the US while the Marshalls stayed in Chiang Mai amazed at how the Lord was working through them?

chapter 11

BLESSERS OR CONVERTERS?

There are undoubtedly a multitude of factors that come into play in determining the results of any activity. Missions and BAM are no different. It is sometimes difficult to discern how or why certain things happen the way they do. Why did *The Purpose Driven Life* sell 30 million copies while other well-written books go by completely unnoticed? (Hopefully, this book will not be one of the latter!) Why do some church plants grow into megachurches while others languish for years until the doors are finally shut for good? The same mystery surrounds BAM enterprises. Why do some succeed and others fail? To answer or at least partially answer that question, I went to Chiang Mai, Thailand, in the summer of 2007 to research various BAM enterprises in a single cultural context. I believe it is difficult to compare and contrast business projects across national and cultural boundaries. Each context is so unique that the differences in results could be explained by the cultural contexts, rather than the model or approach undertaken.

While in Chiang Mai I conducted 128 interviews and researched 12 BAM enterprises. Throughout the process, I noticed some intriguing patterns emerging. The companies that were producing positive ministry and/or business results tended to have four characteristics. Those that were not, tended to have four opposing characteristics.

Listed below are the four unifying characteristics of the high performers.

- a blessing orientation
- openness regarding purpose and identity

- partnership with local churches and ministries
- high cultural adaptation

This model contrasted with the low performers who had four different characteristics.
- a converting orientation
- secrecy regarding purpose and identity
- independence, preferring not to partner with others
- low cultural adaptation

Blessing vs. Converting

When asked the primary motivation for their work, the missionaries who operated sustainable businesses that produced missional fruit tended to give comprehensive, holistic explanations for why they engaged in business as mission. They frequently used the term *bless,* which is why I describe their attitude as a blessing orientation. Their answers reflected a sincere concern for the Thai people, a desire to help people in many aspects of their lives, including financial (income), relational (family), and spiritual (understanding the Christian message and becoming Christ followers). I heard remarks such as, "I want to be a blessing," and, "I'm just here to bless whoever comes my way." This orientation included conversion but only as one aspect of a larger purpose and vision.

In contrast, when asked their primary motivation, the missionaries who operated businesses that were struggling financially and producing little or no missional fruit gave conversion-oriented responses. They would use terms such as *convert* and *evangelism.* I frequently heard the phrase "We have to keep the main thing the main thing," meaning that the business and its corresponding social contribution to the lives of Thai people was only of instrumental value. The purpose of the business was to create an avenue for the missionaries to proclaim the Christian message and produce conversions. Ironically, these missionaries reported far fewer incidences of evangelism than those with a blessing orientation.

Figure 11.1

BLESSERS VERSUS CONVERTERS: COMPARING CONVERSIONS

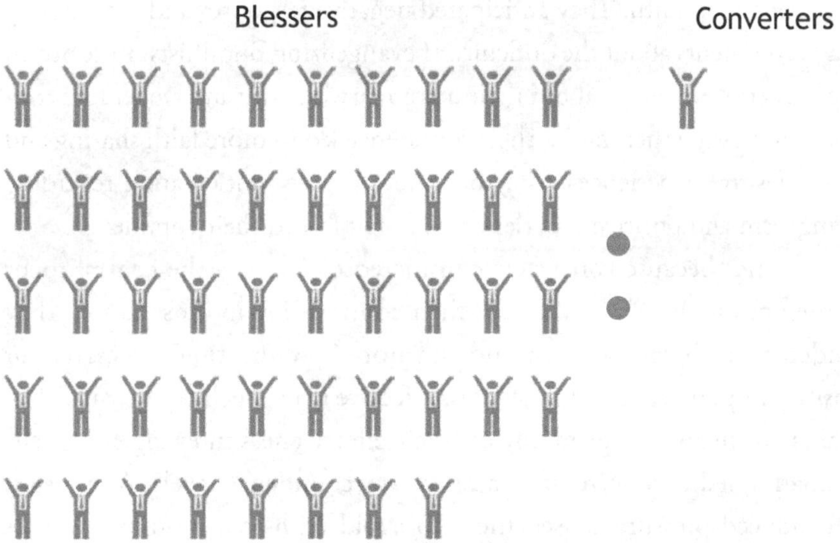

Blessers   Converters

Openness vs. Secrecy

Those with a blessing orientation tended to view themselves as "blessers," while those with a convert orientation viewed themselves as "converters." Both groups believed that the Thais perceived them as they perceived themselves. Therefore, the blessers believed that being a missionary was a positive thing and would be generally viewed as positive by others. For this reason, they tended to be more open about their missionary identity and freely shared their faith with others. In contrast, the converters believed that missionaries would be negatively viewed and wanted to shield their missionary identity. They developed covert strategies. Because sharing their faith brought the risk of blowing their cover, they were very selective concerning whom they talked to about their faith and tended to evangelize quite infrequently.

There are at least three other related factors that could help explain why converters reported fewer incidents of evangelism. First, the converters tended to be insecure about their missionary identity. This insecurity carried over to other aspects of their lives, and they tended to be less confident in sharing their faith. They anticipated negative responses and consistently made comments about the difficulty of evangelizing Buddhists. In contrast, the blessers were secure about their missionary identity and were more confident in sharing their faith. Their confidence led to more faith sharing and more positive experiences. They had more positive anticipation regarding evangelism and positive experiences only reinforced their confidence.

Second, because converters considered conversion the central focus of their ministries, they evaluated their contribution in those terms. They tended to rush the decision and did not allow the time necessary for positive responses, making them less effective in evangelism. Because they evaluated themselves primarily on their effectiveness in evangelism, self-evaluation led to a decrease in already low confidence levels. As a result, self-induced pressure caused them to avoid faith-sharing opportunities because they did not want to fail again or they wanted to wait until just the right time. In contrast, blessers did not tend to rush the decision-making process, but allowed for extensive exposure to the gospel, evangelizing naturally and opportunistically. These factors gave them increased levels of confidence and naturally resulted in more faith-sharing incidents.

Many missionaries were secretive in fear of being exposed as undercover missionaries. But it appears that this fear was not well founded. In three interviews, one with a Thai lawyer, another with a Thai customs official, and another with the family member of another Thai customs official, the interviewees had no desire to crack down on the presence of missionaries. On the contrary, Thailand gives out missionary visas and government policy supports foreign religious activities. One Thai Buddhist employee who did not know that either her managers or I were missionaries told me, "Missionaries are very respected here."

The Thai officials are highly suspicious of people who obscure their reasons for being in Thailand. Their primary fear is pedophilia. In the year I conducted my research, several high-profile cases of pedophilia committed by foreigners emerged in Thailand, particularly in Chiang Mai. Drug trafficking is another focus of concern. They added that they are "cracking down on illegal aliens who are living off the system." Covert missionaries, unfortunately, sometimes fall under these clouds of suspicion. The customs police had, in several incidents, talked to neighbors of secretive BAM practitioners, inquiring as to what they were doing, asking for descriptions of their activities, and if they were truly working or not.

Several missionaries confided in me that they knew that the Thai government was accepting of missionaries but did not feel that they would be effective in converting middle-class Thais if their missionary identity became known. My research indicates that those who are open about their identity are actually significantly more effective in bringing others to faith in Christ.

Comparing six blessing companies versus six converting companies, the ratio difference was 48 to 1 in terms of conversions. (See Figure 11.1.) The converting companies counted 1 conversion after the expenditure of 32 missionary years. In the blessing companies there were 36 conversions after the expenditure of 24 missionary years. (Again, remember there was a very high correlation between blessers and openness and converters and secrecy.) Figure 11.2 illustrates the overall differences I observed.

Figure 11.2

BLESSER VERSUS CONVERTER

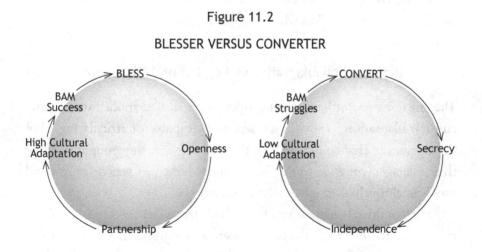

Third, several covert missionaries tended to view work as a distraction from ministry and complained that they did not have time for ministry. They did not see ministry as occurring in the workplace or in the business context; it was just a means to live and work in the country. Ministry in their perspective happened after hours and through leisure activities and conversations with friends.

Partnership vs. Independence

Open businesses also partnered with other local ministries. They brought in local pastors to give devotions and preach in workplace meetings. They donated their finances and sometimes their time to other ministries. When hiring, they went to other ministries, in hopes of finding a future employee who was on a faith journey and needed employment. These steps created multiple opportunities for some employees to hear and see the gospel, thus creating the consistent exposure necessary for them to become Christ followers.

In contrast the converters thought that partnerships would expose their missionary identity and tended to view local ministries with skepticism. Therefore, they preferred to work autonomously. Frequently, these missionaries did not attend public church meetings and sought to minimize their interaction with Thai Christians.

High Cultural Adaptation vs. Low Cultural Adaptation

The missionaries with a blessing orientation also demonstrated higher cultural adaptation.[1] Though not necessarily capable of articulating all of the significant Thai cultural values, they showed that they sought to adapt their management style to the Thai context. This fact was demonstrated most conclusively through employee interviews.

High cultural adaptation firms had far fewer complaints about management, lower employee turnover, and significantly higher levels of employee satisfaction.[2] Those businesses that operated according to a distinct American or Western management style had significant problems. They had high employee turnover, and employee interviews produced sharp negative feedback. In some cases, missionaries appeared unaware that their management style was American, perceiving it rather as "normal." In other cases, they intentionally chose to work from an American management style because they believed that younger, educated Thais responded better to it.

However, my research demonstrates that it is ineffective to reflexively use an American management style without sufficient adaptation to and understanding of Thai cultural values. The belief that one can insert an American or Western management style into an Eastern context emerges in part from a misinformed and exaggerated perception of the impact of globalization and American education.

Many Thai citizens are educated in America and then return to Thailand. Others learn at American universities that have extension centers in Thailand. They become managers, and the result is a trickle-down effect of the American management style. At the same time, American businesses such as McDonald's and Coca-Cola have a significant presence in Thailand leading many American missionaries to assume that globalization and education have made an American management style acceptable and standard. However, this assumption does not take into consideration the deeply ingrained nature of cultural assumptions and practices.

This is well demonstrated by contrasting two companies that I researched. One five-year-old company with low cultural adaptation had 19 employees. They retained no employees from the inception of the business, and the average length of employment was just eight months. The other business, which employed workers of a similar socioeconomic position, was seven years old and had 26 employees. This company displayed high cultural adaptation. In their seven years, only 3 workers had ever left the company and all had returned, for a net loss of 0 employees.

Figure 11.3

ROLE OF EMPLOYEE RETENTION

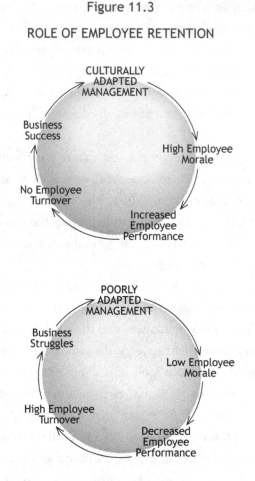

In reality, the changes brought on by globalization and the influence of foreign education are largely superficial. In 64 interviews with Thai employees, not a single one acknowledged any influence of American management techniques, and all strongly reflected commonly accepted Thai cultural values. In other words, neither intentionally nor inadvertently did any Thai employees demonstrate any change in culture as a result of globalization or foreign education. In contrast, they demonstrated quite clearly that they had not changed at all. Nevertheless, several American missionaries operating businesses told me that they could manage according to American management styles because the Thais understood them.

Interestingly, many younger missionaries (under age 35) believed that they were at a disadvantage because Thais more naturally respect elders, but younger managers who managed consistently in accordance with other Thai cultural values did not experience significant problems. Unfortunately, the majority of younger missionaries did not have a firm grasp of Thai cultural values and had significant challenges due to their management style. Without exception, the businesses managed by culturally nonadaptive missionaries had high employee turnover and serious financial problems.

Of course, a natural logical correlation exists between low cultural adaptation management and high employee turnover. The employees in such situations were constantly frustrated, though they could not always articulate what their frustrations were nor were they necessarily aware that they were the result of a cultural problem. Because many of these employees were low-wage workers, they could readily find alternative employment opportunities. As a result of their indirect communication style, Thai employees would not communicate their displeasure directly nor confront managers over their management styles. Expatriate managers with low cultural adaptation would anticipate that any problems would be communicated directly. Therefore, they were frequently unaware that the high turnover rate of their companies was unusual.

Many managers commented to me that high turnover was ubiquitous and unavoidable in Thailand, a belief that is unfounded. Two of my case studies had zero turnover; three others had very low turnover. However, other BAM enterprises that I researched had very high turnover. One company had an average employee term of less than six months.

In contrast to the low employee retention of the low cultural adaptation firms, high cultural adaptation management produced high employee retention as a natural result of fewer cross-cultural miscommunications and frustrations. As they strove to learn Thai culture and adapt to the people, these managers also came across as more humble, a very important Thai cultural trait. Because employees stayed longer, the managers were able to forge stronger relationships with the employees.

Those who demonstrated higher cultural adaptation to Thai culture in their management style not only experienced the benefits mentioned above but also had more incidences of faith sharing, saw more converts, and had employees who reported more respect and trust in managers. These outcomes are natural considered in the context of foundational aspects of Thai culture. Since the Thai Buddhist conversion process generally requires consistent, long-term exposure to the Christian message and witness, it is only natural that conversions would occur more often in businesses with loyal employees who stay long term. Missionaries who had high cultural adaptation could point to changed lives. Low cultural adaptation missionaries experienced very little fruit in terms of changed lives. Simply put, because of high turnover, they did not have the time necessary to influence the Thais positively and spiritually.

Figure 11.4

POSITIVE FEEDBACK CYCLE

Bless
↓
Openness
↓
Partnership
↓
High Cultural Adaptation
↓
Satisfied Employees
↓
Low or No Employee Turnover
↓
Are Exposed to the Gospel Consistently Over a Long Period of Time

Figure 11.4 Continued

NEGATIVE FEEDBACK CYCLE

Convert
↓
Secrecy
↓
Independence
↓
Low Cultural Adaptation
↓
Unsatisfied Employees
↓
High Employee Turnover
↓
Inexperienced and Less Effective Employees
↓
Are Not Exposed to the Gospel Consistently Over a Long Period of Time

High cultural adaptation also resulted in financial success. As a result of the Thai orientation toward interdependence, employees who had a close, positive relationship with their supervisor tended to perform better. High employee turnover means extra cost and time spent on interviewing and training employees. In contrast, low employee turnover means fewer expenses and more time focused on developing a profitable operation. Therefore, cultural adaptation created a natural feedback cycle affecting financial performance.

Typical Thai Buddhist Conversion Process

Understanding the Thai conversion process from Buddhism to Christianity was a challenge for many missionaries. I interviewed 26 Thai Buddhist-background believers. Every convert had two things in common: They had been exposed to the Christian message and lifestyle over an extended period of time, and they had been exposed to the Christian message and lifestyle consistently during that time period.

Through the various businesses, they were exposed to the Christian message on a weekly basis, generally in the workplace, and to the Christian lifestyle on a five-day-per-week basis. The messages or expositions were not always call-to-faith sermons, but were often about broader biblical themes regarding the Christian life. As the seekers moved closer to conversion, they also tended to start attending church and spending free time with Christians, thus increasing their exposure to the message to at least twice a week and exposure to the lifestyle as a daily occurrence. Twenty-two of the 26 Thai Christian converts said the primary reason they became Christians was because they had observed the lives of other Christians. All Thai converts (100 percent) cited this reason in all of the interviews without me first mentioning it.

Figure 11.5

CONSISTENT EXPOSURE TO CHRISTIAN MESSAGE BEFORE CONVERSION[3]

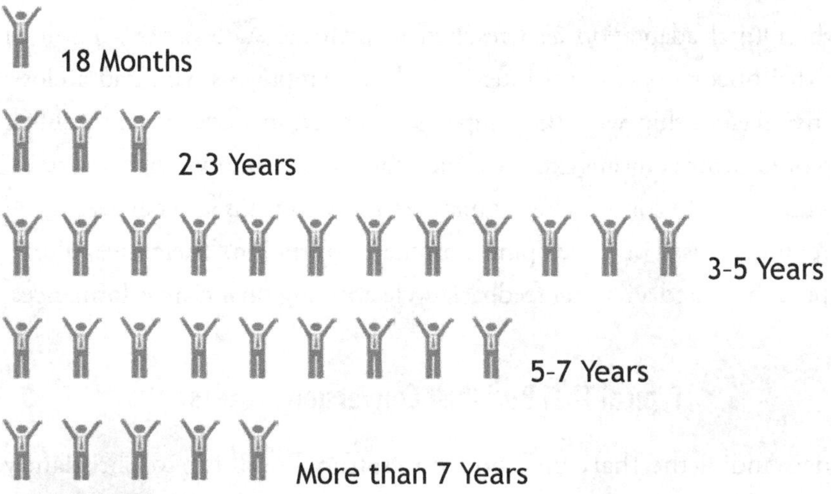

18 Months

2-3 Years

3-5 Years

5-7 Years

More than 7 Years

Figure 11.5 demonstrates the length of time required for conversion of the people I interviewed. Eighteen months was the minimum period of exposure and applied to just one person. Three people needed between two and three years. Twelve people required between three and five years, nine people required between five and seven years, and five people more than seven years. This demonstrates clearly that the Thai conversion process typically occurs over a long period of time, a significant factor being the strong social and cultural pressure of Buddhism. The average convert was exposed 250 to 300 times to a proclamation of the Christian faith before making a personal decision to become a Christ follower.

Cultural Agility

Those who had fruitful ministries and successful businesses had adapted in many respects to the culture but had also intentionally worked to counter certain aspects of the culture. People do not naturally conform to another culture. Culturally shrewd missional entrepreneurs, however, recognize that they must adapt to and respect culture, yet also recognize the need to counter some aspects of the culture.

The most commonly challenged Thai cultural characteristic was their present-time orientation, which can lead to lack of foresight regarding future challenges. In several of the more financially successful companies I researched, the managers told me that they had to consistently emphasize to workers the need to plan ahead and discipline themselves toward a more future orientation. Managers had to teach the Thais to do something that was outside the cultural comfort zone. In these companies, employees regularly mentioned changing their time orientation in the interviews, demonstrating that they were processing the issue.

Those managers who best reoriented their employees did so cautiously, consciously, and consistently. Other managers, who criticized Thai culture and did not expend significant effort in adapting to Thai culture, were not able to effectively reorient their Thai employees. In other words, those who were effective in adjusting their employees away from the traditional

Thai cultural orientation for the sake of organizational performance were focused on what needed to be changed. They did not try to change too much but focused on just one issue. They affirmed and adapted to other Thai cultural values, at least as far as they were aware. So missional entrepreneurs with high cultural adaptation were able navigate the Thai culture and even reorient their employees in limited, yet strategically important, ways.

Another Look at the Kolbowitzes and the Marshalls

Returning to the examples in chapter 10, what may have seemed like a mystifying difference in performance between the two companies is actually not so mysterious after all. The Kolbowitz family and their colleagues made some foundational mistakes that hampered their potential from the very beginning. In contrast, the Marshalls intuitively laid a foundation for positive results.

The Kolbowitzes considered their goal to be the conversion of Buddhists. Ironically, the singular focus on this goal actually prevented it from happening. They considered the business as simply a way to avoid identifying themselves as missionaries. Devaluing the potential social contributions of the business prevented them from evaluating the viability of the model and focusing on its success. Their lack of focus on certain aspects of the business, particularly management style and general cultural adaptation, created a company with high employee turnover. This is of course damaging financially. And, in a context like Thailand where people require consistent, long-term exposure to Christian demonstration and proclamation, it almost completely hinders the process of evangelization.

The Marshalls, on the other hand, considered the business a valuable platform for a variety of reasons. It provided income to unemployed Christians, thus producing more monies for churches and ministries. The business also served as a place for them to develop personal relationships with Christians and non-Christians. The Marshalls recognized the social and spiritual potential of the business and were motivated by both. They also focused on the cultural context, learning the language and intuitively feeling their way through the cultural labyrinth.

In a rush to get to effective evangelism, the Kolbowitz family did not sufficiently learn the language or pay significant attention to their cultural context. Considering the Thai Buddhist conversion process, this was a fundamental mistake that could not be corrected. When circumstances become exceedingly difficult and stressful, it is exceptionally hard to make sense of things that may be readily obvious to an objective outsider. This is especially true on the missions field, in a foreign cultural context. Thus, like the Kolbowitz family, many BAM practitioners get stuck in a rut and do not know how to step outside of their presuppositions to analyze what is going on around them.

Because the Marshalls made some decisions up front, they created a more effective working environment. Since the company was functioning well, Ron had time to pour properly into his employees. This empowered the employees' performance but also helped Ron develop a good relationship with them. This meant no employee turnover and a long time frame in which the employees could observe and listen to Christian behavior and verbal proclamation.

The Kolbowitz family believed it was essential to their mission to avoid being known as missionaries. This caused them to be tentative when sharing their faith. Thus they were caught in a difficult position: Evangelizing may reveal their missionary identity, but their missionary purpose was to evangelize. Their cautiousness also prevented them from interacting with local, Thai-run ministries and from collaborating with them.

The Marshalls, however, were very open about their missionary purpose. They partnered with other ministries and eventually funded several local ministries. They not only distributed resources to other ministries, they also used people from those ministries as resources in their company. Their open partnership model created a win-win situation in which they reduced their own workload and developed more opportunities for their employees to hear and experience the gospel.

Conclusion

Replanting this model in another cultural context may not yield the same results. Every context is unique. Furthermore there is the unquantifiable and often unobservable component of a person's walk with the Lord and his or her sensitivity to His leading on spiritual issues and activity. However, by looking closely at BAM in a single cultural context and comparing multiple organizations, it becomes clear that what businesses do and how they do it can have a tremendous impact on results.

Some cultural contexts may be the exact opposite of Thailand. For instance, perhaps in another country it is not a preference but is fundamentally essential to avoid identification as a missionary. Is business the best vehicle in that situation? Are there other ways to blend into the culture? There are serious consequences to running a nonexistent or poorly performing business.

Maybe in another country people are more spiritually open and do not need years to become Christians. In these cases, other approaches may be warranted. The business model can be adapted, and for many missionaries it may not be necessary or it may even be counterproductive.

BAM practitioners need to understand their local context and discern the right model and approach for that context. What is the typical conversion process there? Does anyone even understand that process fully yet? Has research on business and evangelism been contextualized to the local situation? What produces change in that locale? What are the needs? How can management styles be adjusted to accommodate the local culture? Answering these questions well and not rushing into a predetermined approach will likely help cross-cultural BAM practitioners start from a good foundation and achieve the results that they truly desire.

Questions for Reflection & Discussion

1. What is the difference between a blesser and a converter?

2. What justifications are there for being a "covert" missionary?

3. What benefits are there to being "open" as a Christian?

4. What are some pros and cons of partnership between ministry and business organizations?

5. How can one's level of cultural skills influence the work he or she is trying to do?

part 4

BEST
PRACTICES

chapter 12

SETTING A COURSE

The first step to success in any endeavor is determining what success looks like. That means setting goals. The second step is to determine what needs to happen in order to achieve these goals; this is strategy.

Missional entrepreneurs need to be very strategic in the way they approach their task, because they have a unique mission with multiple goals. Unlike other entrepreneurs who are simply out to make money, missional entrepreneurs need to make money, change lives, and do it all in the right way. This is easier said than done, and a well-honed strategy is necessary.

Casting Vision

While conducting 128 interviews for my PhD research not a single person in a BAM enterprise could cite its mission or vision statement from memory. Ninety percent of respondents either looked to their computer or said it was on their computer when asked. Although several organizations had mission and/or vision statements, very few demonstrated that their statements were actually directing or influencing their operations.

A good first step is to have a mission and vision statement. The second step is to know it and be able to recite it. The third step, the most important, is to know and live the vision and values behind it.

These steps will help missional entrepreneurs understand and articulate clearly what they are ultimately hoping to achieve. They will also help them understand why they want to achieve their mission. Having all of this clear in one's head and at the tip of one's tongue will provide clarity not only for the strategic plan but also for knowing when one can veer from the plan.

My research demonstrates that BAM enterprises often lack relevant, solid mission and vision statements and consequently often lack a robust business strategy as well. Missional entrepreneurs should not only have mission and vision statements, but they should know them, know the values behind them, and continually recite them so that everyone in the organization will know them and live them regardless of whether they are at the top or the bottom of the business, long-tenured, or newly arrived.

The Difference Between Mission and Vision Statements

Put simply a mission statement is the reason a business exists, and the vision statement is the goal towards which the business is moving. The mission is present, and the vision is future. The mission is the reason to be, and the vision is what the business wants to become.

Typically, the shorter and more concise these statements are the better. Consider Google's mission: To organize the world's information and make it universally accessible and useful. A vision statement should also be simple but empowering and exciting and worthy. Consider Microsoft's original vision statement: A computer on every desk and in every home.

While mission and vision statements do not have to have universal or global implications like Google and Microsoft—one can imagine a whole host of similar-sounding statements by businesses that no longer exist—the statements should clarify the purpose of the business and the goals toward which it is moving.

Developing a Business Strategy that Fits

Generally speaking, in my research I have come upon two kinds of missional entrepreneurs: those who tried to start large because they thought that was necessary, and those started small with no vision or strategy for becoming larger. In the former case, they frequently faced ongoing financial challenges that consumed time and energy and produced significant stress. In the latter case, they dealt with small numbers of people and had a relatively minimal impact on the surrounding community. I have found few missional entrepreneurs who aspired to start small and then scale operations over time in a systematic and strategic fashion.

Other BAM operations seem to struggle because they do not have a clear business strategy. For example, one US-based church decided to start ongoing missions in Cambodia. Its members wanted to use a BAM strategy to reach out to poor people in the urban slums of Phnom Penh and to generate funds for other ministry activities. They approached a business consultant, whom I interviewed, who was working for a large, well-respected, multinational company. The consultant was very supportive of the plan but asked if their primary purpose was to help the poor or to generate funds. The church members responded that they wanted the project to employ the unemployed residents of the slum and to be profitable to the point of covering all operating expenses, including expatriate management salaries, and to generate a sufficient profit to support other outreach activities.

The consultant was completely bewildered and explained that if they wanted to operate a profitable business to the extent they intended, they needed to look for skilled and knowledgeable workers who would generally not be found among the unemployed people of the slum. If on the other hand, they wanted to help the unemployed slum residents, then they should not expect the business to generate sufficient income to cover all expenses, much less produce a significant profit capable of supporting other outreach activities. From the consultant's perspective it was clear that the church was not aware that their intended target group—unemployed slum residents—did not have the capacity to carry out their intended business project.

In my research it has not been uncommon to encounter BAM entrepreneurs who are enamored with the concept and potential power of

BAM, but have no actual strategy or idea how to turn that into a reality. This is frequently the case when the entrepreneur's primary intent is to help the poor or some other seriously disadvantaged group. In one instance a group of BAM entrepreneurs tried to find street prostitutes alternative jobs with other BAM operators in Vietnam without even confirming if the prostitutes wanted another job or were remotely qualified for the job.

Of course, most missional entrepreneurs want to help these people in any way possible. However, there often needs to be a training bridge between a person's disadvantaged background and regular, full-time employment. It may be possible in a large or exceptionally profitable company to provide that training internally. It is more likely that this training would require outside consultants, and would probably need to be subsidized through donations. It is difficult for such training to occur in a small, for-profit business that intends to cover all operating expenses. Many missionaries have wonderful dreams that we all want to come to reality. However, it needs to be recognized that BAM is not always the answer and there should be more shared appreciation of various ministry practices and how they can partner together in various hybrid models.

In terms of BAM strategy, entrepreneurs must clarify their purpose. Is it to provide alternative and dignified employment to sex industry workers? Do they want to maximize profits and support other ministries from those profits? If it's the former, they may not be able to do the latter. If it's the latter, then they can support the former from their profits. There is space for both, but determining priorities then determines the scope and financial structure of the company. Once the purpose is clearly defined, there is a need for BAM practitioners to think big but know how to start small and scale smartly.

Think Big

Occasionally there are entrepreneurs who just don't think big. Frequently, these entrepreneurs are "job replacement" entrepreneurs who start up a business in hopes of becoming financially independent, avoiding the corporate world, and generating a living wage from their newly started company. This sounds simple and surely not as risky and complex as say, aspiring to launch a world-changing, immensely profitable multinational corporation. Ironically, these types of small start-ups are generally not successful because they do not generate the movement and energy necessary to sustain a profitable enterprise. In other words, for an entrepreneurial start-up to be successful, it must think big—at least bigger than a simple job replacement.

However, thinking big is not a problem for many entrepreneurs. This is why they are entrepreneurs; they have bigger fish to fry than simply grinding out a six-figure income on Wall Street. Dreams of being the next Steve Jobs, Bill Gates, or Sam Walton dance in their heads at night. The climb-the-ladder career path of corporate America is simply too small and slow for these grandiose-thinking entrepreneurs.

But, there are a couple of potential problems with thinking big. The first is when the focus is purely on the money. I'm not saying that wealth creation and getting rich are bad; they're powerful motivating forces that are foundational to the free market. Many entrepreneurial endeavors, however, take time to generate that dream income. Frustrated by the slow flow of cash coming through the door, many big-thinking entrepreneurs give up before they've really gotten started. Unwilling to cut back on nonessentials and live at a level below what they could make as an employee, they dump their business, head to headquarters, and beg for their job back. The point here is that to make money, you often have to give up money and sometimes for a long time. If money is your only motivation, you'll give up before you get your payout.

A second problem is that many big thinkers cannot distinguish between vision and fantasy. Fantasizers have no problem envisioning themselves leading a magnificent life at the head of a self-created international conglomerate. I know one serial entrepreneur who continually starts new businesses, each one destined to be "the next big thing." It's going to topple Apple, generate more buzz than MTV, or take on Coke. His businesses never take off and before long he's on to "the next big thing." Fantasizers can create the vision, but they cannot ascertain the risks involved, the time needed, or the steps necessary to get the job done. They sound brash and cool, but they really don't know what they're talking about.

Visionaries are different. They, too, have a big vision, sometimes even an outlandish one, like, say to be the next Walt Disney. But they know that this is an immense undertaking, are aware they can't do it alone, are conscious that it will take time, and can create a solid yet flexible plan to get from vision to reality. Unlike fantasizers they don't try to impress people with how big they think — rather they focus on creating real value for real people through a real business.

Start Small

Almost every entrepreneurial endeavor starts small. This is generally by necessity rather than choice. If venture capitalists were willing to fork over seven figures for every idea, many entrepreneurial endeavors would choose to start much bigger. And who wouldn't be tempted to take that money if it were there? Ironically, even if this money were available it likely would impede the eventual success of the start-up.

Numerous researchers have written that starting too big and with too much capital can create an atmosphere of poor performance. You can get away with unnecessary expenses for a while, but eventually there is an end. Starting too big produces the need to generate big returns almost immediately. This often causes a loss of focus and gives rise to an environment in which the company throws mud on the wall to see if it sticks.

In other words, starting small means that you have to be focused. This strategic focus of energy, thought, and resources is what is necessary for a start-up to survive then thrive. Starting too big results in a breakdown of focus before the start-up has sustainable means to generate such a diversified outlook.

Scale Smartly

For many entrepreneurs thinking big and starting small may seem obvious and not altogether very interesting. Plenty of people come with think big, start small, scale fast business plans. However, it is important to be aware that if you get the first two steps right, you may just trip on the third. Instead of seeking to scale fast, entrepreneurs would be wise to focus on scaling smartly.

Consider the contrast of LazyTown Entertainment and Big Idea Productions. LazyTown, founded by Icelander Magnús Scheving, is a children's entertainment company that seeks to educate children about healthy lifestyles.[1] Big Idea Productions, founded by Midwesterner Phil Vischer, is also a children's entertainment company and seeks to teach children important life lessons. It was an industry leader in computer animation in the early and mid-90s. Both Scheving and Vischer had the vision (or fantasy) of being the next Walt Disney. They both founded companies that became quickly successful and garnered a large, loyal, and emotional following. But what they did next made all the difference.

Vischer, with his dream of becoming the next Disney and creating a media company that would compete with NBC, CBS, and ABC, continually pushed for growth. The results were promising. They were rolling in eight-figure annual profits and transitioning from videos to full-length motion pictures. However, the day after the grand opening of *Jonah*, a film that netted a very respectable $6.5 million in its opening weekend ($25 million total), Vischer had to lay off half of his staff.[2]

Scheving, on the other hand, resisted running with his initial popularity. With dreams of being the next Disney prancing through his head, he knew he had to learn the children's entertainment industry. Instead of quickly expanding to more lucrative foreign markets, Scheving focused on his tiny homeland of Iceland. He wanted to test his products on at least two generations of preschoolers before looking to grow. He also knew that it would take more than vision to crack the international market and that he needed to learn how to dance before he showed up at the party. After more than a decade of honing his craft and forming the brand, LazyTown has soared through the international markets.

What happened to Big Idea? The short answer is they pushed too hard. In hopes of retaining their top talent and harnessing talent from other top studios, they doubled their pay scale, and, at the same time, doubled their staff. In one year, they quadrupled their expenses. Despite tremendous growth, profitable licensing agreements, and expanding opportunities, Big Idea was left with too little in the coffer to sustain itself when it faced a lawsuit with a distributor and went into bankruptcy. Though still in existence, it is now a subsidiary of Classic Media. Vischer, its founder and creator, is now a contract consultant for the new owners.

Scheving, on the other hand, was patient and it paid off. LazyTown is now in more than 100 countries, has high ratings among preschool viewers, and has won a batch of industry awards since making its debut in America in 2004. Scaling smartly certainly has its advantages!

A Master Plan

Missional entrepreneurs are unique. They aspire to perform across multiple lines. As a result, a normal business plan is insufficient for what they want to accomplish. In addition to a normal business plan, they need a ministry plan that details their goals, unique mission, purpose, and vision. But this plan cannot be constructed in isolation from the business plan for the two parts are interconnected and should be fully integrated.

For missional entrepreneurs I recommend a business plan and a ministry plan that is merged in what I call a master plan. The master plan is the superior document that clarifies the overall aims of the combined business and ministry endeavors. Missional entrepreneurs should aspire to find win-win situations when there appear to be conflicts between their economic, social, environmental, and spiritual goals. They should seek to create synergy so that their multiple goals do not work against each other but help create a positive feedback cycle. For example, Christ-centered servant leadership can reduce employee turnover and increase employee performance. This is good for the financial bottom line.

Nevertheless, there are times when the goals will work against one another. For example, a missional entrepreneur will choose to pay fair wages to his employees and suppliers. This may raise his costs against competitors who are able to undercut his prices. In this sense, the social-spiritual decision of paying fair wages undermines the financial bottom line. As you read this book on missional entrepreneurialism, the right thing to do may seem clear and obvious, but in the daily pressures of business it can become cloudy and foggy. This is why a master plan is necessary. The master plan presides over the business and ministry plans and helps missional entrepreneurs focus on their vision of who they want to be and what they really want to accomplish.

Questions for Reflection & Discussion

1. What are the values of mission, vision, and purpose statements?

2. What does it mean to think big?

3. Why is it preferable to start small rather than start big?

4. Why is it preferable to scale smartly over growing (too) quickly?

5. How do you envision a master plan?

chapter 13

NAVIGATING CULTURE

Concepts, definitions, and understandings of missions are changing. Missions is not just about working in some faraway place. God is on mission everywhere and has asked us to join Him. As such, it is not necessary to travel to remote places and learn foreign languages to engage in missions. Business as mission is the same. It is not necessary to cross oceans and cultures to engage in BAM. One can be a missional entrepreneur in his or her hometown and be on mission with God through business.

BAM takes many forms and can be practiced in many places. While it is not necessary to cross cultures, many adventurous missional entrepreneurs do. Living and working cross-culturally requires special understanding, training, and skills. Cross-cultural missional entrepreneurs must not only be adept at operating a business, managing people, living with integrity, and sharing God's love, they must do it all within a cultural context that is, at least at first, unfamiliar and where misunderstandings and frustrations can arise without apparent rhyme or reason.

I have lived and worked in several different countries for various periods of time. It is a bit like being lost in an ocean. You look around you and nothing gives you a clear direction for what to do. If you don't take precautions, you could end up nauseous or worse!

This chapter is dedicated to learning how to navigate culture, particularly different, foreign cultures where many missional entrepreneurs find themselves. In order to do that we will use the Thai culture as a case study in cultural dynamics. Missional entrepreneurs will want to go through the same type of cultural analysis for their particular situation.

Foundations of Culture

It is of course very challenging to break down and analyze cultures. Generalizations are often unfair and can be unhelpful. But in order to aid in the analysis of particular cultures, it is first necessary to establish a macro view of culture. Therefore, we will use several tools established by sociologists and interculturalists to understand how we can effectively communicate with, relate to, and work in a different culture. As a tool for cultural analysis we will use the following 15 foundational concepts of culture:[1]

- self
- responsibility
- reality
- time
- past, present, and future
- activity
- control
- communication
- face (reputation)
- power distance
- uncertainty
- work
- productivity
- status
- context

Concept of Self

The concept of self is a critical element of culture and can be evaluated on a continuum between the opposing labels of "individualist" and "collectivist." This concept can be illustrated by how cultures "divide up the spoils."

For example, a collectivist culture would evenly divide a project's revenue among all the people in the group without consideration of time expended or performance. An individualist culture, on the other hand, would weigh the time expended by each member of the group as well as each person's performance. Therefore, if $10,000 is to be divided among a group of five people, the collectivist culture would give $2,000 to each person, but the individualist culture might give $4,000 to one, $2,000 to another, $1,500 to two people, and $1,000 to the person who performed and/or worked the least.

In collectivist cultures the security and well-being of individuals ultimately depend on the well-being and survival of their group. In contrast, in individualist cultures people think that rewards should be directly commensurate with one's level of effort and that the individual is responsible for his or her own security and well-being.

In an individualist culture, people identify first and foremost with the individual self and the needs of the individual are satisfied before that of the group. These cultures value things like independence, self-reliance, and personal freedom. In a collectivist culture, the primary group (usually the immediate family) is the smallest unit of survival, not the individual self. They tend to see the well-being of the individual as based on the survival and success of the group. No culture is exclusively collectivist or individualist, but these definitions serve as a basis for diagnosis and understanding.

How does this play out practically? In one case, a missional entrepreneur living in a collectivist culture set up an incentive system that rewarded employees on an individual basis. This caused serious tension and actually killed employee morale rather than enhancing it as he had hoped.

Concept of Responsibility

The concept of responsibility (personal versus societal) can be evaluated along a spectrum between the opposing labels of "universalist" and "particularist." The term universalist does not refer to the religious concept of universalism, which teaches that all religions lead to God. In cultural analysis, the term refers to the tendency to believe that right is right, regardless of circumstances. In other words, rightness is universally applicable. Particularists, on the other hand, tend to feel that circumstances must be taken into account.

For example, particularists are more willing to perjure themselves if the lies would protect friends; hence, the "particulars" of the case determine the right course of action. Friendship takes precedence over truth telling. Of course, this cultural trait may not find expression in outright lying but in a general willingness to conceal or deceive in order to protect family. Universalists would say that perjury or deception is wrong regardless of whom they are trying to protect, reflecting their belief in absolutes that are applicable in all situations regardless of circumstances. Particularists believe that the circumstances determine how to act in a certain situation and that what is right in one situation may not be so in another.

Navigating the tension between universalism and particularism in international business can be quite difficult for Christian entrepreneurs. In particularist cultures rules and laws are not as objective as they are in universalist cultures. This relates to many ethical situations, such as gift giving and paying apparent bribes. I have seen missional entrepreneurs go to both extremes. One group so emphasizes universalism that they will not distinguish between giving a small gift as a token of friendship—a specific cultural way of doing business in many places—and a bribe. Others, though, view everything as acceptable in the gray area of international business and get themselves in trouble by giving money and gifts to the wrong people. Careful discernment is required here.

Concept of Reality

Another aspect of this distinction is that universalists tend to have an objective view of reality whereas particularists tend to have a subjective view. In universalist cultures, favoritism and nepotism are negative characteristics, and objectivity is held as a positive trait. Particularists view things subjectively rather than objectively. Using connections, favoritism, and working with an "in group" are considered societal norms.

Preferential treatment is expected for friends. Personal feelings should influence decisions. Universalism is sometimes referred to as logic of the head, whereas particularism is called logic of the heart.

Missional entrepreneurs coming from universalist cultures frequently have trouble because employees pressure them to hire family members instead of qualified professionals. While it may not be appropriate to actually hire the family member, the missional entrepreneur would be wise to understand the cultural basis of this request and not be dismissive of that cultural tendency. Finding a creative way to put the right people on the team and respecting the values of the culture would give that company a huge advantage.

For example, I know one missional entrepreneur who was looking for a human resources manager. An employee asked the missional entrepreneur to hire the employee's cousin, who was not qualified. Rather than negatively reacting to the request, he took it quite seriously and said he would try to work something out. Eventually, he offered the cousin a job as a custodian, which was accepted enthusiastically. While the custodial position was an unexpected additional expense, the missional entrepreneur says that the positive impact the job offer made on the rest of the employees more than made up for it. They now saw the entrepreneur as a person who cared for their families; the businessman describes this as a pivotal moment for the success of his company.

Concept of Time

The concept of time, how cultures relate to time, and how they work, can be expressed through the opposite terms of monochronic and polychronic. For example, in monochronic cultures time is perceived as a commodity and a scarce resource that can be spoken of in quantifiable terms. Therefore, it is necessary to use time wisely and not waste it. There is a premium on efficiency, hence a sense of urgency in many matters. People in monochronic cultures tend to be very busy and hurried.

On the other hand, in polychronic cultures time is viewed more abstractly and is considered limitless. Therefore, it is not necessary to hurry or keep to a schedule. Everything happens when it should. I remember watching a documentary in seminary in which a Native American aptly expressed the attitude of polychronic cultures in remarks that went something like this, "Why do these white people allow themselves to be ruled by a watch? It's much smaller than them but it tells them what to do and it puts them in a hurry. The solution is simple. Take off the watch and then you will not be in a hurry. I just don't understand." This is the perspective of polychronic cultures. One day comes after the next. Time is an infinite resource; it is not necessary to stress over its usage.

Time management is difficult everywhere but is exceptionally challenging for people trying to bridge cultures that have significantly different perceptions. I remember one missional entrepreneur who became quite frustrated because he could not get his employees to show up on time for staff meetings. He wisely sought the counsel of a local businessperson, who told him to simply give a time 30 minutes prior to his desired meeting time and say that the meeting would begin with refreshments. This drew people to the meeting place, and the manager was able to start right on time according to his mental clock. This was a more effective response than simply trying to drill into everyone's heads that they should value time like him.

Concept of Past, Present, and Future

Cultures differentiate themselves in how they value the past, the present, and the future. This is measured on a continuum of past, present, and future orientations. Past-oriented cultures tend to value history and put emphasis on their ancestors. They value historic monuments and are more resistant to modern cultural changes as they seek to preserve their traditional way of life.

Present-oriented cultures tend to focus on the present and do not have a strong historical or futurist perspective. Many cultures in underdeveloped settings fall in this category. They do not have a tight connection to their past and any future concerns pale to the tasks of the day. This strong "today" orientation sometimes causes problems because the full consequences of decisions are not considered, perpetuating a negative feedback cycle that prevents development.

The country of Haiti is an illustrative example. Research shows that the farthest many people think into the future is one week. This orientation has contributed to the cutting down of 98 percent of the natural forests on the island. The resulting environmental degradation has increased erosion and decreased agricultural yields, which has perpetuated and intensified the cycle of poverty in that country. The time orientation of a country can have significant consequences for its people.

Future-oriented cultures are ones that are not strongly historical, but are also not focused on today only. They value planning and forward thinking. They seek to construct strategies in order to "control" the future and produce the future they desire.

Missional entrepreneurs need to know what type of culture they come from, what type of culture they are working in, and how they should adapt to it. If it is a past-oriented culture they're working in, then the missional entrepreneur should find ways of respecting that culture's past and use it as a way to bring up historical incidents that have shaped his or her life. Furthermore, any work on future planning should not be done in competition with the past orientation. I know one missional entrepreneur who was so frustrated with the lack of value on future planning among his employees that he stated, "looking back produced failure," in a staff meeting and immediately saw the faces of his employees drop.

Concept of Activity

Cultures also have different ways that they engage in and view activity. This can be seen through the polarization of one thing at a time versus many things at a time. Monochronic people will focus on doing one thing at a time, as they view time and activity in a linear fashion. They are more task-oriented. They accomplish a task, then move to the next task. They don't like interruptions, so it is best not to interrupt them unless it is something of clearly higher priority. They value deadlines to designate the end of a task, and they value punctuality as a designation for the beginning of another task.

Polychronic people, on the other hand, will do many things at a time and have more of a circular view of time and activity; it just kind of swirls around. They prefer to do many things simultaneously. They tend to work in open spaces and work collaboratively on a continual basis. They do not mind interruptions and in fact welcome them. They are more relationally focused and the relationship trumps the task. They will be late for a meeting if a friend interrupts them en route. This excuse would fall on deaf ears to a person from a "one thing at a time" or monochronic culture. But "many things at a time" people will understand this was justifiable.

Concept of Control

The concept of control is expressed through the opposite dimensions of internal locus of control versus external locus of control. Cultures that have an internal locus of control respond affirmatively to the statement, "What happens to me is my own doing." The majority of Americans (89 percent) affirmed this statement, choosing it over "Sometimes I feel I don't have control over the direction my life is taking." This contrasts with just 35 percent of Chinese who agreed that what happens to them is their own doing.[2] Americans have a strong internal locus of control evidenced by American expressions such as "Where there's a will there's a way."

For cultures that hold to an internal locus of control there are very few things or circumstances that have to be accepted as they are. People in this type of culture believe that most things can be changed. In contrast, cultures with an external locus of control believe that the locus of control is outside the individual. Therefore, they view many things in life as predetermined. They see aspects of life as outside of their control. There are limits beyond which one cannot go and certain things that cannot be changed and must be accepted. These cultures have a strong understanding of fate. One Southern Arabian proverb expresses external locus of control: "Caution does not avert the decree of fate."

Concept of Communication

Cultures also have different styles of verbal communication along the spectrum between the poles of direct and indirect. Perhaps more than any other factor, these differences in communication often cause serious cross-cultural misunderstandings. Despite years of experience communicating with people in other cultures, I still face challenges in navigating the different styles of communication and have seen many problems result from this issue.

Direct communication simply means that it is expected that a person will say precisely what he or she means and say it directly to the person who should hear it. In other words, if Bob thinks my emails are sloppily written, he comes to me and tells me that my emails are sloppily written and that he would appreciate it if I smoothed them out a bit.

Indirect communication means that it is expected that a person will not say precisely what they mean, rather they will give hints and indicators. And they will say what they want to say to a third party who then relays the message to the intended recipient. Therefore, if Bob does not like my emails, he will go to another colleague whom he believes will convey the message to me, and ask questions like, "What do you think of Mark's emails?" He'll then give indications like, "I have a hard time understanding them. I wonder if they could be improved, maybe more professional."

Often, indirect cultures are collectivist and particularist, believing what you say and how you say it are largely determined by the particular situation. Direct cultures tend to be individualist and universalist, believing that it is right to say exactly what you mean.

In collectivist cultures, groups are well connected and well established. They share experiences and have an intuitive understanding of one another; therefore, they do not need to be so direct. They can afford to be indirect. In individualist cultures groups are not well connected or well established. People do not share as many experiences and do not have such an intuitive understanding of one another. Therefore, people need to be direct and spell things out for one another.

Collectivist cultures also value harmony, so they avoid direct confrontation with other people. They talk indirectly because preserving group harmony is highly valued and speaking directly to another person could create disharmony and dissension. Individualist cultures do not value harmony as much and, as such, will be more apt to confront another person directly. Due to their value of harmony, people from collectivist cultures will not say no directly but will say yes and perhaps give a subtle hint that it is not really a yes. To a person from a direct culture, this hint can be so subtle that it goes by completely unnoticed. However, a person from an indirect culture would pick up the clue right away and realize the true answer is no.

In direct cultures, people say what they mean and mean what they say. Others do not need to read between the lines. Direct cultures think it is best to tell it like it is. People are less likely to rely on implication or hint around. Rather they are more likely to say exactly what they are thinking; yes means yes.

In contrast, in indirect cultures, people will not say in clear terms what they mean or exactly what they want to say. It is necessary to look for subtle hints and implied meanings. People are more likely to suggest or imply something than to come out and say what they think. Therefore, you have to read between the lines and you can't simply speak directly to other people or tell it like it is. This is frowned upon because it could upset the other person. In indirect cultures, yes can mean yes, maybe, or not a chance!

From my travels, I have a wonderful example of the difference between direct and indirect cultures. When boarding a Thai Airways flight at JFK Airport in New York City, the counter agent, a Thai national, made the unfortunate discovery that my son's passport had expired. Rather than simply telling me that my son's passport had expired and that he couldn't board the plane, she picked up his passport, pointed her finger at the expiration date, and asked sweetly and innocently, "Where is the expiration date on this passport?" While I was not smart enough to check the expiration date prior to going to the airport, I was smart enough to see the expiration date and know exactly what that meant. She then kindly helped us rebook a flight two days later, giving us time to solicit a new passport.

When I arrived in Thailand, I told the story to many American BAM entrepreneurs. The majority made derogatory remarks about the indirectness of Thai culture, such as, "That is so stupid. Why didn't she just say it?" or "These people cannot be trusted as they are never direct." In reality, the Thai agent was communicating according to the indirect style that is embedded in her culture. Rather than telling me directly, she was trying to help me avoid losing face by allowing me to "discover" my own error.

Many of these BAM entrepreneurs dismissed the indirect method as inferior, which reflects a low degree of cultural adaptation. Imagine the response of Thai employees when their mistakes are pointed out to them directly. When that happens they lose face and either become demoralized, resulting in low performance, or they simply leave the job. Dismissing or misunderstanding differences in communication styles can have devastating effects on both the business and ministry aspects of BAM enterprises.

Concept of Face

These styles of verbal communication are related to the importance that a culture puts on "face," a complex concept that is similar to the Western notion of a person's reputation or standing in society. To lose face results in embarrassment and a loss of standing in the community. In direct, individualist cultures, face is not as important. Since the person is viewed more as an individual than a member of a group, losing face does not produce as much ostracism as it does in a group culture. In collectivist cultures, the person is a member of a group so losing face jeopardizes the person's standing in the group. This can be disheartening and even devastating.

In direct cultures, which tend to be universalist, saying the right thing or telling the truth directly is considered superior to concern over someone else's feelings. It is therefore necessary to be honest or even brutally honest. After all, you are telling the truth. This makes it acceptable to say no to invitations and to confront people directly. People as not as concerned about saving face and will not always refrain from hurting someone's feelings. These cultures value the efficient transmission of information. This is the primary goal of every communication exchange.

In indirect cultures, however, face tends to be very important. Preserving harmony, not hurting someone else's feelings, maintaining a good group dynamic, and saving face are primary concerns. Saying the right thing and telling the truth are subservient to these higher goods. Truth is relative; it depends on its impact on others. If the truth threatens harmony or someone's face, then it can and should be adjusted. It is better to say what one thinks the other person wants to hear. It is acceptable, even preferable, to avoid saying no directly and to refrain from confrontation. In communication, the preserving of interpersonal and societal harmony trumps the efficient transmission of information.

To work as a missional entrepreneur in a culture that emphasizes the importance of face, it is critical to respect social mores and to learn how to communicate and interact appropriately. For example, I researched one business in Thailand that had problems with employee turnover. It turns out that the American managers thought it best to deal directly with employee mistakes. They did not realize that every time they did they subjected the employee to a humiliating, face-losing experience that left the employee believing the managers and probably everyone else wanted them to leave. The managers naturally were disheartened that so many employees were leaving, but were unaware of the pain their direct communication methods were causing. Thai employees had tried to indirectly communicate to the managers that their communication style was offensive to the Thai culture. But the American managers did not pick up on the subtle hints and indicators. As a result, both sides had significantly different perceptions of what was going on. The end result was a dying business.

Another business I researched did much better. When an employee made a mistake, instead of approaching them directly with what he or she did wrong, the manager would call in yet another employee. They would have five to ten minutes of routine dialogue. Even though the employee knew that the manager called them in for another reason, it would be inappropriate to immediately launch into the main purpose of the conversation. After this initial small talk, the manager would ask the employee about a particular procedure. The employee would then explain how it should be done. The manager would then respond that he was just checking on everyone's understanding because "it looks like some people, maybe John, don't understand exactly how this procedure works."

The employee would then immediately realize that the entire conversation had been about one thing: John was improperly following a procedure. He would then leave the meeting and go directly to John to re-explain to him how to do it. While this communication chain may seem ineffective or even rude to some people from direct cultures, it is absolutely necessary in indirect cultures and it can be the difference between a dying or a thriving business.

Cultures that put a strong emphasis on face will be very focused on not making mistakes and very sensitive about correction. For example, when I interviewed Thai employees and asked open-ended, general questions about leadership and management nearly all of their initial responses were related to the issue of how a leader should handle an employee's mistake. They have a very definite "mistake" orientation. Therefore, it is vital for an expatriate manager to understand this and be sensitive to this strongly held cultural value.

Concept of Power Distance

Cultures also differ in their perspective on power distance, ranging from egalitarian to hierarchical. Egalitarian cultures have a low power distance. This means that a leader would be approachable, as there is little social distance between the leader and the followers. However, hierarchical cultures have a high power distance. Leaders are not as approachable, and good leaders are considered distant from their followers.

In egalitarian cultures, employees tend to expect to learn from each other, and they expect dialogue. They typically see their bosses as peers and coaches, and they feel free to challenge them and offer counterpoints. They are also generally comfortable with self-directed activities.

In hierarchical cultures, employees expect their boss to be an expert. They expect the leader to provide a clear structure, and they're unlikely to speak up unless called on. They tend to see their supervisor as an authority figure who should be respected. They would almost never challenge or correct their supervisor, even if what the supervisor was doing was obviously wrong to everyone else.

In egalitarian cultures, position or title is not as important. People can communicate across levels and approach the supervisor of their supervisor. However, in hierarchical cultures, the chain of command is critical. Subordinates should never bypass their immediate supervisor and go to a higher level.

Let me give an example. Bob's immediate supervisor was an American but his supervisor's superior was Japanese (a high power distance culture). Bob was frustrated by his immediate supervisor, so he went to speak with the Japanese boss. The Japanese boss was so upset that Bob had tried to go around the chain of command that he threatened him with termination. Bob got so mad that he quit — before he could be fired. This is a classic case of misunderstanding other people's cultural orientation toward power distance. Bob still thinks his Japanese boss mishandled the entire incident while the Japanese boss still thinks of Bob as an insubordinate type and is glad he's gone.

Concept of Uncertainty

Cultures can also be evaluated in how they view uncertainty along the continuum from positive to skeptical. A culture with a positive disposition toward uncertainty will value things like the ability to influence one's future and personal liberties. Cultures with a skeptical view toward uncertainty demonstrate preferences for security and stability.

Understanding a culture's view of uncertainty can be extremely helpful in determining how to communicate with employees. For example, I know one missional entrepreneur who, while working in an Asian country with an extremely negative view of uncertainty, intentionally refrained from letting employees know about their perilous financial situation and the possible necessity of layoffs. He felt that uncertainty would have impeded the employees' performance at a critical time.

Concept of Work

Is the purpose of work achievement or quality of life? Some cultures find achievement, the accomplishment of tasks, and material success to be the primary motivations for work. These cultures place a high value on work and believe that it is important to be successful at work.

Other cultures believe the purpose of work is to create a high quality of life. Work is not about achievement in itself. Rather it is about creating a way of life that one can enjoy. Work serves the purpose of creating that way of life, but the accomplishments of work, especially as an individual, are not as important.

Concept of Productivity

Cultures range from a results orientation to a harmony orientation toward productivity. A results-oriented culture values productivity over harmony and emphasizes tasks and achievement beyond any relationship dynamics. They will sacrifice harmony to obtain results.

A harmony-oriented culture, however, values peaceful personal interaction over particular tasks. They will sacrifice results in order to maintain harmony. Relationships are valued over tasks, and productivity is achieved in a harmonious environment.

Concept of Status

The concept of status refers to whether it is earned through work or some other measure of performance or if it is given through birth or some other means. Is status earned or ascribed? In earned-status cultures one can find concepts like the self-made man. These cultures do not have an entrenched class system and people are able to gain and lose social status rather quickly.

In ascribed-status cultures, there tend to be entrenched class systems. In some cases there is nothing one can do in a lifetime to change his or her class. Royalty is an example of ascribed status that is very difficult to lose. Ascribed-status cultures will value tradition more than earned-status cultures.

Concept of Context

Some cultures are high-context, while others are low-context. This refers to the mental framework (or understanding) from which people are expected to interact. In low-context cultures people are not assumed to share the same framework; high-context cultures assume a shared understanding of the world. In a low-context culture, much of the background information needs to be made explicit in communication. In a high-context culture, background information tends to be implicit.

In a low-context culture people prefer to communicate on a need-to-know basis. If something is outside of a person's immediate job responsibility, then they will not be told about it and that person will probably appreciate not having their mind cluttered with someone else's work. When information is shared, then the hearer will need to be brought up to speed on what has been going on. It is assumed that people have little knowledge of a particular situation unless they are directly involved. Information sharing tends to be done through formal processes such as meetings, conference calls, etc.

Communication in high-context societies presumes a broadly shared, well-understood knowledge of the context of anything referred to in conversation or in writing. Businesses in a high-context culture share information broadly with everyone. When business memos are sent out, there is little background information, for it is assumed that everyone pretty much knows what is going on. Information sharing is done informally, through casual conversations in the hallway for instance, though the sharing of information is done intentionally.

Low-context cultures require direct, active voice expression, and crystal-clear explanations. It is the communicator's responsibility to insure the message is fully intelligible to the target audience. Little, if anything, is assumed. The meaning of the message is in the words. Language is paramount, and the words transmit the information in the form of facts and data.

In high-context cultures, expression tends to be indirect and suggestive, creating an ambiance and relying on historical or cultural references. The receivers of information are expected to do most of the work involved in understanding the full significance of a message. Language is expressive, often emotional. The meaning of the message is in the context, a context rooted in the person and the situation.

Figure 13.1
ANALYSIS OF THAI VERSUS US CULTURE

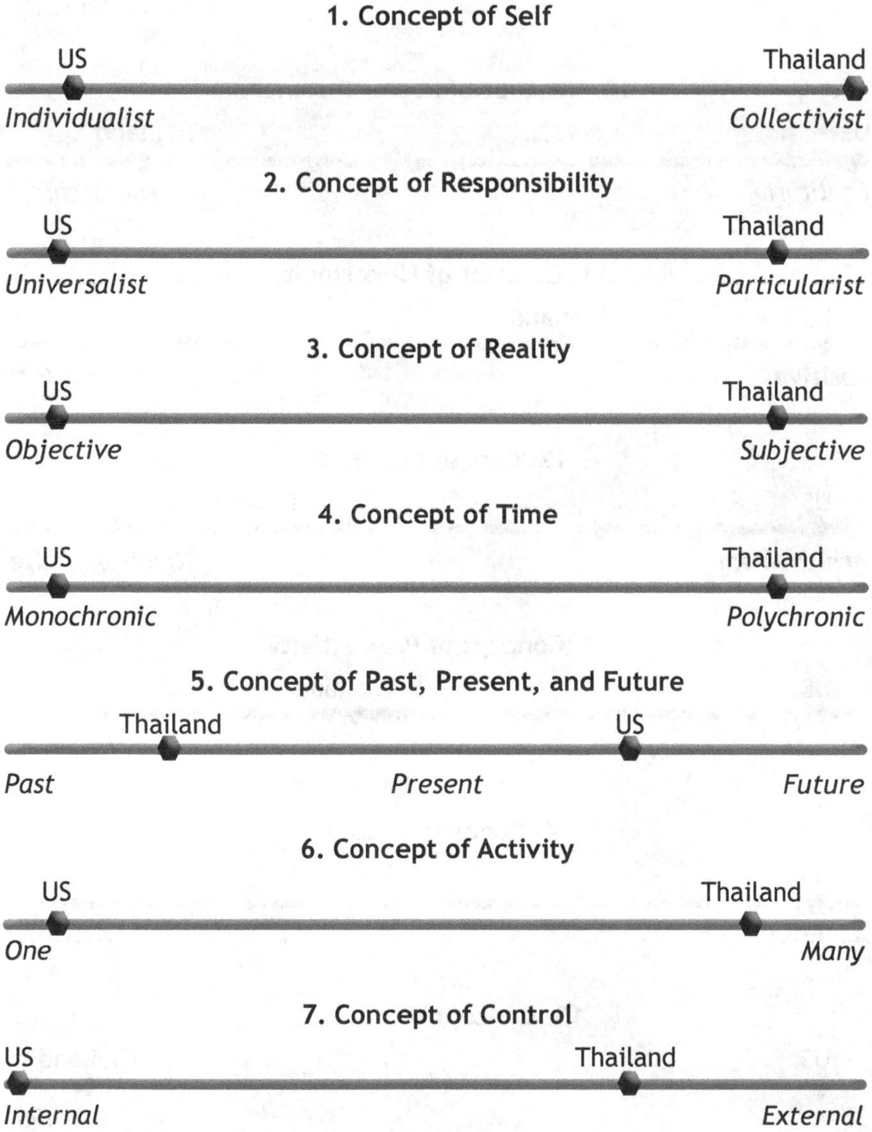

1. Concept of Self

US   Thailand

Individualist   Collectivist

2. Concept of Responsibility

US   Thailand

Universalist   Particularist

3. Concept of Reality

US   Thailand

Objective   Subjective

4. Concept of Time

US   Thailand

Monochronic   Polychronic

5. Concept of Past, Present, and Future

        Thailand   US

Past   Present   Future

6. Concept of Activity

US   Thailand

One   Many

7. Concept of Control

US   Thailand

Internal   External

8. Concept of Communication

US   Thailand

Direct   *Indirect*

9. Concept of Face

US   Thailand

Less Important   *Very Important*

10. Concept of Power Distance

US   Thailand

Egalitarian   *Hierarchical*

11. Concept of Uncertainty

US   Thailand

Positive   *Skeptical*

12. Concept of Work

US   Thailand

Achievement   *Quality of Life*

13. Concept of Productivity

US   Thailand

Results   *Harmony*

14. Concept of Status

US   Thailand

Achieved   *Ascribed*

15. Concept of Context

US   Thailand

Low   *High*

The Challenge of Crossing Cultures

Cultural differences can sometimes seem exotic, charming, or quaint, and for tourists they are often an interesting, exciting, yet easily dismissed aspect of their short journey. However, for those living and working cross-culturally, these differences can be a daily challenge. When one considers the magnification of cultural differences across these 15 concepts, it can seem amazing that anyone ever succeeds at doing anything cross-culturally, much less run a successful business.

For example, when I compared Thai culture to US culture across these 15 concepts, I discovered that the US and Thailand were on the same side of the continuum in only one of them. (See Figure 13.1.) On 8 of the 15, both were near the extremes, reflecting a near opposite perspective on these issues. On one concept, communication (degree of directness), the US demonstrates a strong but not extreme preference while Thailand still reflects an extreme preference for indirectness. In other areas such as locus of control, uncertainty, work, productivity, and source of status, the US demonstrates an extreme preference while Thailand reflects a moderate preference toward the opposite. In 14 of the 15 areas, at least one of the cultures reflected an extreme preference.

These findings indicate that cross-cultural interactions between the two cultures are very difficult to navigate. Yet, in my research I found very few people who could articulate how the cultures were distinctly different and how a person should alter their normative behavior for the cultural differences. This astounds me. It is critical that missional entrepreneurs engage in careful cultural analysis rather than simply jump to conclusions, prejudge the other culture, or just do what seems right to them.

Missional entrepreneurs should seek to understand the culture in which they find themselves and then adapt in appropriate ways. If they choose to act counterculturally in some instances, they should at least have thought through the issues. This type of analysis is hard work, but is likely to bear positive fruit in many areas.

Questions for Reflection & Discussion

1. Of the 15 foundational concepts of culture, list two or three you regard as most important and why.

2. Which cultural concepts could directly influence the success of a business?

3. Which cultural concepts could influence the process of sharing Christ?

4. If you could change the positioning of your culture for one of these concepts, which would it be?

5. Choose another culture and compare it to mainstream US culture along these 15 continuums.

chapter 14

CHALLENGES AND COMPETITION

All human activity takes place in multiple social and cultural contexts. Business and missions activities are no different. To be effective, missional entrepreneurs must be aware of the critical importance of the multiple external environments in which they must function. We live in a new time for business and for missions. Globalization is radically changing social structures and government policies. Business and missions must adapt to these new realities.

Missional entrepreneurs must establish enterprises that are financially sustainable, socially sustainable, culturally sustainable, and missionally sustainable. There is an interconnectedness of activity. Despite BAM's promise and potential, it also carries significant challenge and risk. These must be acknowledged and understood in order to be handled and leveraged appropriately. In addition to what we have already reviewed, there are several other factors that must be seriously considered in order to operate a BAM enterprise that is effective across multiple bottom lines.

Business Is Hard

One of the first things that missional entrepreneurs have to realize (if they haven't already) is that business is challenging. Doing business in a cross-cultural context or a developing country compounds the complexity. I have had the opportunity to peek behind the curtain of some well-known BAM operations in several countries (not cited in this book) and saw that they were confronting serious challenges that are not publicized in newsletters and other published reports. This is, for better or worse, a normal occurrence in other businesses as well as other types of ministry activities.

There is a veil over much of what we do. Generally, people prefer to work out difficulties on their own and don't want to wash their dirty laundry in the town square. Other times, people are incentivized to conceal challenges from investors or other supporters. Sometimes, people are just trying to protect their reputation. At the end of the day, aspiring missional entrepreneurs should know that their chosen journey includes many unique challenges. The vast majority of missional entrepreneurs whom I have interviewed said that their task has proven far more difficult than they imagined, and if they had known how hard it would be, they probably would not have started.

A couple of comments continue to ring in my mind. One entrepreneur who had won awards for his entrepreneurial ventures in the US said, "I thought starting a business in the States was hard. This is much harder!"

Most of the people I have interviewed have experienced significant challenges maintaining their businesses. Many times the challenges were personal, such as extended working hours and loss of personal savings. Other times the challenge was simply trying to figure out the laws and processes of a different culture whose structures are not overly supportive of foreign entrepreneurs. Cash flow is another real difficulty for entrepreneurs everywhere.

Flexibility, adaptability, and perseverance are necessary traits of BAM entrepreneurs. They need to have flexible attitudes that embrace change as a challenge that they can overcome. They need to have the ability to adapt to changing circumstances, evolving business plans, and market shifts. Finally, they need to have a persevering spirit that understands what good can be done if they stick to it and see their vision through.

That being said, not every BAM endeavor is meant to be. Around the world, there are aspiring BAM entrepreneurs who have held on too long to their dream. Instead of adapting and creating a new plan or just realizing that it is not meant to be, they have become a member of the walking wounded. Therefore, while perseverance is a necessity, so are realism and objectivity.

Responding Positively to the Challenges

Paradoxically, people who succeed at BAM tend to be very comfortable with failure. They know and understand the difficulty of business and embrace it as inevitable and something to be overcome, not something to become discouraged about. I talked to a successful missional entrepreneur in East Asia who had seen tremendous spiritual fruit through his business, as well as financial profit. However, three of his previous businesses had failed miserably. By persevering he has built a BAM enterprise that serves as a role model for many others in the region.

In addition to being able to stomach failure, successful business entrepreneurs are calculated in their risks and comfortable with them. They are not fearless and reckless risk takers, as they are sometimes caricatured. Missional entrepreneurs need to know their risks and understand how to ascertain those risks. When possible, they should seek to minimize their risks to protect the overall mission. However, completely eliminating risk is not possible and missional entrepreneurs need to develop the capacity to live at peace with the fact that the life path they have chosen is not for the faint of heart.

One successful BAM entrepreneur wanted to start a printing company, but the up-front costs were quite expensive. To minimize his risks he secured printing contracts and then subcontracted out those contracts until he eventually got a contract large enough to justify purchasing the needed equipment. While this took more time and produced some unique challenges, it reduced his risk significantly and presently he has a successful operation.

Handling Competition

Frequently, missional entrepreneurs find themselves in competition with one another. Many complain that certain competitors use donations to lower prices and steal clients. In other cases, I've had BAM entrepreneurs make accusations against their fellow BAM competitors ranging from corporate espionage to character slander.

Missional entrepreneurs who work in parts of the world that receive a lot of missionaries frequently complain in general about an unlevel playing field or unfair competitive advantage. One of the more common complaints is that other missionaries are using donated funds to support a business. They claim this creates a fake economy that hurts local businesspeople—by driving them out of business—as well as other missionaries who do not have access to donor subsidies. Frequently, this is a case of the pot calling the kettle black as the complaining missionaries do not consider their salaries as subsidies even though their salaries frequently come from fund-raising and not from the business.

Others complain of government subsidies. For example, as a part of their foreign aid policy, the British government gives stipends to British citizens who teach English in various countries. This allows British citizens to charge lower prices than other English teaching competitors, driving down the market rate and making it nearly impossible for companies completely reliant on generated income to make ends meet.

In all actuality, business is never on a perfectly level playing field. Business schools and business textbooks teach about "competitive advantage," the concept that a business should seek to construct a "playing field" that is not level but in fact benefits them. Businesses do this in a number of ways, such as the use of technology, superior knowledge, or higher financial investment.

In saying that, however, BAM operations do need to ensure that their overall economical impact is beneficial. For example, one missional entrepreneur told me that his Christian employees encouraged him to use his subsidies to lower his prices dramatically. Their logic was that this would run his competitors—all locals—out of business. He could then use his monopolistic position to increase his prices and earn more profits with higher margins. When he initially resisted the idea, the employees countered that he could then hire more local workers, expand his business operations, and be able to influence more people with the gospel. The business owner did not follow their advice, insisting that this was an unfair and unethical business tactic and would violate their missional purposes.

Coffee Shops and English-Teaching Businesses

The topic of a so-called level playing field is a hot one primarily because competition is so high in so many BAM situations. The high competition stems from the fact that missionaries tend to go into industries that have low barriers to entry. *Barriers to entry* is a term that comes from competition theory. Economists invoke it to describe obstacles in the path of a firm that wants to enter a given market. The term can also refer to hindrances that an individual may face while trying to gain entrance into a profession or trade. It more commonly refers to hindrances that a company (or even a country) may face while trying to enter an industry or trade grouping.

Opening an English-teaching business or a coffee shop are two perennial favorites with missionaries. There are good reasons for this. For example, a native English speaker is almost automatically qualified to teach English in a developing non-English speaking country. Granted, they may need to get a certificate, but for a native English speaker this is not overly difficult, expensive, or time consuming.

In the case of the coffee shop, though it is more complex than many people realize, it is learnable, not tremendously expensive, and fairly doable by most people. In both cases, these businesses provide a natural context for conversation and relationship development, which is another reason why so many missionaries pursue them.

However, the ease and inexpensiveness of opening these businesses qualifies them as low-barrier-to-entry industries. This actually makes them very difficult businesses to operate in a financially sustainable manner. For example, in a city like Chiang Mai, where there is a high missionary population, several missionaries have opened these types of businesses. They are then in de facto competition with each other. Some receive subsidies from their missions agencies or outside donations to fund operations and are therefore able to charge lower prices. This means other missionary-operated businesses have to lower prices to attract clientele. A potentially vicious cycle is begun. And it is worth noting that these BAM entrepreneurs are not only in competition with other missionaries, but also other expatriates and local citizens.

The gravitational pull to find something inexpensive and easy to do puts many missionaries in low-barrier-to-entry businesses with high levels of competition. This means that BAM entrepreneurs should be forewarned that competition is likely and aware of the need to handle competition appropriately. In my research, many BAM practitioners seem very frustrated with the level of competition without acknowledging that they were also a competitor to others. In other words, they wanted to operate a low-barrier-to-entry business with little or no competition. This is simply not how things work.

Missionaries have tried at least two ways to deal with competition in low-barrier-to-entry industries. Some have called for greater levels of investment. In other words, they believe that in order to operate effectively in their business climate, it is important to make a large initial investment. However, high-capital investments carry a great deal of risk to those doing the funding. Other missionaries have taken a different approach, shunning large investments and retreating to an even smaller business. These smaller businesses often involve a low barrier to entry and minimal financial investment, but also generate minimal financial returns. However, the missionaries point out that such businesses still enable them to build relationships and have a presence in the marketplace. They also say they are not risking a lot of "kingdom" money in a startup company.

Alternative Response: Collaboration and Competition

Radical collaboration is an emerging trend in global business. Many years ago, the milk and beef industries overcame competitiveness in order to join forces and cooperatively promote their industries. It's happening in other places as well. For instance, Gannett Company (*USA Today*) and Tribune Company (*Chicago Tribune, Los Angeles Times*) share major stakes in CareerBuilder.com, despite the fact that these two news organizations could be considered competitors. Longtime rivals are realizing that holding grudges and battling to the bitter end makes for a lose-lose scenario. Working together can be quite effective in creating a win-win situation.

Societal stereotypes caricaturize big business in the image cast by Gordon Gekko (played by Michael Douglas) in the 1987 movie *Wall Street*: the greedy corporation that would devour any competitor that stands between them and the almighty dollar. However, it is actually the bigger, wealthier businesses that are more likely to engage in these forms of radical collaboration. For instance, I recently met with the head of the department of commerce for a US state and in the meeting he told me small- and medium-sized businesses in his state desperately needed outside help but were inherently skeptical. Paradoxically, he said the bigger and more successful a company is the more likely they are to be open to sharing services and seeking external help.

What does this have to do with BAM? Unfortunately, the same phenomenon is true in BAM operations. Entrepreneurs and missionaries are in many cases strong-willed people with a healthy do-it-yourself attitude. This is what empowers them to start risky new businesses or move to foreign countries or both. However, this attitude also causes them to compete when they should be collaborating or cooperating. While there is no surefire way to solve this challenge, it is worth recognizing that a Christian is called to love a competitor as himself or herself. Missional entrepreneurs should seek ways to grow sustainable businesses that look out for the best of all involved and work for the common good, even in the midst of competitive industries.

Questions for Reflection & Discussion

1. How should a missional entrepreneur prepare for the inherent challenges of doing business?

2. How should Christians view competition?

3. What can missional entrepreneurs do when they realize they are in competition with one another?

4. How can companies collaborate with and compete against one another?

5. Do you think competition among ministries is completely destructive or can it also be helpful? What are some possible pros to competition?

chapter 15

INSIGHTS FOR MISSIONS AGENCIES

In my travels and research I have seen that missions agencies worldwide are becoming increasingly excited about the possibilities of BAM and are seeking to utilize the energy and momentum created by missional entrepreneurs. However, many missional entrepreneurs are electing to forgo relationships with missions agencies, viewing them as unnecessary and troublesome rather than vital and helpful. Part of this can be attributed to the personalities of those who are attracted to entrepreneurial endeavors, particularly those entrepreneurs who are brave enough to launch off into distant and sometimes dangerous lands.

As someone who has worked both with and independent from missions agencies, I share many of the concerns of my fellow missional entrepreneurs. But I also understand that if we all work together, we can accomplish a lot more and benefit from each other. My goal in this chapter is to point out some of the common points of contention between agencies and entrepreneurs and suggest possible resolutions.

The Role of the Missions Agency

Obviously not all BAM enterprises are affiliated with a missions agency. However, many are started and funded by a missions agency, and missionaries sent by agencies or boards operate many BAM companies. One of the biggest issues faced by missional entrepreneurs is the amount of external control exerted by the missions agency on day-to-day operations.

Several BAM businesses have ceased to function due to missions agency intervention. This is either because the missions agency wanted to shut down the company over disagreements or the BAM missionary became frustrated with the level of intervention and shut down the business. In some instances, the entrepreneur resigned from the missions agency and continued working independently.

In cases where a business maintains an ongoing relationship with a missions agency and continues operations, the relationship neither appears to hurt nor facilitate financial success. So, though there are real pros and cons to partnering with an agency, the measurable financial ramifications are a wash. My personal research on this is limited, so I would not want to draw any conclusions.

It appears that BAM enterprise-missions agency relationships can be great, terrible, or somewhere in between. What are the potential benefits? Missions agencies can provide missional entrepreneurs with access to cross-cultural training, counseling, biblical teaching, ministry strategies, potential partners, group insurance, and a connection with a like-minded body of believers. In general, missionaries underestimate the challenges of running a business, but businesspeople underestimate the challenges of working cross-culturally. This is where a missions agency can provide real value.

The potential cons include unwelcome, direct intervention into business affairs, micromanagement of ministry activities, and even demoralizing criticism regarding associated expenses. Obviously, these problems are not universal, but they do occur. And when missions agencies engage in these behaviors, it can quickly kill the enthusiasm of missional entrepreneurs and cause many to leave or recommend to other missional entrepreneurs that they not seek official relationships with missions agencies.

Suggested solution: Missions agencies with missionaries operating businesses should develop documents explicitly stating the relationship of the agency to the business and the missionary. These documents should address such questions as who has control and ownership of the business and who reports to whom on what issues.

Different Visions

Many missional entrepreneurs have become frustrated with the approach they feel some missions agencies take toward business. These entrepreneurs believe the agencies in question consider business as solely a means for access. Many of these business missionaries have discontinued working for or in partnership with these missions agencies.

One missional entrepreneur said to me, "I refuse to accept money from either missions agencies or churches. They view business simply as a way to get into a country rather than a ministry in itself. They are more trouble than they are worth." While I don't agree with this blanket assessment, his comments show the depth of concern out there.

There are many good reasons to run a BAM enterprise. Before doing so, the missions agency and the missional entrepreneur need to think through their purpose and vision. Many people view access as a primary motivator and that is a good reason. Some countries are open for business but closed for missions. Other countries are open for business and open for missions. In both these cases, the missions agency should consider the various issues involved and decide if BAM is a strategy they want to pursue there. Other countries, like the Democratic Republic of Congo, are closed for business, but open for missionary work. Is BAM appropriate there? These are the kinds of perspectives that missions agencies need to consider.

What is the purpose of BAM? In this book I have laid out my view. Nevertheless, I recognize that not all people engaged in BAM always see it the same way. There are many conflicting views of the purpose of BAM, especially related to the aforementioned access issue and BAM's usefulness in creating relationship networks, etc. Many missions agencies view BAM through the lens of "traditional ministry," meaning that they view the goal of missions primarily as church planting and evangelism and they see BAM as an effective model to achieve those goals.

However, many missional entrepreneurs have slightly different aspirations, focusing on the social contribution of creating jobs, fostering social justice, and the like. At times the two groups sound like they are saying the same thing—that BAM is a powerful tool for missions—but they are actually speaking different languages because they have vastly different views of missions and as a result differ greatly on the purpose of BAM. I have seen strategy documents for major missions organizations that explain their view of BAM, and they did not take these foundational elements into consideration.

Suggested solution: Missions agencies with missionaries operating businesses should develop documents clearly articulating the agency's view of the purpose of BAM (including the issue of access) and the relationship of BAM to its broader organizational mission.

Figure 15.1

ACCESS/BUSINESS VIABILITY GRAPH

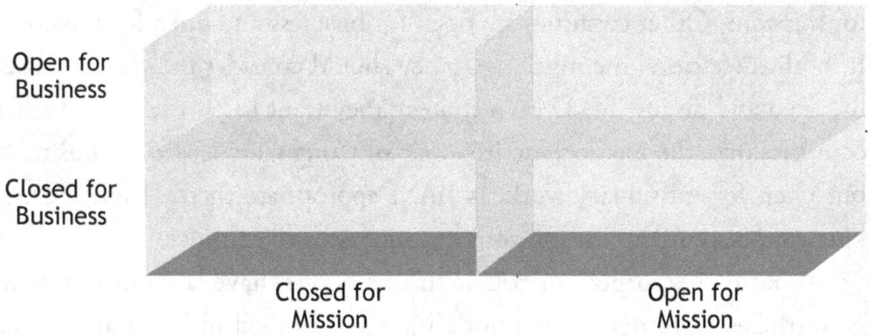

Open for Business

Closed for Business

Closed for Mission

Open for Mission

Muddy Financing

The primary culprit for meltdowns between missions agencies and missional entrepreneurs is the lack of a clear agreement regarding the financing of the business. Conflicts between missional entrepreneurs and their agencies over funds and ownership are not uncommon. Generally, there is no written agreement, and both sides assume the other shares their understanding. Often there is controversy over who controls the profits and decides how they will be spent. There is also commonly a lack of clarity over what would happen if the company were ever purchased.

The typical scenario is that the BAM entrepreneur has put some personal savings into the company and assumes that these savings will be recovered through the generated income of the business. Sometimes the BAM entrepreneur not only assumes that he or she will regain the personal money but will also control at least some of the profits earned in part from using his or her personal money. On the other hand, missions agencies often have the understanding that financially profiting from a ministry activity is not appropriate. They operate from the assumption that others feel the same way.

Since there is frequently no clear communication on this key point, things can melt down quite quickly. Missional entrepreneurs argue that they have invested their savings or retirement and want and deserve to get it back plus appropriate earnings. Missional entrepreneurs often interpret the missions agency's negative reaction as a lack of trust, and the situation deteriorates with both sides viewing the other suspiciously until there is complete collapse.

Other times, the problem is that the missions agency has invested funds without clarifying that it is only an investment, sometimes with the expectation of an additional return on their investment, i.e. interest and/or profits. This becomes problematic not only when the business starts making money, but also if the business loses money. One thing that missions agencies and missional entrepreneurs must acknowledge is that there is always the possibility of losing money. Both parties can be unhelpfully idealistic at times and not recognize the financial risks to entrepreneurial start-ups.

The situation is made more complex since many businesses are incorporated as a legal entity in the country of operation and not in the country that sends the missionaries. In order to purchase land or to counter the difficulties of being a foreigner, many BAM entrepreneurs choose to have multiple shareholders in their businesses, many of whom are nationals. Therefore, missions agencies actually have little control and simplistic solutions cannot be found. It is, therefore, problematic that a minority of all businesses I have researched have even discussed these potential challenges with their missions agencies. Some agencies have developed policy guides and some businesses have signed statements of intent or memorandums of understanding. However, in general there is a dearth of preventive planning regarding these potentially deal-breaking challenges.

To prevent these problems, missions agencies should develop policy that creates a variety of options for various scenarios. Agencies and their BAM entrepreneurs should discuss financial arrangements and determine in advance what form the business will take. For example, they should decide whether or not it is acceptable to pursue personal profit through the business. If not, they should decide if it is appropriate for the missionary and others to invest money with the expectation of having it returned later.

If it is acceptable to recoup the money later, then it should be determined if interest will be added. If interest can be added, it should be determined whether it will be equal to, less than, or greater than inflation. There are no right or wrong answers on this. However, I have observed in a number of cases that the parties involved have dramatically different assumptions about how the money should be handled. In many instances it led to a complete meltdown in which the BAM missionary left the missions agency and retained the business, the missions agency fired the missionary and retained the business, or the business was shut down.

Initial agreements of understanding should be as detailed as possible, and the process should be conducted in such a manner as to allow everyone to express their honest desires. In several cases, it was clear to me that BAM missionaries had not informed supervisors of their personal stake in the business nor their desire to earn back that stake with profit because they were fearful of a negative reaction. This fear prevented open and honest discussion that could have offset a plethora of later problems.

Missions agencies should consider special shared ownership structures with missionaries. It is certainly a valid point to consider that many missionaries may become lax about finances when they have no personal stake. This is actually quite natural, which is why in general business endeavors venture capitalists seek to fund people whose personal finances and futures are intertwined with the business. This is also why banks evaluate loan risks for home purchases based on the amount of down payment a person makes. They know that if people are invested in something, they'll see it through. Otherwise, they may just walk away. It is reasonable to expect that missionaries will be more likely to see a business through if they have a personal stake in it, even though most of them are not doing what they are doing for financial reasons. It is worth thinking about some of these possibilities.

Suggested solution: Missions agencies should develop thorough and well-researched policies regarding businesses operated by their missionaries. Both the agency and entrepreneur should agree to transparent and comprehensive memorandums of understanding that address the issues of ownership, the amount of shares, expected return on investment, and caveats for instances of financial loss.

The Question of Sustainability

There are a wide variety of opinions when it comes to funding a BAM enterprise and the relevant importance of profit. Some people feel that "real" businesses do not allow people to receive subsidized salaries, i.e. missionaries who receive a stipend from their missions agency. Others note that such stipends are acceptable since these people would otherwise be susceptible to tremendous financial pressure and risk. Many BAM enterprises are started with donated funds, while other people consider that a "fake" way to launch a business. There are a number of BAM leaders who strongly feel that if missional entrepreneurs are to be successful, then they need to earn their salaries from the business itself and raise capital from investors who expect a reasonable return on their investment. This does, on the surface, seem to be the most natural way of doing business.

However, the situation for most BAM enterprises is more complex than for a normal business. Many missional entrepreneurs choose a location because of a particular location's need, not because of its lucrative potential. Raising capital for entrepreneurial start-ups can be a difficult and elaborate process. Trying to convince investors to invest in risky parts of the world is that much harder.

On the other side of the argument, however, is the idea that it is not very wise to set up a company that will be funded by an indefinite supply of donations. Venture capitalists generally look for entrepreneurs who have a lot to lose, believing that this makes the entrepreneur sufficiently incentivized to find innovative solutions and produce a profitable enterprise. Therefore, it could be counterproductive to unleash entrepreneurs who have no personal financial incentive to the success of the business. Surely, establishing scores of mediocre to bad businesses around the world is not what we mean when we talk about missional entrepreneurialism!

Discussing profits and subsidized salaries can be quite confusing. With regard to financing, the most important issue in my understanding is whether or not the plan is sustainable. Unlike some traditional entrepreneurs, missional entrepreneurs are not motivated by the money. They are focused on creating a better world that follows Christ and glorifies God. As such, some creative solutions are appropriate.

Many social business ventures seek grants from foundations and government entities that want to promote innovative business solutions to social problems rather than return on investment. Missions agencies, churches, Christian foundations, and Christian individuals can look at missional entrepreneurialism in the same way. It's something to support because of the missional cause, not because of the financial return.

On the other hand, it is also appropriate to view some missional ventures as investment opportunities that can provide a solid financial return. It's just that not all missional entrepreneurial ventures will be well suited for that, and there is a place for donor support in this field as there are in others.

In any case, the implications and strategy of the funding process should be carefully considered. If missions agencies are going to provide or encourage donations to a business, then they should be clear how long they are going to financially support it and what financial benchmarks need to be reached for ongoing support to continue. If donations are used to fund the initial or ongoing expenses of a BAM enterprise, this should be built into the business plan.

The salaries of missionaries operating businesses are an expense that should be addressed separately. They are an employee of a missions agency and simultaneously a manager of a business, so it is an unusual position. One possibility is to build in a declining scale of donations for expenses, including salaries, demonstrating the expectation that the business should be generating sufficient income to cover the expenses as time moves on. It is important to establish very clear benchmarks (time frame and amount) for this sliding scale for salary. And, if donations are ever used to subsidize expenses and/or salaries, there should be clearly written guidelines on ownership and dispersion of profits.

Another possibility is that the missionary's salary should come from the missions agency for the long haul. This also should be determined clearly beforehand. There are several missional entrepreneurs who receive salaries from missions agencies and donate what would be their salary from their business to local ministries or simply reinvest it into the business. These are both plausible options to consider in cases when a missional entrepreneur is also the employee of a missions agency.

Below I have outlined some of the several possible, sustainable business models.

- *Traditional Business Model:* Investments and generated income cover all expenses and salaries.
- *Subsidized to Profitability Model:* A mix of investments, donations, and generated income sustain the company until its cash flow is positive, then the company operates under the traditional business model.
- *Missions Agency Employee Subsidized/Investment Partnership Model:* Investments and generated income cover all expenses, excluding the salaries of missions agency employees, which are covered by the missions agency. This is the only subsidy.

- *Missions Agency Employee Subsidized/Mixed Partnership Model:* A mix of investments, donations, and generated income cover all expenses, excluding the salaries of missions agency employees, which are paid by the missions agency.
- *Donor Subsidized Model:* A mix of investments, donations, and generated income cover all expenses and expatriate management salaries.
- *BAM Donor Model:* Donations and generated income cover all expenses and expatriate management salaries.

For some businesspeople, it undoubtedly raises concerns that there would be any business model that allows for ongoing donor subsidies. In looking through these six models, missional entrepreneurs would be wise to start at the top and only move down as justified.

Soup kitchens, thrift shops, and other social business ventures frequently have employees who are paid by an umbrella organization rather than by any profits. But this is sometimes a reason for the presence of inefficiencies. There are probably acceptable reasons for having a business covered by donations for an extended period of time, such as trying to establish a presence in a conflict-ridden and hostile country, but it would be wise not to rush into that model. A great deal of reflection and outside input are needed.

Suggested solution: Missions agencies with missionaries operating businesses should develop documents that include transparent business models and consider the ramifications and need for donated subsidies to cover expenses and salaries.

A Matter of Priorities

Missional entrepreneurs and missions agencies sometimes have divergent understandings of BAM and its priorities. This is often related to the issue of the purpose of BAM, as addressed above.

One missions agency, for example, has a policy guide that states BAM enterprises should not become overly time consuming and that BAM missionaries cannot allow time spent on the business to distract their focus from "ministry." This guide seemingly demonstrates that this missions agency does not view the business as a ministry in itself, but rather as a potential distraction to ministry. This can be frustrating to missional entrepreneurs who view their business work as a ministry.

For some, business is simply a means to another end, and it can be disposed of if that end goal can be achieved through an easier, less expensive, less time-consuming alternative. For most BAM entrepreneurs, however, running and operating the business is the mission and ends such as evangelism, relationship building, and helping the poor can be met within it. Therefore, it is worthwhile for BAM entrepreneurs to ensure that a particular missions agency is affirming of their approach to the BAM enterprise before launching a start-up in a foreign country.

Suggested solution: Missions agencies and missionaries operating businesses should develop documents that include transparent business plans explicitly stating the purpose, mission, and vision statements of the business as well as examples of best practices for a variety of scenarios.

Workable Ministry Strategies

Business creates a web of relationships. However, some of these relationships are short-term or consist of very brief interactions. Furthermore, some businesses are not overly conducive to developing relationships. Some businesses require a minimal time investment per relationship in order to be profitable. Others, such as Internet-based and technology-based businesses, have very little human interaction. Many businesses simply do not create an atmosphere in which the Christian workers have extended contact with non-Christian clients or customers. This produces frustration for many BAM entrepreneurs, particularly those who emphasize evangelization in their ministries. This frustration is exacerbated in a culture like Thailand where long-term, consistent exposure to Christian demonstration and proclamation is generally necessary to produce conversions.

There are at least two ways to handle these potential issues. First, the BAM entrepreneurs should consider these factors when determining what type of business to start. They can seek to develop a business that allows them to have long-term, consistent interaction with non-Christians. From my research, it appears many BAM entrepreneurs have taken this into consideration in Chiang Mai, but this has also put many of them in competition against one another.

Choosing a business that allows for long-term relationships is not always possible. Many times BAM entrepreneurs have a specific skill set that pushes them toward a particular type of business. Other times it is not possible to find a sustainable market niche in a certain industry. So, in many circumstances, option one may not be preferable. In these cases, missions agencies can be valuable allies in thinking through missiological approaches. For example, the missions agency can train the missional entrepreneur in progressive evangelism or the idea that people take steps toward Christ over time.

Many businesspeople (perhaps from their sales experience) still view evangelism as a conversion-only experience, meaning that some of them tend to push for a decision. This can be counterproductive depending on the setting and the non-Christian's current spiritual state. Missiologists, however, have expressed several different ways to move people in the right direction so that they will one day be receptive to becoming a Christ follower.

My wife, Laurie, and I have developed the following evangelism scale, based on the well-known Engel scale, to illustrate a non-Christian's progressive receptivity to the gospel. In this scale there are two groups of non-believers. The first we call *situational*, meaning that they are unbelievers because they have never heard the gospel, or they live in a country where highly distorted perceptions of the gospel exist. Buddhists in Thailand would be an example. The second group we call *intentional*. These are people who have grown up in Christian contexts or are very familiar with the gospel message but for whatever reason are not followers of Christ. People in both groups have to progress in their understanding of the gospel to become a potential believer. They will be unresponsive to direct evangelism until they have reached that point.

Figure 15.2

RUSSELL EVANGELISM SCALE

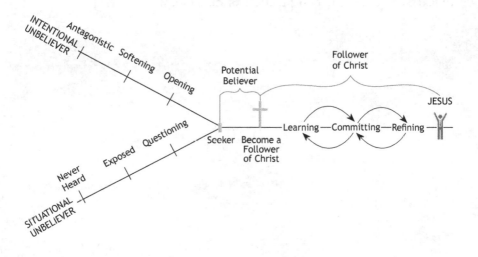

In a business that is not conducive to sustained long-term interaction with non-Christians, it would be appropriate to adopt an evangelism-scale strategy for having a spiritual influence through the business. Each business can adapt the evangelism scale according to its particular situation. So, instead of making conversion the sole evangelistic focus, it would be appropriate to seek to influence people to move down the evangelism scale to where they are closer to becoming a Christ follower.

When I asked a missional entrepreneur in Thailand how many people had become Christians in his company, I believe he rightly responded, "I do not think counting the number of conversions is an appropriate way to monitor our spiritual effectiveness. We have seen literally hundreds of people become open to Christ and make steps toward Him. That's how we define success."

Missions agencies can provide missional entrepreneurs with both teaching and tools to increase their understanding of the intricacies of evangelistic ministry in many parts of the world. This should decrease frustration and increase effectiveness.

Suggested solution: Missions agencies with missionaries operating businesses should develop a training plan enabling missional entrepreneurs to learn and apply the best practices of missiology.

Questions for Reflection & Discussion

1. Should missions agencies promote BAM?

2. Should missional entrepreneurs seek to have official relationships with missions agencies?

3. What are the pros and cons of business-missions agency partnerships?

4. When a missional entrepreneur starts a company while working for a missions agency, who should "own" the company?

5. What if the missional entrepreneur starts that company with his/her money?

part 5

SPECIAL
TOPICS

chapter 16

MISSIONAL LEADERSHIP

The more I am around business enterprises, entrepreneurial start-ups, social ventures, Christian ministries, and churches, the more I am convinced that everything is dependent upon leadership. If leaders do not know their way, then no one finds the way there either. Personal leadership is foundational to success; that's why I am addressing it in this chapter.

Few people would dispute the importance of leadership. However, I have noticed in entrepreneurial start-ups and BAM enterprises that not as much attention is given to it because the madness of business and other matters pushes it aside. This is a mistake. It is necessary to take time out and consider the principles and implications of good leadership for BAM. That is the purpose of this chapter.

I want to explore a paradigm for effective leadership as a missional entrepreneur that will lead to success across multiple bottom lines. Success in the common vernacular generally pertains to the gaining of fame and prosperity. However, for our purposes it means the achievement of something desired and planned, namely the integration of leadership, faith, and work in a way that skills, gifts, talents, passions, and faith strengths are seamlessly integrated.

Leadership is the ability to influence the actions of others. It is not necessarily being in a position of authority. Someone can be a leader and not in a position of authority. And most definitely, as we all know, someone can be in a position of authority and have no leadership capacity or influence.

I define missional leadership as the ability to positively influence others in matters of faith and work in the context of an organization that is not patently religious in nature. Ultimately, missional leadership is not just about positively impacting an organization in terms of its organizational goals, but also about being a positive influence on others in their own faith journeys.

Seven Principles for Missional Leadership

Becoming a missional leader is a holistic, all-encompassing endeavor that takes a lifetime. While the process takes time, missional entrepreneurs can become effective missional leaders. To aid in that process I have developed a paradigm that ensures that leadership is approached as a spiritual and comprehensive endeavor. The seven steps of this paradigm are:

1. *Spiritual:* missional leadership, work, and employment should be viewed as a spiritual reality.
2. *Scriptural:* Scriptures inform and form missional leadership.
3. *Solidarity:* missional leadership is governed by an ethic of solidarity between clergy and laity, between people of faith and people of no faith or other faiths, and between people in varying levels of authority in the organization.
4. *Serve:* missional leadership is motivated by a desire to serve supervisors, subordinates, peers, owners, customers, followers, employees, etc.
5. *Sustainable:* missional leadership is exercised in such a way that high standards can be maintained in all areas for a long time.
6. *Situational:* missional leadership recognizes the inherent complexity to life and treats each situation as distinct with its own answers and solutions.
7. *Strategic:* missional leadership is approached with an intense focus that is marked by intentional planning, execution, and reflection.

Spiritual
In the earlier chapters of this book, we discussed the spiritual mission of business. Leadership has a deep spiritual foundation, too. The Bible starts

with God working, as well as governing and leading. When He called Adam and Eve to "rule over the fish of the sea and the birds of the air and over every living creature that moves on the ground" (Genesis 1:28), He was putting them in a position of leadership, one that they were expected to handle wisely and carefully.

As the story of God moves through the Old Testament, you observe that the story is focused primarily on God's work with particular leaders, such as Noah, Abraham, Moses, Nehemiah, etc. Jesus is, of course, the quintessential servant leader, who, during His time on earth, also showed a preference for working with leaders rather than the masses.

In the Book of Revelation, the images of God's future kingdom demonstrate that it is not a place absent of leadership. Christ is viewed as the ultimate leader but we are to lead in partnership with Him (Revelation 20:4,16; 22:5). Leadership is built into God's purposes for this world. He leads and calls us to lead with Him. Leadership will not pass away and is not a temporary necessity; it is an eternal reality. Leadership is something that is innate to God's design and desire for the world. He has led from the beginning, continues to lead, and will lead forever. He called humans to exercise leadership before the Fall, works with leaders after the Fall, and has given us a picture of a future world that also includes leadership.

Leadership has a spiritual mission and if you are a missional entrepreneur, God is calling you to view your leadership role as a spiritual one. Leadership is not about being the head honcho, calling all the shots, being in charge, or anything else. Leadership is an opportunity to serve God and neighbor and to influence others to do the same.

Spiritual leaders are led by an inner compass that is shaped by their relationship with God. This compass — not popularity or profits — directs them. I know one BAM entrepreneur whose employees approached him with a strategy to gain significant market share in a competitive market by leaking to locals information about a competitor. The information would have reflected badly on the competitor and locals would have flocked to them. While it was possible that the information was true, it could not be proven and the leader felt he could not build up a business by bringing down others. Though it would have been hard to trace the leaked information back to the leader, he would have won his employees' affection, and he may have gained profits, he chose not to give out the information, simply because he did not believe the move was spiritual. That's the way a spiritual leader thinks and operates.

Scriptural

The Bible is the most widely sold book in the history of the world. The Scriptures contain true story after true story of people through the centuries and how they loved, hated, cared for, and neglected one another, and how they feared, revered, respected, and rejected God.

What becomes obvious when one reads through the Scriptures without any preconceptions is how so many of its primary figures were not prophets or priests but people who worked a job and served God in varying degrees. Many of the Old Testament figures were people who worked. Noah, Moses, Abraham, and Job were all people who had careers and spent most of their lives working in various roles. Jesus spent the vast majority of His life as a carpenter. As we have seen, Paul continued and further developed his trade as a tentmaker after his conversion and during his missionary journeys.

Far from being a philosophical treatise pertaining merely to abstract ideas, the Scriptures are full of insights, warnings, commendations, and, most of all, stories of the normal, routine things of life. They are about life, leadership, and all that comes with it. Therefore, the Scriptures can be confidently read by the missional leader for insights and direction derived from proverbs, commands, and principles that pertain to common, workplace situations. The Scriptures are not essentially theoretical as some might suppose; rather they are fundamentally practical. The practicality of the Bible is what makes it so essential to successful missional leadership and entrepreneurship. It should not only shape our moral and ethical decisions and behaviors, but it is full of models and examples for us to follow in our routine work lives.

Scripture should not only be shaping the lives of missional leaders, but missional leaders can also use the Scriptures to influence others. In most parts of the world people still respect and often revere the Bible, even if they are not Christians. I have seen and experienced this in Hindu, Buddhist, and Muslim cultures. Sometimes these very same people did not respect the church or Christians, but they respected the Bible.

I know of many missional entrepreneurs who routinely quote from the Scriptures as a source of wisdom, which in turn has influenced employees over a period of time to the extent that the employees began asking deeper questions about the Christian faith. In one Middle Eastern country a profitable BAM enterprise successfully teaches leadership principles using biblical passages, stories, and characters. The employees there value the scriptural component and benefit from the teachings.

Solidarity

Missional leadership should be marked by an ethic of solidarity. This ethic should be embodied in all of the relationships of the various spheres of the missional leader's life. The first sphere that deserves attention is one faced by the church at large: the clergy/laity divide. There can no longer be a division between clergy and laity in terms of ecclesiastical importance. The spiritual landscape is shifting and will probably be less and less based in the setting of local congregations. Therefore the church has really no choice but to empower lay leaders for spiritual service. But the issue is more fundamental than such a pragmatic approach would suggest.

Through the centuries as Christianity has become a world religion, the church has struggled with the various ways it should be structured and governed. One of the necessary developments was that of remunerated clergy, or people who received financial stipends and/or support for their service to the church. Christ justified this development by commissioning Peter and Andrew to leave their fishing trade behind to become "fishers of men" (Matthew 4:18–20). He also said, "the worker deserves his wages" (Luke 10:7). Paul referred to this statement as a commandment, saying, "The Lord has commanded that those who preach the gospel should receive their living from the gospel" (1 Corinthians 9:14). So, there definitely is a place in the church for remunerated ministers or clergy.

However, just what place paid ministers and priests should have in current and future structures is the difficult question. As a means of "quality control" and perhaps in order to maintain control, there have been large sections of the church that have essentially turned ordained ministers into mediators between God and man. This is despite the clear New Testament teaching regarding the uniqueness of mediation. Paul wrote, "For there is one God and one mediator between God and men, the man Christ Jesus" (1 Timothy 2:5).

Even in churches and denominations that claim to advocate for the priesthood of every believer, there is a sense that those who are paid, do true ministry and others have the ministry of supporting the "true ministers." Paul seems to state the opposite in his letter to the Ephesians. He wrote the purpose of pastors and teachers is "to prepare God's people for works of service" (Ephesians 4:11–12). This seems to imply that the laity are the ones who do the good works and the clergy are there to prepare them for it. Catholic missionary and theologian Vincent Donovan writes:

> The 'priesthood of all believers' has often been used as an empty slogan by Catholics and Protestants alike. Catholics do not want to apply the priesthood to all believers, to the *laos*, the people of God, the laity. Protestants often use the phrase in a negative way. By stressing the second part of the phrase, they in fact deny the first part, or at least put a brake on the deepest sacramental, sacrificial and incarnational meaning of the priesthood of Jesus Christ. If only the Catholic meaning of the priesthood could come to live with the Protestant meaning of the faithful in the church, we might yet arrive at a new understanding of the power and glory of Christianity.[1]

The ethic of solidarity does not apply simply to the missional leader but to all in the church so that clergy and laity mutually affirm and support one another in their respective missions. Howard Snyder put it well when he wrote:

In fact, the unbiblical use of the terms 'ministry' and 'laity' is the most extensive and oppressive form of exclusive language in the church. When we use gender-exclusive language, we exclude about 50 percent of all Christians. But when we use the minister/layman distinction, we exclude 90–95 percent of all Christians! It is time to be truly inclusive by referring to all Christians as ministers and banning the term 'layman' whenever it means Christians who are not ministers.[2]

Another sphere touched by the ethic of solidarity is that of Christian cooperation. Missional leaders should aspire to work in solidarity with other Christians of different backgrounds. Consider Christ's prayer on behalf of all His followers:

"I do not ask on behalf of these alone, but for those also who believe in Me through their word; that they may all be one; even as You, Father, are in Me and I in You, that they also may be in Us, so that the world may believe that You sent Me. Their Future Glory the glory which You have given Me I have given to them, that they may be one, just as We are one; I in them and You in Me, that they may be perfected in unity, so that the world may know that You sent Me, and loved them, even as You have loved Me."

— John 17:20–23

Throughout this prayer, Christ shares His vision for unity and the purposes for that vision. Note the clear link between Christian unity and the unity of the Trinity. Twice He prays for us to be unified and twice He parallels our unity to the union between God the Father and Himself, God the Son. This shows the enormous theological value of solidarity among Christians. There should be no division among us. We should be one.

Through our unity we can enjoy in the human dimension the joy of communal unity that the three Persons of the Godhead enjoy at the divine level. Lack of unity prevents us from imitating God in this way and inhibits us from enjoying the fullness of human relationships for which He has created us. Furthermore, an absence of solidarity among believers presents an image of God as a God not united, but rather divided. If we recognize the theological paradigm for Christian solidarity, perhaps this will help us avoid unnecessary strife and division and choose the higher path of love so that we may enjoy unity just like God the Father and God the Son.

Additionally, Christ makes quite clear what can result from our unity. Twice He says, "so that the world may know [or believe] that You sent Me." True unity provides a clear picture among the peoples of the world that Christ is true and that the gospel is real. This is the clearest strategy for worldwide witness given by Christ in the Bible. Perhaps we shouldn't spend so much time with various strategies and methodologies and simply seek to live in solidarity with our siblings in Christ. Solidarity is a foundational pillar for success in missional leadership. Christ's strategy for world evangelization was the unity of all believers. This should be realized at all levels and in all locations, including the global marketplace.

Missional leaders should work in solidarity with people of other races, ethnic groups, national origins, gender, and even with people of other faiths whenever possible. Christian leaders should not succumb to pressures and prejudices that diminish the importance of working in solidarity with other people. Instead of following the trends of the day, missional leaders should be paving the way in the development of paradigms that reflect the inherent dignity and value of all people.

The difference that an ethic of solidarity can make in terms of ministry impact cannot be underestimated. While researching one BAM enterprise we noticed a significant increase in the responsiveness of employees and clients to the gospel during a certain period of time. That period of time occurred 18 months prior to our analysis. When we tried to isolate the variables to determine what caused the jump, we realized the only one that changed was that 6 months prior they had intentionally started working in partnership with local churches and ministries.

On the other hand, I have talked with numerous BAM entrepreneurs who, perhaps because of their entrepreneurial impulse, prefer working in isolation from others. I have actually never met an entrepreneur who worked in isolation who actually saw significant long-term spiritual fruit.

Serve

Leadership and business management literature has been dominated in recent years with the concept of servant leadership, a term coined in the 1970s by Robert Greenleaf in an essay titled "The Servant as Leader." In 1977 Greenleaf wrote, "Part of the problem is that *serve* and *lead* are overused words." If that was true in 1977 then it is even more so now. But Greenleaf followed up with some good advice, "Not everything that is old and worn, or even corrupt, can be thrown away. Some of it has to be rebuilt and used again. So it is, it seems to me, with the words *serve* and *lead*."[3] This has led to a revolution in corporate literature as business leaders have scrambled to discover the practical benefits of a service orientation.

Other leadership and corporate management writers have also given significant focus to the concept of servant leadership. In Stephen Covey's paradigm of principle-centered leadership, he captures many of the essential components of servant leadership. He says that every morning principle-centered leaders "'yoke up' and put on the harness of service, thinking of others."[4]

Service-oriented business professionals are taught to not only seek a win for themselves or their companies but to operate under a paradigm that seeks to help as many people as possible come out on top. This means business professionals should strive to help customers, clients, supervisors, janitors, and peers succeed in their respective dealings. Such leaders operate in a spirit of innovation and creativity to find new solutions that will help us all. This is effectively done only if the servant leader seeks to understand the other person's perspective. When this understanding is achieved, then it will be easier to arrive at a newly developed solution that helps all involved.

This sort of creative service orientation leads to a more effective organization. Increasingly secular business literatures points out that in order for employees to release their creative energy, the business must serve them. Companies do not need to impose goals from on high, but rather it is increasingly believed that the most efficient way to achieve strong financial results is for leaders to serve their employees. While secular business literature focuses on the economic bottom line, the missional entrepreneur will recognize that a servant style of leadership reflects Christ's character, helps us become more like Christ, and has the potential to produce results across multiple bottom lines.

Even Christ came to serve and not to be served: "The Son of Man did not come to be served, but to serve, and to give his life as a ransom for many" (Matthew 20:28). Therefore an attitude of service should permeate the missional leader. In order to illustrate practically what it means for missional leaders, particularly those in positional authority, to serve others, I have turned the word into an acronym. SERVE means to support, empower, release, verify, and encourage.

- *Support:* Missional leaders have an attitude of working below people and lifting them up. We do not work in such a way that others must work below us. Just as pillars of a building support it and hold it up, so we should support others and hold them up as higher than ourselves.

- *Empower:* This means quite simply to give power. Our rhetoric will be equaled by our action. We will not only say that we exist to support people, but we will also empower them to serve others in a meaningful way. This means providing resources as well as decision-making powers. An atmosphere of trust is necessary; this strengthens people.

- *Release:* After people are empowered they are free to use that power. They are truly released and not kept on a short leash that bruises their emotional neck and gives them whiplash as they are "pulled back" by the master of the resources.

- *Verify:* An appropriate accountability system in place. There is a time and place for a system that helps people reconsider their options in moments of temptation and to ensure that objectives and directives are carried out properly. Blindness to the human potential to do wrong is not empowering to people. We need accountability; we should verify that everyone is doing what they should be doing.

- *Encourage:* After people have been supported, empowered, and released, and their actions verified, they need little else other than to be encouraged. Encouragement is something often sought but rarely given in the lives of most people. Developing a lifestyle of encouragement is crucial to being a successful leader amidst the reality of life's trials and challenges.

I once spoke with a BAM entrepreneur named John (not his real name) who was working for another BAM company during a difficult financial crunch. The leaders began to pressure the workers repeatedly to increase performance in order to weather the difficult time. As a result of the financial challenge many of the workers could not deliver as the leaders wanted and when they didn't perform they received a pay cut. All the while the leadership kept the same pay. John saw the proverbial handwriting on the wall and realized he was in for some difficult times. He resigned, taking a job at another BAM company.

A few months later John's new company also experienced a financial crisis and called an emergency meeting, informing the employees of the challenging circumstances. Then the leaders announced that in an attempt to make payroll the members of the executive team were going to take deep pay cuts. The employees so appreciated the gesture that they worked harder and did all they could to help the company. In just a couple of months, the company had recovered financially, and no one outside the executive team experienced a pay cut. At the exact same time they were rebounding financially, John's first company had to shut down operations.

We shouldn't serve simply to benefit. But God's way of serving does create a positive feedback cycle in many cases whereas living for oneself can keep others from helping you when you most desperately need them.

Sustainable

Many organizations seem to have a fascination with quick fixes and short-term gains. A sense of urgency has led many to continually focus on what needs to be done right now without much concern for long-term planning and future vision. Accompanying this attitude is the belief that the primary barrier to the full attainment of the company's objectives is something the organization is doing wrong. This sense of urgency and "we are the barrier" mentality produces an unproductive atmosphere. The constant analysis and incessant scrutiny stresses many and kills off areas of potential growth, both personal and organizational, before they've had a chance to breathe.

In *Good to Great* Jim Collins discusses the pipe dream of many organizations to find a quick-fix solution to their mediocrity. His conclusions are summarized in the following statement:

> In each of these dramatic, remarkable, good-to-great corporate transformations, we found the same thing: There was no miracle moment. Instead, a down-to-earth, pragmatic, committed-to-excellence process — a framework — kept each company, its leaders, and its people on track for the long haul. In each case . . . it was the victory of steadfast discipline over the quick fix.[5]

The chief problem with an intense, quick-fix oriented approach to leadership is that it is not sustainable. Many leaders who have high standards for excellence expect their people to perform and have little patience for poor work. Pushing others can in certain cases help them become more successful. But if all the people involved are highly competent and need little direction, then such an approach is best used sparingly as it tends to poison the environment. This poisoning is generally due to the emotional costs involved, and this leadership style is particularly disruptive when a leader relies on it too much. Pushing others can be effective at times, but its weakness is that it is not sustainable. Missional leadership should ensure people are edified and encouraged rather than burdened and burned out.

Missional leaders should not seek quirky, quick fixes but should focus on long-term, quality work. They should not overly rely on pacesetting and should avoid creating high intensity environments that foster burnout over positive human development. Good leaders should not borrow strength from others but should develop internal strength so that others will be strengthened through them. Furthermore, missional leaders should also seek to work in an environmentally sustainable way that does not reduce natural resources, but rather creatively expands them. Missional leaders should also be committed to financial profitability, for through the ethical creation of wealth the business, the employees, the relationships, and many other things can be sustained.

Situational

In the late 1960s, through the 70s and into the 80s, Hersey and Blanchard developed what they called situational leadership.[6] Blanchard and Johnson adapted this model for their book, *The One Minute Manager*, which has sold more than 12 million copies.[7] The model calls for the leader to examine the needs of a unique situation, and then adopt the most appropriate leadership style. Its popularity is probably due to the fact that it passes two basic tests of such models: it is simple to understand, and it works in most environments for most people.

The model calls for four different types of leadership style, namely, directing, coaching, supporting, and delegating based upon the development level of the follower. There are four development levels, which are:

1. high competence and high commitment,
2. high competence and variable commitment,
3. some competence and low commitment, and
4. low competence and low commitment.

The beauty of the model is its simplicity. All models are an attempt to reduce complexity into understandable and workable paradigms. However, there is a need to develop situational leadership beyond what Blanchard and others have developed. Situational leadership should not be merely consumed with an attempt to simplify the complex; rather, it should embody an ethos that recognizes the inherent complexity of leadership situations and be driven by creativity and innovation toward answering questions and solving problems. Missional leaders will need to adapt their leadership style to their followers' competencies and also to what type of day the follower is having, the pressures of a certain situation, the reality of deadlines, etc. Attention needs to be paid and sensitivity given to gender and intercultural issues. Missional leaders will also need to adapt their style depending on the position of the person with whom they are interacting. Is it a new employee or their supervisor? Missional leaders should exert influence up, down, and across the organization, but to do so effectively their leadership style will need to be tailored to numerous contexts.

Applying situational leadership principles, missional leaders will develop intuition about when it is good to speak about one's faith and when it is best to simply live out the ideals of one's faith. Paul, speaking from personal experience as a missional leader, said, "Be wise in the way you act toward outsiders; make the most of every opportunity. Let your conversation be always full of grace, seasoned with salt, so that you may know how to answer everyone" (Colossians 4:5–6). St. Francis of Assisi reportedly said, "Preach the gospel always and if necessary use words." Situational leadership will help the missional leader develop sound judgment to make on-site decisions about when and how to share one's faith in an appropriate and respectful manner.

The reality of the need for situational leadership affects how missional leaders should be trained. Instead of giving them a blueprint that should produce results, we should train them to study their situations, analyze people's needs, reflect upon their observations, consult with one another and mentors, pray, and then, based on this process, determine the best long-term path. Situational leadership means that the person in the situation is best suited for determining the necessary leadership approach. Adaptability and flexibility are key factors in missional leadership.

Strategic

There is an old axiom, "If you fail to plan, plan to fail." This is why missional leadership must be strategic. If the missional leader does not seek to intentionally live out the above principles in a planned and calculated way, experience says that it will not happen.

In view of the aforementioned complexity of life and leadership situations, it would be inappropriate to speak of strategy in any universal sense. Despite the uselessness of universal strategies, it does pay to be strategic in missional leadership. However, in developing strategies it is well worth the time to pay attention to some notes of caution. First, the task should not be defined too narrowly. While a particular organization or person simply cannot do everything, it is important to avoid the tendency to task reduction. For example, I worked in Russia through a consortium of more than 80 educational, humanitarian, and religious organizations. I was able to see the emphasis of the various groups and the way they perceived their task. Many of them were indeed strategic, but many had such a narrow strategic focus that it affected their understanding of human nature and their ability to function effectively in unique situations. We must beware of reductionism in our philosophies and theologies when we select a strategic focus.

Second, in developing strategies we must be careful not to set our goals too high. In one sense, we must envision doing great things. Frequently, a limited vision is the chief reason for poor performance. However, high goals sometimes can produce an intense environment that engenders the feeling of the greyhound running around the track after a rabbit that is designed to stay one step ahead. This atmosphere can lead to burnout and ineffectiveness because of the pressure and stress.

There is a tension between setting goals too high and too low. The best solution is to encourage people to develop their own strategies and goals after going through an in-depth, on-site critical analysis process. Strategy should hinge on two factors primarily: the needs of the local situation and the gifting and skill set of the missional leader and team.

Specifically, the missional leader needs to develop a strategy that reflects the spiritual nature of the task, is consistent with Scripture, promotes solidarity with others, focuses on serving, is sustainable, and appropriate to the particular situation. A strategy based on these principles will tend to be more successful than alternatives.

Conclusion

The world is changing and religious leadership needs to change with it. In order to adapt, the church will need to deconstruct the old clergy/

laity model and move to a partnership paradigm that understands the importance of missional leadership. Despite much work and glimpses of success, progress is still needed to close the persistent faith-work gap. The missional leader can best work out his or her calling by living from a model that acknowledges the spiritual nature of the missional task and recognizes the Scriptures as a book of stories of ordinary people who lived their faith in an authentic way in everyday life. The model will also reflect an emphasis on working in solidarity with different people and groups of people, characterized at all times by an attitude of service. For genuine life success any leadership approach must be sustainable and adaptable to specific situations. Finally, in order for the paradigm to be effectively implemented, missional leaders will have to be strategic and intentional.

Questions for Reflection & Discussion

1. How can leadership be reflective of God and His character?

2. Of the seven steps for missional leadership success, which is the most important to you?

3. How can missional leaders practically and realistically serve others in their organizations?

4. How can missional leaders express unity or destroy unity with other Christians?

5. How can missional leaders be true to their faith in Christ but demonstrate solidarity with those of other faiths?

chapter 17

REFLECTIONS ON OFFSHORING

Many view increased global connection as a new and legitimate opportunity for serving God and influencing others towards Christ through business. To that end, numerous BAM entrepreneurs/adventurers have packed up their lives and moved to faraway lands and started new business ventures.

Through the years I have also talked to several US-based business owners who have said that they would love to go overseas and establish a business, but the responsibilities and commitments of their current business keep them at home. To some of these people I have recommended offshoring a part of their business as a way to lower costs, increase profits, and create potential avenues for influencing people in other countries with God's love. I have encouraged these entrepreneurs to enlarge their vision of business so that they can increase their reach for the sake of the kingdom of God.

As nations open up to doing business with other nations, the practice of offshoring has dramatically increased. This has become a controversial topic, commonly discussed in mainstream media and political debates. Many of the entrepreneurs I talk to, as well people in the general public and in churches, express concern about offshoring. There are two main critiques of offshoring heard in the US: a perceived loss of American jobs, and a perception of worker exploitation in the developing countries.

Some blame corporate greed for these two alleged problems. Others counter by pointing to the power of the "invisible hand" and say that a rising tide lifts all boats. But what is a Christian to do? Does the Christian faith compel people to work for or against offshoring?

The premise of this chapter is that Christians can engage a globalized economy, and their engagement can be a legitimate means to spread God's blessings and to love and serve our global neighbors. If approached correctly, offshoring has the potential not only to help those in other countries, but Americans as well.

Outsourcing is a world-changing phenomenon. According to the International Association of Outsourcing Professionals, US companies spent $4.2 trillion on outsourcing in 2006, more than a 30 percent increase from the $3.1 trillion spent in 2003.[1] One type of outsourcing is called offshoring. This is when work is not only contracted outside of a company, but also outside of its country. Offshoring is transforming the way many do business and is producing significant change around the world. In the best seller, *The World Is Flat*, author Thomas Friedman cited offshoring as one of the ten "flatteners" that is creating a more level and more competitive playing field around the world. Although this form of outsourcing is immensely popular, it is also hotly debated and controversial.

God Bless America

Not a day goes by that I do not see a bumper sticker or hear a politician saying "God bless America!" For those of us who grew up singing the song, it resonates within us. We do want God to bless America. That is, after all, much better than God not blessing us! Upon reflection, however, it is clear that by itself this is an inadequate and narrow view of whom God aspires to bless.

God told Abraham he would be a blessing to the nations (Genesis 12:1–3). God desires to bless the nations and has a truly global view of humanity. He values an employee in India in the same way that

He values an employee in America. God rejoices when an Indian is hired. God rejoices when an American is hired. God desires to bless all people in all nations, not just us and our country. By offshoring business, we are spreading the blessing of income generation and dignified employment.

Stories Jesus Told

We have a moral responsibility to be an integral and instrumental part of spreading the blessing of God to the nations. Jesus said that we should love God and neighbor (Luke 10:27). To explain what this meant, Jesus told the parable of the good Samaritan. This is the story of a wealthier person providing for someone else in need. We know that the Samaritan was wealthy for two reasons: he was riding on a donkey (not walking like the others in the story), and he had the financial means to pay for the victim's hotel bills and other needs.

Since God is a global God, His call to love our neighbor is a global call. In other words, we are to love our global neighbors. The wealthy can do this by passing economic blessing to those in need. God does not desire for anyone, American or not, to remain involuntarily unemployed. Some people consider offshoring a zero-sum situation, meaning an American loses his/her job and a foreigner gains it. However, as will be explained later, this is not generally an accurate assessment of offshoring. Nevertheless, many Christians would still insist that we should focus our efforts on job security for people of our own country. I will argue that this is not an appropriate economic posture, but regardless of that, it is definitely not the right spiritual approach. This perspective is more in line with the people who crossed the road to avoid the injured man, rather than the Samaritan who stopped to help a person of a different race who was in need.

Jesus also told the parable of the workers in the vineyard (Matthew 20:1–16). This is the story of several workers who had worked all day in the fields. At the end of the day they complained because several workers who joined at a late hour were paid the same amount. One possible applied principle of this story could be the importance of involving people in economic processes from which they have been previously shut out. In the context of globalization, God wants us to create an economic context so that as many people as possible can actively participate. Through meaningful employment and sufficient income they will be given the opportunity to flourish.

The Reality of Poverty

Many American Christians are oblivious to the lives of billions of people. Recently, I read an article that cited people's complaints about trying economic times. One disgruntled American grumbled that the family eats out only once or twice a month rather than weekly as they previously had. While there are undoubtedly people in great need in the US, it would be helpful for more people to understand the harsh conditions under which many people of the world live.

Throughout the developing countries of the world, I have personally seen people who live on trash heaps. They earn meager incomes by processing garbage, salvaging what they can, and selling it. Economic compulsion is a powerful force that pushes some people to do whatever they can to survive. Besides living in landfills, many participate in illegal and degrading activities, such as prostitution, because they feel it is their only option.

When there is a legitimate and positive economic alternative, people flock to it. On a daily basis one can find thousands of people lined up at offshoring facilities in the developing world in hopes of work. Many of these same factories have been inaccurately and falsely criticized as abusing people's basic human rights. If people had better options, they would not be lining up en masse for the slim chance of finding work. This explains why people in other countries tend to view globalization significantly more positively than Americans. The truly poor like offshoring. According to David Dollar:

The Pew Center for the People and the Press surveyed 38,000 people in 44 nations, with excellent coverage of the developing world in all regions. In general, there is a positive view of growing economic integration worldwide. But what was striking in the survey is that views of globalization are distinctly more positive in low-income countries than in rich ones.[2]

Christians should be excited to see the redeployment of resources into poor countries, improving the quality of life for people who live in poverty. The positive impact of globalization and how it increases the standard of living in many countries is something we should all support. This is positive not only from a spiritual standpoint, but from an economic one as well.

The Economic Benefits of Offshoring

Offshoring has repeatedly been proven to bring benefits back to America. N. Gregory Mankiw, a Harvard professor then serving as chairman of the White House Council of Economic Advisers, once said offshoring is only "'the latest manifestation of the gains from trade that economists have talked about at least since Adam Smith. . . . More things are tradable than were tradable in the past, and that's a good thing.' Although Democratic and Republican politicians alike excoriated Mankiw for his callous attitude toward American jobs, economists lined up to support his claim that offshoring is simply international business as usual."[3]

There have been two basic waves of offshoring: the offshoring of manufacturing and the offshoring of services. Although Americans have become acclimated to having products provided from offshore locations, such as coffee from Brazil or plastic toys from China, they react more aggressively towards the offshoring of services, a more recent phenomenon. In large part, this is because consumers can directly see that shirts from China only cost $5 instead of $15 for a US-made shirt. Or they can appreciate that a plastic toy only costs $4 at Walmart instead of $15 at a "Made in the USA" store. These numbers are merely illustrative, but the anger directed at the offshoring of production is largely tempered by the benefits accrued directly to the consumer. Services are a different matter. Any benefits of their offshoring cannot be felt as directly and their relocation tends to anger Americans a bit more.

To understand this issue, first it is necessary to put the job relocation in perspective. It has been predicted that by 2015 roughly 3.3 million US business-processing jobs will have moved abroad. That sounds like a lot, but to put this in perspective, in 1999 *alone*, 1.15 million jobs were lost as part of mass layoffs with in the US. And 1999 was a very prosperous year for the growing US economy.[4] The US economy is dependent upon flexibility and adaptability in its workforce. It also has the highest reemployment rate in the world, which is one of its biggest strengths.

Second, although the benefits of locating services offshore cannot be seen or felt as directly by the consumer, the benefits to the consumer are just as great. According to *McKinsey Quarterly*, "It [offshoring] directly recaptures 67 cents of every dollar of spending that goes abroad and indirectly might capture an additional 45 to 47 cents—producing a net gain of 12 cents to 14 cents for every dollar of costs moved offshore."[5] This is true for manufacturing or services. Excess protection of a closed US economy not only hurts the US economy, it hurts the global economy.

Additionally, although it is nice that benefits accrue to Americans in the form of cheaper products and services, we do want to point out that it is not a zero-sum game. Offshoring is an act of a mutual-economic benefit where the pie is larger for both the offshorer and the offshore provider. They are better off than before; this means it is a truly beneficial economic transaction.

Here is a list of some of the benefits to Americans of offshoring:[6]

- *Corporate savings.* This money can be reinvested into new business opportunities (factories, technology, etc.) that create US jobs. Or corporate savings can be passed to the shareholders who will then use the extra profits to consume more (which is good for the economy) or create additional savings to be used for little Johnny's college education (which is also good for the economy).
- *Better deals for consumers.* Americans like low prices.

- *Additional exports.* Offshore service providers frequently need American technology.
- *Repatriated profits.* Often the profits earned in India and the like are brought back into the US creating additional tax revenue and additional earnings for US shareholders.

Benefits to the offshore provider include:

- *Infusion of direct foreign investment.* Again *McKinsey Quarterly* notes how foreign direct investment benefits India:

> Foreign direct investment played a key role in the creation of these industries: the fast-growing Indian companies that now dominate the global sector got started only after multinational companies pioneered the approach, showed the world that India was a viable outsourcing destination, and trained a critical mass of local employees. . . . Today foreign companies continue to provide healthy competition that forces Indian companies to improve their operations continually.[7]

- *Job employment and training.* The former chairman of Wipro/Spectramind, for instance, worked for American Express and GE, and the CEO of Daksh came from Motorola. Nike alone employs about 800,000 workers throughout developing countries in Asia, such as China, Vietnam, and Indonesia. And as a further benefit to society, Hannah Jones, the Nike vice-president of corporate responsibility, points out: "On average, the workers are 18- to 24-year-old women, many of whom are the first women in their families and their communities to work in the formal economy and have economic independence. So we have a huge opportunity to affect these women . . . [and] to have a multiplier effect on their communities."[8] These young women, in developing countries such as Thailand, are incredibly susceptible to abuse, sex trafficking, and other atrocities. Being gainfully employed reduces their risk of being caught up in these things.

- *Raises local competition.* The presence of multinationals raises the competitive landscape for local firms. Often, local firms in developing countries
  enjoy monopoly status and can exploit their workers and consumers.

Many social commentators and Christian theologians do not really
understand the way business works. Methodist theologian Donald E.
Messer critiqued Nike this way:

> Here is another rather remarkable example of how unevenly the benefits of world trade
> are distributed: the American basketball star Michael Jordan annually makes more
> money for endorsing Nike shoes than the combined income of all 22,000 Indonesian
> women who make the shoes. It is not surprising that many of these women are hungry,
> despite their day-long toils at the assembly line. I do not object to Jordan getting rich.
> He has for years brought pleasure into our lives with his matchless athletic skill. What is
> objectionable is the near-starvation wages paid Indonesian working women.[9]

Messer's criticism does not acknowledge: how many Indonesian workers
want these jobs, the dynamics of supply chain economics, and the
complexities of wage comparisons. In Indonesia you can see more than
3,000 Indonesians waiting each day outside a large footwear factory in
hopes of a single day's work. The wages paid to these women are not
near-starvation wages; they are decent and fair wages with appropriate
buying power for the Indonesian economy. Multinational companies
often offer up to 25 percent premiums over local factories. The working
conditions in multinational factories typically far exceed the conditions
of local factories. Although much of American's indignation is targeted at
our large US multinationals, much more effort should be concentrated on
the smaller local players who participate in a far higher rate of abuse. If
our popular press truly cared about the Indonesians who suffer most, why
do they target a factory that has more than 3,000 people a day standing
outside hoping for work?

We should care deeply about economic disparity. But it is not
appropriate to assess the situation through wage comparisons between

countries. In reference to such calculations, Jagdish Bhagwati, professor of economics at Columbia University and senior fellow for international economics at the Council on Foreign Relations, said, "These numbers are totally meaningless. . . . Households in outer Mongolia are not thinking about what households on Park Avenue in New York are doing. So what's the point of putting them together and comparing the wealth of one group to the wealth of another group?"[10] Wealth needs to be fairly distributed to all parties responsible for its creation. This includes the factory workers in Indonesia. However, for criticism to be constructive, one needs to analyze each context and avoid arbitrary and sensational numeric comparisons.

Offshoring and Small Town, USA

In some cases poor management of offshoring justifies criticism to it. Layoffs are a very delicate matter and should be done in an affirming way. This is not always done. For example, RadioShack fired 400 staffers via email with a message that read, "The work force reduction notification is currently in progress. Unfortunately your position is one that has been eliminated." Bank of America announced plans to outsource tech support jobs to India and told 100 American workers that they had to train their own replacements before they could get their severance payments.[11] Such incidents of poor management not only get one's company onto "101 Dumbest Moments in Business" lists, but also fuel a building backlash against offshoring.

To be sure, offshoring does not produce uniform results. For some people it has resulted in involuntary job loss and serious personal problems. Most people tend to view offshoring through the lenses of their personal experiences or of the experiences of someone close to them. Many Americans are suspicious of offshoring and view it negatively because they know people who have apparently suffered as a result of it.

This is true of one small town that I researched in the eastern United States. In 2005 three large furniture factories closed their doors resulting in more than a thousand layoffs, approximately 16 percent of the town's workforce. The factory owners were unable to compete with Mexican and Chinese offshore competitors. Rather than using offshore labor, they hung on until there was simply no more money. Understandably many of the people of this town are not positively disposed to offshoring, and globalization could be considered the longest four-letter word in town.

However, as I researched the aftermath of this situation, I found that the town took important steps to alleviate the problems caused by offshoring. For some people what was a negative situation turned positive.

By way of a unique partnership between educational institutions and economic developers, as well as state, local, and federal government agencies, an entrepreneurial institute was established to serve the area in June 2005. The institute has three strategic centers to ensure the welfare of the town's people: 1) a business incubator facility that offers business assistance and consulting services; 2) a technology-enhanced educational center, which includes high-demand technical curricula and occupational programs for high school and college students, transfer programs, and a university center; 3) a continuing education center for workforce skills including literacy, GED, workforce, and corporate training. In addition to these three centers, the institute subsidizes rental space for new business ventures and brings in development experts, such as Suzanne W. Morse, author of *Smart Communities: How Citizens and Local Leaders Can Use Strategic Thinking to Build a Brighter Future*, to give presentations to local civic leaders, entrepreneurs, business owners, and the unemployed to educate them regarding future possibilities.

After being laid off, one interviewed worker took advantage of these rental subsidies and unemployment payments to start a picture framing and gourmet coffee business. Two years later, he has moved out of the subsidized rental and into a large storefront downtown. Though not wealthy, he has been able to grow his business and has generated sufficient income to purchase a new home, significantly larger than the one he lived in before.

Being laid off clearly causes difficulty in people's lives, but by responding proactively and having access to tangible tools to help, individuals can rise to the challenge. For many workers, the difficult times were short-lived, and they are better off now than they were before. Offshoring has helped many people move to a higher level position as it forced them to be innovative and proactive.

Despite an ongoing negative sentiment toward offshoring in the area, the response of the town government appears to have truly helped. A year after the layoffs unemployment had returned to pre-layoff rates. Though there are some people who have had difficulty finding new jobs and still others who are working at lower wages, it would be hard to say that the community has been as negatively impacted as original prognostications argued it would be.

Unfortunately, some people are still not taking full advantage of the new possibilities offered to them. A call center moved into town and was prepared to hire 250 workers. The job required for the workers to be trained, a service that was provided free of charge by the institute. Despite this opportunity, the call center had tremendous difficulty hiring 250 people, because many people do not want to hassle with more training. Furthermore, they have a very high turnover rate, a common problem with US-based call centers. I think this illustrates two things: people in town have other employment options and Americans don't like working at call centers.

The experience of the town I researched demonstrates several things. First, layoffs are difficult for the individuals being laid off. Therefore, sensitivity (contra RadioShack and Bank of America) is of the utmost importance. Second, America is much better equipped than other countries to handle layoffs. In many other countries there are simply no viable options when one's job falls through. Third, If we respond positively, proactively, and intelligently, Americans will be better off as they move into higher level positions. Fourth, the attitudes of many Americans toward offshoring are contradictory. Phil Knight has reportedly explained that Nike offshored shoe production because Americans did not want to make shoes.[12] The same is seemingly true with call centers. Whether, when push comes to shove, this is actually the case may be up for debate, but it is certain that if Americans will not take certain jobs, then many people in other countries will be glad to get them.

Love Your Neighbor

Offshoring is a controversial topic, and it should be approached with sensitivity and genuine care for all involved. However, offshoring is not something that Christians or Americans should resist and fight against. Offshoring creates an avenue for us to embrace and love our global neighbor. Despite claims to the contrary, offshoring is not a zero-sum game that takes from Americans and gives to others, though shortsightedness and passive responses by some people have resulted in ongoing hardships. When approached correctly, offshoring can lift all people, both domestic and abroad, to a higher socioeconomic status, create human prosperity, and serve as a powerful change agent in areas that most need one. The primary hindrances to future positive developments in offshoring are misunderstandings as a result of distorted information or poorly developed theories and ideas. I hope this book will help overcome some of those hindrances and will serve as a conversation starter, so that we can love God and neighbor through current global processes.

Questions for Reflection & Discussion

1. How can offshoring benefit people in developing countries? How can it harm them?

2. How can offshoring benefit people in America? How can it harm them?

3. How can the refrain "God bless America" prevent us from seeking that blessing for people in all countries?

4. How can Christians ensure that offshoring benefits all people?

5. Does an American desire for cheap goods conflict with the desire to prevent offshoring?

ENDNOTES

Foreword

[1] "Sphere Sovereignty (1880)," in James D. Bratt (ed.), *Abraham Kuyper: A Centennial Reader* (Grand Rapids, MI: Wm. B. Eerdmans, 1998), 461.

Chapter 1

[1] R. Paul Stevens, *Doing God's Business: Meaning and Motivation for the Marketplace* (Grand Rapids, MI: Wm. B. Eerdmans, 2006), 80. The author lays out several of these categories in his work. I must give him credit for stimulating my thinking. To his excellent framework, I have added the not-so-excellent business as a cover for missions simply because it is so prevalent. I also added business in missions because that is so often what BAM is assumed to be.

[2] George Barna, *Revolution: Finding Vibrant Faith Beyond the Walls of the Sanctuary* (Carol Stream, IL: Tyndale House Publishers, 2005), 13.

[3] Ibid., 33.

[4] Ibid., 49.

[5] Ibid., 62.

[6] Ibid., 63.

Chapter 2

[1] Robert Wuthnow, *God and Mammon in America* (New York: The Free Press, 1994), 55–56.

[2] Laura Nash and Scotty McLennan, *Church on Sunday, Work on Monday: The Challenge of Fusing Christian Values with Business Life* (San Francisco: Jossey-Bass, 2001), 141.

[3] The Hebrew word for work in Genesis 2:2 is *melaka*. It is also used in Exodus 20:9, 1 Chronicles 4:23, and Haggai 1:14. *Maaseh* is another Hebrew word for work used in the Bible (Genesis 5:29, Exodus 5:13, Proverbs 16:3, Ecclesiastes 1:14). Another Hebrew word for work in the Bible is *avodah*. Interestingly enough this word is sometimes translated *work* (Genesis 29:27,

Exodus 34:21, 1 Chronicles 28:21, Psalm 104:23) and other times *worship* (Exodus 3:12, 8:1; Numbers 8:11; Deuteronomy 10:12; Joshua 24:15). This has very powerful implications as the same word for working in the fields was used for worshipping God. It seems the Israelites understood that work was not just a way to supply their physical needs, but also a way to spiritually worship God.

4 Karl Marx, "The Grundrisse" in Gilbert C. Meilaender (ed.), *Working: Its Meaning and Its Limits* (University of Notre Dame Press, 2000), 29.

5 Karl Barth, *Church Dogmatics*, Volume III, Part 1 (Edinburgh: T&T Clark, 1956), 184 and 185.

6 Miraslov Volf, "God at Work," 16. Lecture given at Yale Divinity School, transcript available at http://www.yale.edu/faith/esw/centerReadings.htm (accessed on July 29, 2009).

7 http://www.answersingenesis.org/creation/v16/i1/wonders.asp (accessed September 1, 2009).

8 Peter F. Drucker, *Landmarks of Tomorrow* (New York: Transaction Publishers, 1996), 180.

Chapter 3

1 www.globalaidsalliance.org/page/-/PDFs/OVC_factsheet_new.pdf (accessed September 1, 2009).

2 http://www.worldvision.com.au/Libraries/3_3_1_Aid_Trade_and_MDGs_ PDF_reports/Globalisation_The_Poor_Must_Come_First.sflb.ashx (accessed September 1, 2009).

3 http://findarticles.com/p/articles/mi_m1309/is_3_37/ai_70654234/ (accessed September 1, 2009).

4 Thomas H. Naylor, William H. Willimon, and Rolf Österberg, *The Search for Meaning in the Workplace* (Nashville: Abingdon Press, 1996), 75.

5 There are literally mounds of literature devoted to how to create community in a corporate or business environment. To discuss this literature is outside of the scope of my intent here, as I am just pointing out that this is an inherently spiritual facet of business. If interested, pages 75–92 of the book cited above (*The Search for Meaning*) are a good read for practical insights on building community in business from a Christian perspective.

6 Victor Hamilton, *The Book of Genesis: Chapters 1-17: New International Commentary on the Old Testament* (Grand Rapids, MI: Wm. B. Eerdmans, 1990), 178.

[7] Peter F. Drucker, *Concept of the Corporation* (New York: Transaction Publishers, 1993), 193.

Chapter 4

[1] C. William Pollard, *Serving Two Masters? Reflections on God and Profit* (New York: HarperCollins Publishers, 2006), 2.

[2] Rose Marie Berger and Brian Bolton, "Trickle Up Economics," *Sojourners*, http://www.sojo.net/index.cfm?action=magazine.article&issue=sojo0401&article=040142f (accessed August 8, 2009).

[3] Graef C. Crystal, "CEOs are Overpaid" in Tamara L. Roleff (ed.), *Business Ethics* (San Diego: Greenhaven Press, 1996), 62.

[4] Jim Collins, *Good to Great* (New York: HarperBusiness, 2001), back cover.

[5] Ibid., 10.

[6] Jürgen Moltmann, "Der Sinn der Arbeit" in Jürgen Moltmann (ed.), *Recht auf Arbeit, Sinn der Arbeit* (München: Chr. Kaiser, 1979), 77. (Author's own translation.)

Chapter 5

[1] F. F. Bruce, *Paul: Apostle of the Heart Set Free* (Grand Rapids, MI: Wm. B. Eerdmans, 1977), 37–38.

[2] Ibid., 126.

[3] *Acts of Paul* appears to have been written by a presbyter in Asia Minor in the late second century. Though there appears to be reason to believe that some of the accounts recorded in the book are legendary, the description of Paul's appearance is most likely accurate. In *Paul: Apostle of the Heart Set Free*, F. F. Bruce concurs with Sir William Ramsay who wrote, "this plain and unflattering account of the Apostle's personal appearance seems to embody a very early tradition." Hippolytus, bishop of Rome in the early third century and the greatest scholar of Western Christendom at the time, appears to have accepted the work as a genuine record of events (though not as holy Scripture; something it was never intended to be considered).

[4] F. F. Bruce, *Paul: Apostle of the Heart Set Free* (Grand Rapids: Wm. B. Eerdmans, 1977), 468.

[5] Ben Witherington III, *The Paul Quest: The Renewed Search for the Jew of Tarsus* (Downers Grove, IL: InterVarsity Press, 1998), 43.

[6] Ben Witherington III, *Conflict & Community in Corinth: A Socio-Rhetorical Commentary on 1 and 2 Corinthians* (Grand Rapids, MI: Wm. B. Eerdmans, 1995), 21.

[7] Ibid., 12.

Chapter 6

[1] Ramsay MacMullen, *Roman Social Relations: 50 B.C. to A.D. 284* (New Haven, CT: Yale University Press, 1981), 74–75.

[2] Ibid., 76–77.

[3] Martin Hengel and Anna Maria Schwemer, *Paul Between Damascus and Antioch: The Unknown Years* (Louisville, KY: Westminster John Knox, 1997) 160.

[4] F. F. Bruce, *Paul: Apostle of the Heart Set Free* (Grand Rapids, MI: Wm. B. Eerdmans, 1977), 291.

[5] Ronald Hock, *The Social Context of Paul's Ministry: Tentmaking and Apostleship* (Minneapolis: Fortress Press, 1980), 93.

[6] From L. Gregory Bloomquist, *The Function of Suffering in Philippians.* Cited in Ben Witherington III, *Friendship and Finances in Philippi: The Letter of Paul to the Philippians* (Valley Forge, PA: Trinity Press International, 1994), 123.

[7] Ronald Hock, *The Social Context of Paul's Ministry: Tentmaking and Apostleship* (Minneapolis: Fortress Press, 1980), 92.

[8] F. F. Bruce, *The Book of the Acts: The New International Commentary on the New Testament* (Grand Rapids, MI: Wm. B. Eerdmans, 1988, rev. sub. ed.), 346.

[9] F. F. Bruce, *Paul: Apostle of the Heart Set Free* (Grand Rapids: Wm. B. Eerdmans, 1977), 269–270. Perhaps Paul was a widower. Or perhaps his wife left him after his conversion and he did not remarry.

[10] William J. Webb, *Slaves, Women & Homosexuals: Exploring the Hermeneutics of Cultural Analysis* (Downers Grove, IL: InterVarsity Press, 2001). This source provides a very helpful, in-depth, and insightful look at the issue.

Chapter 7

[1] E. A. Judge, *The Social Pattern of the Christian Groups in the First Century: Some Prolegomena to the Study of New Testament Ideas of Social Obligation* (London: Tyndale, 1960), 60.

[2] Ben Witherington III, *Conflict & Community in Corinth: A Socio-Rhetorical Commentary on 1 and 2 Corinthians* (Grand Rapids, MI: Wm. B. Eerdmans, 1995), 20.

[3] Ben Witherington III, *The Paul Quest: The Renewed Search for the Jew of Tarsus* (Downers Grove, IL: InterVarsity Press, 1998), 128.

[4] Roland Allen, *Missionary Methods: St. Paul's or Ours?* (Grand Rapids: Wm. B. Eerdmans Publishing Co., 1962), 49.

[5] Eckart Schütrumpf, "Credibility," in Thomas O. Sloane (ed.), *Encyclopedia of Rhetoric* (New York: Oxford University Press, 2001), 178.

[6] George A. Kennedy, *Aristotle on Rhetoric: A Theory of Civic Discourse* (New York: Oxford University Press, 1991), 37.

[7] Eckart Schütrumpf, "Credibility," in Thomas O. Sloane (ed.), *Encyclopedia of Rhetoric* (New York: Oxford University Press, 2001), 178.

[8] James S. Baumlin, "Ethos," in Thomas O. Sloane (ed.), *Encyclopedia of Rhetoric* (New York: Oxford University Press, 2001), 265.

[9] Ibid., 264.

[10] In the Corinthian situation it seems there were those who would not listen to him because he would not receive pay. Therefore, Paul's decision to work or not work was not based simply on the notion of gaining credibility for the message. But it was a benefit in many cases.

[11] Eckart Schütrumpf, "Credibility," in Thomas O. Sloane (ed.), *Encyclopedia of Rhetoric* (New York: Oxford University Press, 2001), 178.

[12] George A. Kennedy, *Classical Rhetoric & Its Christian and Secular Tradition from Ancient to Modern Times*, rev. 2nd edition (Chapel Hill, NC: The University of North Carolina Press, 1999), 149.

[13] As mentioned before, Paul's working as a tentmaker did not establish credibility with the upper class people but actually garnered criticism. However, working as a tentmaker would have helped him gain credibility with *more* people than the alternative of patronage. So, despite the fact that there was a cost to this decision, there would have been a greater cost had he chosen to go the route of patronage.

[14] Ben Witherington III, *1 and 2 Thessalonians: A Socio-Rhetorical Commentary* (Grand Rapids, MI: Wm. B.Eerdmans, 2006), 124.

[15] T. G. Soares, "Paul's Missionary Methods," *Biblical World* 34 (1909), 326–336, esp. 335. Cited in Ronald Hock, *The Social Context of Paul's Ministry: Tentmaking and Apostleship* (Minneapolis: Fortress Press, 1980), 88.

[16] Oscar Broneer, "The Apostle Paul and the Isthmian Games," *Biblical Archaeologist*, Volume 25 (1962), 2–31.

Chapter 8

[1] Neal Johnson and Steve Rundle, "Distinctives and challenges of business as mission," Tom Steffen and Michael Barnett (eds.) *Business as Mission: From Impoverished to Empowered* (Pasadena, CA: William Carey Library, 2006), 24.

[2] Heinz Suter and Marco Gmür, *Business Power for God's Purpose: Partnership with the Unreached* (Switzerland: VKG, 1997), 21.

[3] Samuel Moffett, *A History of Christianity in Asia, Volume 1: Beginnings to 1500* (Maryknoll, NY: Orbis Books, 1998), 297.

[4] Dwight P. Baker, "William Carey and the Business Model for Mission," *Between Past and Future: Evangelical Mission Entering the Twenty-First Century* (Pasadena, CA: William Carey Library, 2003), 167–202.

[5] http://www.businessasmissionnetwork.com/2006/10/rich-history-of-business -as-mission.html (accessed September 2, 2009).

[6] Steven Pointer and Michael Cooper, "Seventeenth Century Puritan Missions: Some Implications for Business as Mission," in Tom Steffen and Michael Barnett (eds.), *Business as Mission: From Impoverished to Empowered* (Pasadena, CA: William Carey Library, 2006), 170.

[7] Karl Rennstich, *Mission und Wirtschaftliche Entwicklung: Biblische Theologie des Kulturwandels und Christliche Ethik* (Munich: Kaiser Verlag, 1978), 247–250.

[8] http://www.gsb.columbia.edu/honor/ (accessed August 21, 2009).

[9] http://mbaoath.org (accessed August 21, 2009).

[10] http://www.fairtradefederation.org/ht/d/sp/i/8447/pid/8447 (accessed August 21, 2009).

[11] Ibid.

[12] http://www.palletenterprise.com/articledatabase/view.asp?articleid=2226 (accessed August 24, 2009).

[13] http://www.hopeinternational.com (accessed August 21, 2009).

[14] http://www.youreasyoffice.com (accessed August 21, 2009).

[15] J. Gregory Dees, "The Meaning of Social Entrepreneurship," http://www .fuqua.duke.edu/centers/case/ (accessed August 21, 2009).

[16] Jim Collins, *Good to Great and the Social Sectors: A Monograph to Accompany Good to Great* (New York: HarperCollins, 2005), 5. (emphasis in original)

[17] William Foster and Jeffrey Bradach, "Should Nonprofits seek Profits?" (Harvard Business Review, February 2005), 5–6.

[18] J. Gregory Dees and Beth Battle Anderson, "For-Profit Social Ventures," *International Journal of Entrepreneurship Education* 2 (1) (Senate Hall, NY: Senate Hall Academic Publishing, 2002).

Chapter 10

[1] The two models in this chapter are composites based on international research I conducted for my PhD dissertation at Asbury Theological Seminary, Wilmore, Kentucky. The stories are realistic and could easily and accurately fit the experiences of numerous BAM enterprises. However, the names of all persons and organizations have been changed. Any similarity in names is not intended.

Chapter 11

[1] Nantachai Mejudhon, *Meekness: A New Approach to Christian Witness to the Thai People* (D. Miss. dissertation, Asbury Theological Seminary, 1997). See also Mejudhon's chapter, "Meekness: A New Approach to Christian Witness to the Thai People," in David Lim, Stephen Spaulding, Paul De Neui, *Sharing Jesus Effectively in the Buddhist World* (Pasadena, CA: William Carey Library Publishers, 2005), 149–186. High cultural adaptation means congruency with at least seven of the eight cultural categories and five of the six contextualization categories as proposed by Mejudhon. Low cultural adaptation reflects congruency with three or less of the eight cultural categories and two or less of the six contextualization categories proposed by Mejudhon. The eight cultural categories (broadly) are: time, work and play, youth vs. age, equality vs. hierarchy, materialism vs. spirituality, change vs. tradition, independence vs. dependence, and confrontation vs. indirection (avoidance). These categories were originally outlined by scholar Paul Fieg, an American Peace Corps volunteer in Thailand for many years. Mejudhon suggests six contextualization categories that communicate meekness in the Thai context (with slight modification by M. Russell): displaying humble attitudes toward Buddhism and Thai culture, developing genuine and sincere relationships with Buddhists, presenting the benefits of the gospel in a nonconfrontational manner, allowing time for the diffusion of the gospel, using indigenous strategies for communicating the gospel, and becoming insiders by playing credible, appropriate roles within Thai culture. Overlap is possible.

[2] Though many of those interviewed inherently understood some of the cultural differences between Thais and Americans, very few could articulate clear categories. This demonstrates a need for increased focus on Thai culture and strategies for managerial adaptation.

[3] Figure 5 seems to suggest there is an ideal "tipping point" between two and three years of exposure. However, the age of the companies I researched contributes to the apparently diminishing rate of return of conversions

for the longer time periods. The oldest company I looked had only been operating for nine years. This company, for obvious reasons, was the only one to report conversion after more than seven years. Furthermore, they have added numerous employees through the years meaning only a few employees have been with the company longer than seven years (virtually since its inception). More research is needed in this area.

Chapter 12

1 *The Economist*, "Fit for Purpose," March 31–April 6, 2007. 76. See http://www.lazytown.com/pdf/PR_USA_Economist_Apr2007.pdf (accessed August 31, 2009).

2 Phil Vischer, *Me, Myself, and Bob: A True Story About Dreams, God, and Talking Vegetables* (Nashville, TN: Thomas Nelson, 2006). See also philvischer.com (accessed August 31, 2009).

Chapter 13

1 In this chapter I rely heavily on the work of cross-cultural theorists such as Edward T. Hall Jr., Geert Hofstede, Alfred Kraemer, Fons Trompenaars, Charles Hampden-Turner, Craig Storti, and Harry Triandis.

2 Craig Storti, *Figuring Foreigners Out: A Practical Guide* (Yarmouth, MA: Intercultural Press, 1999), 66.

Chapter 16

1 Vincent J. Donovan, *Christianity Rediscovered* (Maryknoll, NY: Orbis Books, 1978), 159.

2 Howard A. Snyder, *Global Good News: Mission in a New Context* (Nashville, TN: Abingdon Press, 2001), 230.

3 Robert K. Greenleaf, *Servant Leadership: A Journey into the Nature of Legitimate Power and Greatness* (New York: Paulist Press, 1977), 6. (Italics in original.)

4 Stephen R. Covey, *Principle-Centered Leadership* (New York: Fireside, 1990), 34.

5 Jim Collins, "Good to Great," *Fast Company* Issue 51, October 2001, 90.

6 Paul Hersey, Kenneth Blanchard, and Dewey E. Johnson, *Management of Organizational Behavior: Leading Human Resources* (Upper Saddle River, NJ: Prentice-Hall, 2001); *Management of Organizational Behavior: Utilizing Human Resources,* (Englewood Cliffs, NJ: Prentice-Hall, 1977).

[7] Kenneth Blanchard and Spencer Johnson, *The One Minute Manager* (New York: HarperCollins, 2003).

Chapter 17

[1] "Outsourcing Trends to Watch in 2007," *Fortune*. September 3, 2007.

[2] David Dollar, "The Poor Like Globalization," *Global Envision* http://www.globalenvision.org/library/23/504/ (accessed August 19, 2009).

[3] Alan S. Blinder, "Offshoring: the Next Industrial Revolution?" *Foreign Affairs*, March/April 2006, http://www.foreignaffairs.com/articles/61514/alan-s-blinder/offshoring-the-next-industrial-revolution (accessed August 19, 2009).

[4] *McKinsey Quarterly*, "Who wins in offshoring?", CNET News.com, October 26, 2003, http://news.cnet.com/Who-wins-when-jobs-move-offshore/2030-1014_3-5096283.html (accessed August 25, 2009).

[5] Ibid.

[6] Martin N. Baily and Diana Farrell, "Exploding the Myths of Offshoring," *McKinsey Quarterly*, http://www.databazaar.biz/press/offshoring.pdf (accessed August 19, 2009).

[7] Martin N. Baily and Diana Farrell, "Exploding the Myths of Offshoring," from *McKinsey Quarterly* on CFO.com, July 14, 2004, http://www.cfo.com/article.cfm/3015027/1/c_2984273?f=bc (accessed August 25, 2009).

[8] Jim Phills, "15 Minutes with Hannah Jones," *Stanford Social Innovation Review* http://www.ssireview.org/articles/entry/726/ (accessed August 19, 2009).

[9] George McGovern, Bob Dole, and Donald E. Messer, *Ending Hunger Now: A Challenge to Persons of Faith* (Minneapolis, MN: Fortress Press. 2005), 40.

[10] Jagdish Bhagwati, *Hoarding the Wealth*, Marketplace Public Radio Interview, http://marketplace.publicradio.org/shows/2006/12/05/PM200612052.html (accessed August 19, 2009).

[11] Adam Horowitz, David Jacobson, Tom McNichol, and Owen Thomas, "101 Dumbest Moments in Business," http://money.cnn.com/galleries/2007/biz2/0701/gallery.101 dumbest_2007/index.html (accessed August 19, 2009).

[12] http://www.answers.com/topic/phil-knight (accessed August 25, 2009).

GLOSSARY OF TERMS

Most of these terms are foundational to this book. Some are not, but are commonly used terms in other BAM literature and worth knowing for further research.

Business *and* mission: business is distinct and separate from mission(s)

Business *as a cover for* missions: establishing a business purely for the means of obtaining access; no real business activities are performed

Business *as a platform for* mission: business as a vehicle for engaging in external missions activities, such as church planting and evangelism

Business *as* mission: business as a vehicle of the mission of God in the world

Business *for* mission: business with a primary focus of funding mission(s) with its profits

Business *in* missions: business as an approach and strategy for church planting and evangelism in cross-cultural settings, with a preference for working in unevangelized parts of the world

Community development: a set of values and practices that plays a special role in overcoming poverty and disadvantage by improving various aspects of local communities

CPE missions: a missions paradigm that prioritizes church planting and evangelism

Environmental sustainability: providing for the needs of this generation without doing harm to the next

Faith at Work: a growing movement focused on the relevance of faith to one's work and how Christians can live out and express their faith at work

Frontier missions: cross-cultural missions to previously unevangelized peoples

Great Commission company (GCC): a parallel term to BAM, referring to a "socially responsible, income-producing business managed by kingdom professionals and created for the specific purpose of glorifying God and promoting the growth and multiplication of local churches in the least-evangelized and least-developed parts of the world." (See Steve Rundle and Tom Steffen, *Great Commission Companies*, p. 41. Full bibliographical information is listed on p. 306.)

Holistic missions: a missions paradigm that values church planting, evangelism, service to the poor, and other social development interventions

Kingdom business: a parallel term to BAM, referring to business ventures designed to be vehicles of the coming kingdom of God. The goal is to transform people and nations by integrating gospel proclamation and social service.

Marketplace ministry: intentionally integrating ministry, such as counseling, chaplaincy services, and evangelism into a marketplace or workplace setting

Microenterprise development (MED): a common strategy for income generation in developing nations, which involves activities such as funding, training, and mentoring to promote the development of business among the poor. Typically defined as a business started with less than $1,000.

Microfinance: the provision of loans, savings accounts, and other basic financial services to the poor, those without access to traditional financial services

Mission: God's overarching purposes in the world

Missions: the local outworkings of Christians partnering with God in His mission

Mission *in* business: seeking to engage in missions activities, such as church planting and evangelism, within a business

Overseas private equity (OPE): the development of large and established companies. OPEs are businesses started with an investment between $50,000 and $100,000 or more.

Quadruple bottom line: the triple bottom line refers to reaching financial, social, and environmental goals. The quadruple bottom line adds distinctly spiritual goals.

Small and medium enterprise (SME): businesses that are started with a loan or capital investment between approximately $1,000 and $50,000. SMEs form the bedrock of most modern economies. The World Bank estimates that SMEs contribute an average 51.5 percent of GDP in high income countries—but only 15.6 percent in low income countries. By contrast, the "informal" micro-enterprise sector accounts for an average 47.2 percent of GDP in low income countries, but just 13 percent in high income countries. (See http://www.brookings.edu/papers/2007/03development_de_ferranti.aspx [accessed September 3, 2009].)

Tentmaking: marketplace ministry, specifically in an international cross-cultural setting.

Triple bottom line: a term in business literature referring to the multiple goals of a business. A response to the conventional wisdom that a business has one bottom line, namely financial profits. Typically the new triple bottom line is focused on reaching financial, social, and environmental goals.

RECOMMENDED RESOURCES

Books:

Bakke, Dennis. *Joy at Work: A Revolutionary Approach to Fun on the Job* (Seattle, WA: PVG, 2005). In this memoir-like work, Dennis Bakke, the founder of global power company AES Corporation, focuses on the nature of work through the lens of his committed Christian perspective.

Eldred, Ken. *God is at Work: Transforming People and Nations Through Business* (Ventura, CA: Regal Books, 2005). An overview of God's purposes for work and how it relates to BAM by a successful Silicon Valley entrepreneur.

Grudem, Wayne. *Business for the Glory of God* (Wheaton, IL: Crossway, 2003). A concise summary of how business and its various aspects, such as profit, ownership, money, competition, and lending can glorify God. Written by a theologian with an economics degree from Harvard, this book is deep, yet short and accessible, making it a unique resource.

Hicks, Douglas. *Religion and the Workplace: Pluralism, Spirituality, and Leadership* (Cambridge, UK: Cambridge University Press, 2003). This book addresses issues of managing faith-related issues in a multifaith or pluralistic workplace. It contains helpful principles for how to live and relate one's faith.

Hock, Ronald. *The Social Context of Paul's Ministry: Tentmaking and Apostleship* (Minneapolis: Fortress Press, 2007). Originally based on Hock's dissertation at Yale University, this work takes a unique and in-depth look at the relevance of tentmaking to Paul's strategy as well as to the social contexts of his business as mission work.

Miller, David W. *God at Work: The History and Promise of the Faith at Work Movement* (New York: Oxford University Press, 2007). This book takes an historical and theological look at the faith at work movement. It is balanced, thorough, and objective with helpful frameworks. For the serious reader.

Nash, Laura and Scotty McLennan. *Church on Sunday, Work on Monday: The Challenge of Fusing Christian Values with Business Life* (San Francisco: Jossey-Bass,

2001). A good look at the faith-work gap inherent in churches and practical ways that this gap can be bridged.

Novak, Michael. *Business as a Calling: Work and the Examined Life* (New York: Free Press, 1996). Novak is a Catholic moral philosopher who draws from a wide variety of traditions. This work provides a helpful look at how business can be a unique calling from God.

Rundle, Steven, and Tom Steffen. *Great Commission Companies: The Emerging Role of Business in Missions* (Downers Grove, IL: InterVarsity Press, 2003). A short and helpful book compiled by an economics professor (Rundle) and an intercultural studies professor (Steffen) with interesting case studies.

Stevens, R. Paul. *The Other Six Days: Vocation, Work, and Ministry in Biblical Perspective* (Grand Rapids, MI: Wm. B. Eerdmans, 2000). This excellent work looks at the relevancy of the Christian faith to our work and explores concepts of ministry as it relates to work.

—. *Doing God's Business: Meaning and Motivation for the Marketplace* (Grand Rapids, MI: Wm. B. Eerdmans, 2006). This book is a companion and follow-up to the earlier work by Stevens, looking at the divine purposes for work and service in the marketplace.

Thomas, Sir Keith (ed.). *The Oxford Book of Work* (Oxford University Press: 1999). A dense 656-page book that looks at historical, philosophical, and theological views of work.

Yamamori, Tetsunao, and Kenneth A. Eldred (eds.). *On Kingdom Business: Transforming Missions Through Entrepreneurial Strategies* (Wheaton, IL: Crossway Books, 2003). An early compilation of case studies looking at BAM as it was practiced in the late twentieth century.

Web sites:

Global Envision: dedicated to dialogue on globalization and poverty alleviation. http://www.globalenvision.org

GreenBiz.com: a popular Web site with up-to-date information on environmental developments and how they relate to business. http://www.greenbiz.com/

Fair Trade Federation: comprehensive information on all things related to fair trade. http://www.fairtradefederation.org/

Social Entrepreneurship Organizations

Ashoka: supports social entrepreneurs worldwide with resource funding, access to expertise, and peer support. http://www.ashoka.org

Easy Office: A for-profit social business venture that provides affordable finance, accounting, and bookkeeping services tailored to nonprofits nationwide. Their goal is to help nonprofits reduce costs and focus their energies on their distinct missions. http://www.youreasyoffice.com

HOPE International: A Christ-centered nonprofit organization focused on alleviating physical and spiritual poverty through microenterprise development. http://www.hopeinternational.org/

Opportunity International: A Christian network of microfinance and formal financial institutions that take the form of commercial banks, development banks, or credit unions and can accept deposits. http://www.opportunity.org/

Academic Centers

The Chalmers Center for Economic Development at Covenant College: a research and training center with the mission of helping the church worldwide to minister to the poor in their community without creating dependency. http://www.chalmers.org/

Princeton University Faith and Work Initiative: an initiative directed by David Miller with the mission to generate intellectual frameworks and practical resources for the issues and opportunities surrounding faith and work. http://www.princeton.edu/csr/current-research/faith-and-work/

INDEX